The Rough Guide
History of

Egypt

Rough Guides online
CPL
www.roughguides.com

credits

Rough Guides series editor: Mark Ellingham
Text editor: Andrew Dickson
Production: Link Hall, Julia Bovis, Katie Pringle
Design: Henry Iles
Cartography: Maxine Repath, Ed Wright
Proofreading: David Price
Picture research: Lisa Pusey

Cover credits

Front – Tutankhamun's death mask, Cairo Museum
Back – Mohammed Ali mosque, Cairo

publishing information

This edition published May 2003 by
Rough Guides Ltd, 80 Strand, London WC2R 0RL

distributed by the Penguin group

Penguin Books Ltd, 80 Strand, London WC2R 0RL
Penguin Putnam, Inc. 375 Hudson Street, New York 10014, USA
Penguin Books Australia Ltd, 487 Maroondah Highway, PO Box 257,
Ringwood, Victoria 3134, Australia
Penguin Books Canada Ltd, 10 Alcorn Avenue,
Toronto, Ontario, Canada M4V 1E4
Penguin Books (NZ) Ltd, 182–190 Wairau Road,
Auckland 10, New Zealand

Typeset to an original design by Henry Iles

Printed in Spain by Graphy Cems

A catalogue record for this book is available from the British Library.
ISBN 1-85828-940-8

The Rough Guide
History of

Egypt

by Michael Haag

series editor
Justin Wintle

To the memory of my father

Contents

Introduction

E gypt appears on the map as a large rectangle at the northeast corner of Africa with Sinai as a small triangular
peninsula at the southwest corner of Asia. Through Sinai
runs the Suez Canal, which provides the shortest link
between the Mediterranean and the Indian Ocean via the Red
Sea, while Sinai itself is the only land bridge between Africa and
the remainder of the Eastern Hemisphere. Egypt therefore controls a great international crossroads, so that even if it did not
share a border with Israel, its geographical position would ensure
it a major role in the politics of the Middle East. To this must be
added Egypt's qualities of endurance and stability in a region of
conflict and flux – well illustrated by the fact that this paragraph
as accurately describes Egypt's place in the world during the first
millennium BC as in our own third millennium AD.

In the course of those thousands of years, Egypt has known
many empires that have come and gone – Persian, Greek,
Roman, Arab, Ottoman, British – so that today it is **America**
which cajoles and courts the ancient nation on the Nile. With the
aim of ensuring Egypt's cooperation in the task of maintaining
stability in the region, the United States has been pouring nearly a
billion dollars a year into the Egyptian economy since **Anwar
Sadat** signed a peace treaty with Israel in 1979, making Egypt
along with Israel the world's largest recipients of American aid –
and this is not to mention further contributions from the
International Monetary Fund, the World Bank, the European
Union and Japan.

Egypt's desperate need for financial assistance arises in large
part from the failure of its bureaucratic state-directed economy,
an inheritance from the centralized socialist regime of president
Gamal Abdel Nasser during the 1950s and 1960s, and which
is only very slowly being reformed. Egypt also suffers from rapid

population growth, which strains its ability to provide adequate educational and health facilities and employment to its people, and threatens to exhaust natural resources, in particular the supply of water.

Though nearly twice the size of France and a third the size of the United States, Egypt is an almost entirely rainless country of dry and barren desert where only a few oasis-dwellers and nomadic Bedouins can survive. As the **River Nile** is the only perennial water source in Egypt, nearly all the nation's seventy million inhabitants are confined to that three percent of the country taken up by the Nile Valley and the Delta. The very existence of the Egyptian people depends on the Nile – which throughout their history has been both their provider and taskmaster.

Egyptians began recording their history five thousand years ago when King Menes, in one of the earliest examples of writing in the world, commemorated his unification of **Upper** and **Lower Egypt** – that is, the Nile Valley *up*river from his new capital of Memphis and the Nile Delta *down*river to the north. Strong centralized rule organized the resources of a united Egypt and unleashed its potential with sudden and startling effect, so that within four hundred years King Cheops was building his Great Pyramid, still the largest building (by volume) standing on the face of the earth.

Architectural, cultural and political patterns established at the beginning of pharaonic history served Egypt for three thousand years and more, into the period of **Greek rule** following the invasion of Alexander the Great, and Egypt's incorporation into the **Roman Empire** after the death of Cleopatra. During this Graeco-Roman period, it is no exaggeration to say that **Alexandria** on the Mediterranean coast of Egypt was the cultural and intellectual capital of the world. In Alexandria, too, with its mixed Egyptian, Jewish and Greek civilization, **Christianity** was developed and transformed into a universal faith – not least because of Egypt's contribution of a powerful imagery to the new religion, such as the Virgin and Child and the Cross and the Resurrection, symbols that can be traced back to the earliest notions in Egyptian belief.

The great discontinuity in Egyptian history was the **Arab invasion** of the 7th century and the introduction of **Islam**. Through its abjuration of images, its conviction that nothing worth acknowledging preceded the teachings of Mohammed, and by its subjection and persecution of the Copts, the native inhabitants of the country, Islam destroyed much of Egypt's cultural inheritance. Yet in place of Alexandria, and not far from the crumbling ruins of Memphis, the Arabs' own foundation of **Cairo** became one of the great medieval cities, a magnificent treasure trove of Islamic architecture arising amid the rich and exotic caravanserai of trade linking East and West, the fabulous city of *The Thousand and One Nights*.

From Cairo in the late 1100s, **Saladin** launched his campaign against the Crusaders in Palestine and Syria, as a century later the **Mamelukes** rode out from the city to destroy the Mongol hordes that had been ravaging the Middle East and Europe. But Mameluke power weakened when European ships found their way round Africa to India and the Far East, bypassing the trade counters of Cairo, and the **Turkish invasion** in 1517 reduced Egypt to a provincial backwater of the Ottoman Empire.

The ancient idea of a canal linking the Mediterranean with the Red Sea was revived by **Napoleon** when he invaded Egypt in 1798 with the intention of undermining Britain's command of the ocean route to India. The encounter marked the beginning of Egypt's often turbulent relationship with the West, as an impoverished and benighted backwater became forcibly exposed to the modern – if imperfect – world of science, industry, capital and secular thought.

In the last half-century or so, an independent Egypt has moved from a landed oligarchy under a constitutional monarchy to socialism within a police state and now to an increasingly privatized and free market economy under a veiled military dictatorship, which permits a cautious freedom of public expression. Yet if this is progress, it is also true that the Egypt of today is almost unrecognizable from that of even thirty years ago, when secular trends were still paramount. Now Islamic fundamentalists operate within the political system, where they press for the full adoption of traditional Islamic law and work for the complete **Islamization** of Egyptian society. Their aim is to reinstitute a 'golden age' enjoyed during the earliest days of Islam in the 7th century; but to outside eyes, and indeed in the eyes of many Egyptians, they want to return Egypt to something more like the Dark Ages.

Religiosity has always played a powerful role in Egyptian society, not least when it has disguised from Egyptians themselves the great changes their seemingly changeless world is undergoing. As much as Islamization may appear to be a rejection of secular progress, in fact it may be the means by which necessary and inevitable changes are accepted and legitimized in the name of holy law.

A note on the chronology of Ancient Egypt

Starting from the unification of Egypt, the ancient Egyptians counted the years by the duration of the reigns of kings, with each new king beginning a new cycle of years. **Manetho**, an Egyptian priest in the 3rd century BC, arranged the kings into thirty dynasties. To these dynastic divisions of what we call the **Dynastic** or **Pharaonic Period**, Egyptologists have added a further system, grouping the dynasties into distinct periods – so that for example the **Old**, **Middle** and **New Kingdoms** refer to periods of strong centralized authority, while the **First**, **Second** and **Third Intermediate Periods** refer to those times when centralized authority dissolved. As often as not kings, monuments and artefacts are dated in books and at museums and sites not by year but by dynasty or kingdom or period.

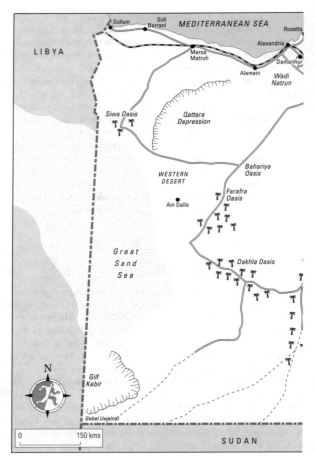

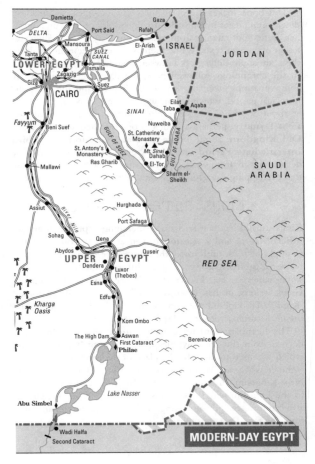

MODERN-DAY EGYPT

This book makes use of all these chronological systems. For determining dates by our calendar, Egyptologists rely on a number of methods ranging from radiocarbon dating to the interpretation of ancient texts. While there is broad agreement on dates, there are some differences between one authority and another. In the chronology followed here, the dates for prehistory are approximations given in very round figures, and those for the historical period, which begins with the introduction of writing at about 3000 BC, are subject to margins of error as follows: **First Dynasty**, perhaps as much as one hundred and fifty years; **Old Kingdom**, about fifty years; **New Kingdom** and **Third Intermediate Period**, about ten years. Dates from 664 BC are derived mostly from written Greek sources and are precise. Note that overlapping dates for kings indicate regencies or joint rule.

Kings' names and titles

Kings usually had several names, including a **praenomen** (an official name) and a **nomen** (given at birth); following the example of most authorities they are referred to here by their nomens. Sources, however, give different spellings, and also some names are best known to us in the form used by ancient Greek writers, so that 'Cheops' is the Greek form of the nomen 'Khufu'. Throughout this book an attempt has been made to use the most familiar version and spelling of a king's name.

The Egyptian word for king was **nesu**; the term 'pharaoh' derives from the hieroglyphic *per-o*, meaning 'Great House', which was used to describe the place of the royal administration – much as we say 'Whitehall' or 'the White House'. From the New Kingdom onwards (after 1550 BC), the word was applied to the king himself. Egyptologists, however, though guilty of anachronism, happily use 'king' and 'pharaoh' interchangeably from the First Dynasty onwards.

List of maps

List of illustrations

1: From Prehistory to the Old Kingdom

c.30,000–c.2160 BC

The Nile Valley has probably been home to human life since two million years ago, when **early man** first passed this way into Asia and Europe from his birthplace in East Africa. The first significant traces of occupation, however, date to around 30,000 BC, when a dramatic warming of the climate, accompanied by a change in wind and rainfall patterns, drove hunter-gatherers from their drought-stricken grasslands in northern Africa towards the river. The passing of a renewed wet phase in the Western Desert around 6000 BC ended a last attempt at subsistence there and confirmed Egypt's total dependence on the Nile.

Though Egyptian skies were virtually rainless and the forbidding desert encroached on either side, the Nile was an oasis of perennial life. The river was all the more remarkable for the surge in flow that came precisely at the hottest time of year, when from July to October it inundated the land and then receded, leaving behind a deposit of fertile silt. The first distinct **farming cultures** appeared in the Valley, the Delta and the Fayyum around 5450 BC, and over the coming millennia marshes and untamed floodplains were transformed into fields, which, planted in autumn, brought abundant harvests in spring. The huge agricultural surpluses supported the growth of an increasingly skilled and stratified society – a process that was carried furthest in southern or Upper Egypt. It was from here that the impetus came to unify the whole of Egypt, a process that was accomplished by about 3000 BC.

In the two centuries preceding unification and the four centuries that followed (when its population rose from about 750,000 to about one and a half million), Egypt underwent more accelerated change than it was to experience again until very recent times. By the end of what we call the **Early Dynastic Period** in about 2686 BC, a divine kingship presiding over a centralized administrative system – with the unquestioning support of a hierarchical society – had given Egypt a remarkable degree of security, order and prosperity. By its very nature, much of this achievement was intangible and has left few remains, but its effects would be felt during the Old Kingdom across a wide range of activities including trade, conquest, art and architecture. For example, within the first hundred years of the Old Kingdom – in no more time than it took our own fast-moving age to travel from the beginnings of the Industrial Revolution to the Eiffel Tower – Egypt invented architecture in stone and went on to construct the most massive building still standing on the face of the earth, the **Great Pyramid of Cheops**.

Yet 400 years further on, the Egyptian state collapsed into chaos – possibly the victim of its excesses, but also more than likely from a failure of the Nile's annual flow. A 'dark age' called the **First Intermediate Period** had begun.

Settlement along the Nile and the Predynastic Period c.30,000–c.3000 BC

In Egypt the migrants from the dessicated savannahs lived on the desert's edge, descending to the river to hunt, fish and gather edible wild plants. But towards the end of the last Ice Age (around 11,000 BC), monsoon conditions and huge discharges of water in the African interior caused bouts of catastrophic flooding in Egypt, making the Valley during this 'Wild Nile' stage a difficult refuge. The return of modest seasonal rains to the Western Desert led to its repopulation from about 9300 BC, and it was here, not along the Nile, that pastoralism and crop cultivation first evolved in Egypt around 7000 BC. Only with the return of arid conditions around 6000 BC was the desert abandoned for the last time, and agriculture was introduced to the Nile Valley reluctantly and late – a full two-and-a-half millennia after it had been established in the Fertile Crescent of the Near East (Palestine, Syria and Mesopotamia).

Between about 5450 and 4000 BC, a number of **farming-based cultures** arose in Upper and Lower (northern) Egypt. Though localized, these had much in common: Emmer wheat (whose grains do not thresh free from the chaff) and barley were grown, while domesticated cattle, pigs and goats were reared. Fishing was important, too, while hunting was far less so. Arrowheads, scrapers and blades were still made of flint; though the Near East and southwest Europe had learnt how to smelt copper by 6000 BC, Egypt remained in the Stone Age for a further 2500 years.

Despite these similarities, there were significant differences between the cultures of Upper and Lower Egypt, and after 4000 BC these became more pronounced. The most important for the future development of Egypt was the development of the **Badari** and **Naqada** cultures of Upper Egypt. These steadily became more socially stratified, formed political units led by autocratic princes who celebrated domination of their foes and emphasized the cult of the dead through elaborate rituals. Being further from the Near East, they were also less subject to foreign influences either through immigration or trade, and developed a worldview and a cosmology tightly bound to the limits of the Nile Valley. These traits were to become characteristic of ancient Egyptian civilization after the princes of Upper Egypt had brought the entire country under their control by 3000 BC.

c.30,000–c.9300 BC A change in the earth's climate introduces more temperate conditions in Europe and North America, culminating in the end of the **last Ice Age**. In the once-fertile lands of northern Africa and the Near East, grasslands turn into deserts, and hunters and gatherers migrate towards the few remaining rivers. In Egypt they are established along the desert escarpment overlooking the **Nile Valley** and also on the fringes of the **Fayyum** and the **Nile Delta**, where they hunt, fish and adapt their flint tools to gathering wild cereals. But settled agricultural life does not yet exist – rather a more intensive use of depleting resources.

c.9300–c.6000 BC A period of **rainfall** occurs in the Sahara, resulting in a temporary greening of the desert. Evidence of this is found at **Gebel Uweinat**, an oasis at the southwest corner of Egypt 700km west of the Nile and 1000km south of the Mediterranean, where rock carvings depict the teeming wildlife of the grasslands.

MICHAEL HAAG

Rock drawings of giraffes, gazelles and other grassland animals were discovered in 1923 at Gebel Uweinat, deep in the Sahara

> ❝ There was nothing beyond the drawings of animals, no inscriptions. It seemed to me as though they were drawn by somebody who was trying to compose a scene. Although primitive in character, they betrayed an artistic hand. The man who drew these outline figures of animals had a decorative sense. On their wall of rock these pictures were rudely, but not unskilfully carved. There were lions, giraffes and ostriches, all kinds of gazelle, and perhaps cows, though many of these figures were effaced by time. ❞
>
> Ahmed Hassanein, describing his discovery of Gebel Uweinat in *The Lost Oases* (1925)

c.7000 BC **Agriculture** evolves in the moist conditions of the Western Desert, where cattle, sheep and goats are grazed and barley and dates are cultivated.

c.6000 BC As the grasslands turn to desert once more, its pastoralists and cultivators migrate to the **Nile Valley**, the **Delta** and the **Fayyum**, where agriculture is established 2500 years after becoming widespread in the Near East.

c.5500 BC The **Predynastic Period** begins with the development of settled agriculturally based cultures in Lower and Upper Egypt.

c.5450–c.4400 BC The Fayyum, a fertile depression in the Western Desert fed by the waters of the Nile, sees **Fayyum culture** established on the northern shore of Lake Qarun, its economy the first within the reaches of the river to be based on agriculture and animal husbandry. Wooden sickles with flint blades are used for reaping, and finely woven fibre baskets are made for carrying and storing.

c.5000–c.4100 BC The people of **Merimde culture** live in mud and wickerwork huts at the boundary of the Western

> **❝** It is clear to any intelligent observer, even if he has no previous information on the subject, that the Egypt to which the Greeks sail nowadays is, as it were, the gift of the river. **❞**
>
> Herodotus, *Histories*, 5th century BC

Desert and the southern Delta. Their economy is similar to that of the Fayyum, but they also grow flax, which is spun into thread and woven into linen on a crude loom. Human figurines make their first appearance in Egypt.

The earliest Egyptians were buried in sand pits with pots and other simple grave goods for use in the hereafter

The annual inundation of Egypt

The cause of the Nile's yearly flood was long a mystery and has been understood only in modern times. There were two breakthroughs: the discovery by James Bruce in 1770 of the source of the **Blue Nile** at Lake Tana in Ethiopia and that of the **White Nile** at Lake Victoria in central Africa by John Hanning Speke in 1862. The two Niles meet to form a single mighty stream in **Sudan**, the White Nile flowing steadily year round but despite its greater length contributing only twenty percent to the volume of the Egyptian Nile – which alone would be insufficient for the country's needs. But the Blue Nile swells to a torrent as the summer rains wash down from the Ethiopian highlands, carrying with them their precious silt. At ancient Memphis (near present-day Cairo), the Nile's rise would reach its full height towards the end of September and would begin to subside a fortnight later. Sowing could begin towards the end of October or early November, with harvest time following in late March or early April.

In earliest times, the effects of the inundation were evened out by digging basins that captured the water and held it for some time after the river had receded. **Basin irrigation** was probably practised by 3000 BC and was managed locally. And yet the Egyptian state did not arise out of a collective need to control the river; indeed, there is no evidence of centralized irrigation projects until those initiated for the Fayyum over a thousand years later by the Twelfth Dynasty kings of the Middle Kingdom.

c.4600–c.4350 BC The small domed houses of **El Omari culture**, located just south of modern Cairo, are set in plots surrounded by reed fences, each home to a self-suffi-cient farming family which is the equal of its neighbours (social distinctions do not exist within Omari society). The deceased are given simple burials within the village and are laid out in a contracted position facing west, which in Dynastic times would become associated with the Land of the Dead.

c.4400–c.4000 BC **Badarian culture** (it is named after finds initially made by archeologists at El Badari near Sohag) extends as a series of Nile-side villages from Assiut in the north to Esna in the south and is the first agricultural society in Upper Egypt. A high degree of craftsmanship is exhibited both in its pottery bowls – which are worked by hand to a thinness never again equalled in Egypt – and in its burial offerings of clay and ivory female figurines and small objects made of copper.

The predominant motif of Naqada II pottery is the boat, shown here with cabin and standard. Ostriches in the desert are also depicted

c.4000–c.3500 BC Naqada I culture develops, named after the site of Naqada in Upper Egypt between Qena and Luxor. Although it is perhaps only a more advanced continuation of the Badarian culture (which has penetrated further south, close to the First Cataract in present-day Aswan), unlike Badarian culture it displays no foreign influence. A greater variety of grave goods indicates a diversified and structured society with an incipient hierarchy. Decorated pottery displays a delight in the observation of nature, but humans – when represented at all – appear as stick-figure hunters and warriors in attitudes of domination. The first towns appear, among them **Hierakonpolis** on the west bank of the Nile between modern Esna and Edfu.

c.4000–c.3200 BC Maadi culture, named after the southern suburb of modern Cairo where the finds were made, is unique in the Predynastic Period for its entrepreneurial society, which welcomes foreign contact. It carries on an extensive trade with Sinai and the Near East, makes advances in metallurgical technique and

Wealth and trade along the River of the Gods

The expansion of Naqada II culture northwards into Lower Egypt and southwards to the Nubian border was partly the consequence of an appetite among hierarchical society for prestige goods. Surplus cereal production on the floodplains of the Nile, as well as mineral resources such as gold, stone and beads from the Eastern Desert, were channelled through the growing Upper Egyptian towns of **Abydos**, **Naqada** and **Hierakonpolis** and taken downriver to Lower Egypt. There they were exchanged for copper, oils and other luxury goods from Sinai, Palestine, Syria, Mesopotamia and Persia, and for lapis lazuli (whose sole source was Afghanistan). Trade was also established with **Nubia** in the south, from where ivory, ebony, incense and the skins of wild cats were imported.

Powerful local principalities formed at Abydos, Naqada and Hierakonpolis, which – along with other towns in Upper Egypt – saw increasing social stratification and became centres of craft production. Copper was now sufficiently common to be substituted for stone when making such substantial objects as blades and axes. Stoneworkers, too, sharpened their skills, paving the way for the great achievements in sculpture and architecture of the Old Kingdom.

Naqada's extraordinarily wide-ranging trade was made possible by the large boat, which in turn required supplies of cedarwood brought overland from Lebanon (Egypt was a virtually treeless country). The pottery of Naqada II reflects this: its predominant motif was the boat, which became a status symbol as well as a means of trade. More tellingly, perhaps, in this pottery the Nile begins to be portrayed as a mythical river upon which the first gods sailed – establishing the link between the human and cosmic orders which was to become a pervasive feature of Egyptian ideology in Dynastic times.

extends its commercial influence across much of Lower Egypt.

c.3500–c.3200 BC Naqada II culture spreads over the whole of the Nile Valley from the First Cataract at the Nubian border in the south to the eastern edge of the Delta and also into the Fayyum in the north.

" " The falcon god Horus leads captive the inhabitants of the papyrus country. **" "**

The Narmer Palette (c.3000 BC), one of the earliest examples of Egyptian writing

PRIVATE COLLECTION

The Narmer Palette conveys in symbols and images the unification of Egypt and marks the beginning of hieroglyphic writing in about 3000 BC

c.3200–c.3000 BC With **Naqada III culture** the indigenous material culture of Lower Egypt disappears and is replaced by that of Upper Egypt. Naqada III is sometimes called **Dynasty 0** as a line of kings now rules in Upper Egypt and perhaps beyond. The power of Naqada is eclipsed but Hierakonpolis remains important, while kings are buried in elaborate tombs at Abydos. A simple form of **hieroglyphic writing** combining pictographs and phonetic signs is employed in royal circles for economic and administrative purposes and in commemorative art. According to mythology, Horus, the protective falcon god of Hierakonpolis, gives the throne of Egypt to **Menes**, to whom tradition gives the credit for the **founding of Memphis** and the **unification of Upper and Lower Egypt** – though in reality this may have come about gradually, perhaps through intimidation rather than a campaign of conquest.

The Early Dynastic Period (First and Second Dynasties) c.3000–c.2686 BC

The **Early Dynastic Period** was a time of cultural, economic and administrative consolidation, an era when the foundations were laid for a civilization that would endure for three thousand years. Most important in this process was the authority of the king, who, as the increasingly godlike head of the state religion, legitimized the new political order and its hierarchical society. From his capital in Memphis, he ruled over a united Egypt extending for a thousand kilometres from the First Cataract to the Mediterranean. It seems likely that centralization was assisted by a common spoken language (though nothing of it survives), and administration was facilitated by hieroglyphic writing. Although irrigation was generally left in local hands, land was the king's to dispose of as he pleased, trade was a royal monopoly, and he was able to command military campaigns. Through a literate bureaucracy, the king operated an efficient system of taxation, organized state building projects and recruited the labour necessary for the state's needs. Architecture symbolized the political order through the large tombs of high officials and monumental royal tombs, their construction and decoration the work of full-time craftsmen and artisans supported by the Crown.

Evidence for the Early Dynastic Period is almost entirely funerary but nonetheless revealing. Ordinary Egyptians were buried in pits dug in the sand, but for people of rank a large pit was cut from the bedrock and divided into chambers, and a rectangular single storey flat-roofed mud-brick structure called a mastaba was built on top of it – this too divided into chambers, which were filled with grave goods to see its inhabitants through the afterlife. Apart from having more imposing tombs and separate funerary shrines where rites could be performed, kings were distinguished from the rest by being buried at **Abydos**. High officials were buried at **Saqqara** on the desert plateau overlooking Memphis, though during the Second Dynasty some kings were also buried there.

First Dynasty kings enjoyed another distinction at death: royal burials were accompanied by sacrificial humans – probably officials, priests, servants and women from the royal household, who were strangled with the intention that they should continue to offer the king their services in the afterlife. Lions were sometimes sacrificed to provide the king with game for hunting, as were dwarfs to keep the king amused. Human sacrifice, however, must have had something of a dispiriting effect on the royal court; at any rate, the practice was abandoned by the beginning of the Second Dynasty.

The wealth of Second-Dynasty high officials is illustrated by their elaborate tombs, which amounted to entire houses for the afterlife, the largest having 27 rooms and containing men's and women's quarters complete with bathrooms and toilets. But the ancient Egyptians believed that it was impossible for the dead to enter the afterlife unless their bodies were preserved, which had previously occurred naturally from the dehydrating effects of burial in the sand; now the growing fashion among the wealthy for burial in wooden coffins required that their bodies be wrapped in resin-soaked linen to prevent decomposition.

This use of wooden coffins and resin points to an increased trade with cedar-rich Lebanon, the old overland route via Palestine replaced by the sea route to **Byblos** – where the first inscription referring to an Egyptian king, **Khasekemwy** of the Second Dynasty, has been found. And the grave goods of tombs at Saqqara and Abydos also reveal much about the Second Dynasty's culture and trading links: the presence of copper indicates access to mines in the Eastern Desert, Sinai and the Negev and the expansion of copper-working in Egypt; many of the jars found in these tombs probably contained wine (the vine was first domesticated in Egypt); other ancient jars have preserved, even after five thousand years, the scent of aromatic oils imported from Palestine and Syria. Possibly by Khasekhemwy's time at the end of the Second Dynasty the Egyptians had installed a trading post and garrison, perhaps even an administrative centre, at **Buhen** by the Second Cataract (near present-day Wadi Halfa). This gave them direct control over exotic African goods.

Writing, meanwhile, answered the developing needs of trade and administration, and by the end of the Early Dynastic Period **hieroglyphics** had become sufficiently flexible to convey a continuous narrative.

First Dynasty (c.3000–c.2890 BC)

c.3000 BC Though Manetho (see p.xi) listed **Menes** as the first king of the First Dynasty, scholars now place him in Dynasty 0 and begin the First Dynasty with **Aha**. That king's high officials are the first to be buried at **Saqqara** near Memphis, but in the tradition of the Predynastic kings Aha builds his tomb at **Abydos**, where at his death he is joined by 33 strangled courtiers and servants to wait upon him for eternity.

Djer, second king of the dynasty, conducts military campaigns against 'the Setje' (probably in Sinai) and as far south as the Second Cataract in Nubia, obtaining **turquoise** from the former and **gold** from the latter. Along with **lapis lazuli** obtained by trade from Afghanistan, these are among his grave goods at Abydos, where also he is joined by 338 human sacrifices – though hereafter the practice declines.

The **double crown**, combining the conical white crown of Upper Egypt and the flat-topped red crown of Lower Egypt, is introduced during the reign of **Den**, fourth king of the dynasty, perhaps in confirmation that the process of centralization is well and truly complete. Den's tomb at Abydos is paved with red and black **granite** brought downriver from Aswan and indicates the advances made in working with harder stone.

c.2890 BC **Qaa** is the eighth and last king of the First Dynasty. Inscribed labels describe large amounts of aromatic oils among his grave goods, probably imported from Syria or Palestine and indicating the extensive foreign trade controlled by the crown.

Second Dynasty (c.2890–c.2686 BC)

c.2890 BC **Hetepsekhemwy** is the first king of the Second

Dynasty. There is some evidence that he and his two immediate successors choose to be buried at Saqqara near Memphis, not at Abydos.

c.2686 BC Significant **technological innovations** are made during the reign of **Khasekhemwy**, the seventh and last king of his dynasty. He is the first king of whom a copper statue is made; at Abydos his tomb chamber is the first large-scale construction in stone; and at Saqqara, where he builds a walled funerary enclosure, he erects a mound of sand and gravel covered with mud brick, the earliest suggestion of a pyramid. Though Khasekhemwy reverts to the old tradition of royal burial at Abydos, his will be the last.

> The Egyptian state was not a man-made alternative to other forms of political organisation. It was god-given, established when the world was created; and it continued to form part of the universal order. In the person of Pharaoh a superhuman being had taken charge of the affairs of man. And this great blessing, which ensured the well-being of the nation, was not due to a fortunate accident but had been foreseen in the divine plan. The monarchy then was as old as the world, for the creator himself had assumed kingly office on the day of creation. Pharaoh was his descendant and his successor. The word 'state' was absent from the language because all the significant aspects of the state were concentrated in the king. He was the fountainhead of all authority, all power and all wealth.
>
> Henri Frankfort, *Ancient Egyptian Religion* (1948)

The Old Kingdom (Third to Eighth Dynasties): c.2686–c.2125 BC

More than anything the Old Kingdom is defined by its architectural accomplishments, most especially by the grand line of **pyramids** running along the edge of the Western Desert. Their construction was to bring profound changes to Egypt's economy and society, for the great burst of pyramid-building during the Third and Fourth Dynasties probably became the means by which those who were close to the king and initially dependent on him began redistributing his power and wealth among themselves.

The **Step Pyramid** built for **Djoser**, the second king of the Third Dynasty, marked the beginning of the new pyramidal form that was to be pushed to its limits during the first century of the Old Kingdom. Its architect was Djoser's vizier Imhotep, who was also Chief of the Observers, the title borne by the high priest at what the Greeks would later call **Heliopolis** (City of the Sun), now overbuilt by the northern suburbs of Cairo. Despite Heliopolis' name, in Imhotep's time star cults were probably pre-eminent, his title referring to astronomical observations generally and not yet to a cult of the sun. Symbolically the Step Pyramid was the means by which Djoser could ascend to the heavens, a star among eternal stars.

Whether true pyramids with smoothly sloping sides – first built by **Sneferu**, the first king of the Fourth Dynasty – evolved naturally out of the earlier stepped form or were induced by a change in religion is not known, but certainly the two ideas were to coincide. The sun cult eventually became predominant at Heliopolis, where it was associated with the creation myth of the primal hill. This hill rose from the chaos of the waters bearing the sun god **Ra**, just as after the Nile's annual inundation the waters subsided and the sun drew the harvest from the mud. Heliopolis also claimed a primal hill, the **benben**, a word whose root was bound up with the notion of 'shining' and 'ascending'. The benben had already been depicted in Second Dynasty inscriptions; now in Sneferu's true pyramids it was manifested architecturally — at once symbolizing the reborn sun rising above the land and the rebirth of the king himself.

Sneferu's works were a gigantic undertaking. He completed the fifth largest pyramid, that of his father Huni at **Meidum**, and went on to build the fourth and second largest pyramids, the Bent and Red pyramids at **Dahshur** between Meidum and Saqqara. The ever-closer relationship between king and sun god was stated plainly by **Chephren** and **Mycerinus**, who incorporated Ra into their names (**Khafra** and **Menkaura**) — a practice that would recur throughout the rest of ancient Egyptian history. Autocratic power was in their hands, their pyramids at **Giza** at least as much an assertion of their authority as a symbol of the sun cult.

Things would change, however, with **Userkaf**. Before ascending the throne as the first king of the Fifth Dynasty, he had most likely been high priest at Heliopolis, and it was during his reign that the cult of Ra was raised to the official state religion. Userkaf and his Fifth Dynasty successors all built modestly sized pyramids, but diverted considerable resources to building elaborate sun temples too. This represented a significant transfer of power and wealth to the priesthood of Ra — a multiplication of guardians and priests, sustained by a rising level of royal donations and by endowments of land exempted from taxation in perpetuity.

As the king surrendered his monopoly on divine power, members of the royal family withdrew from the highest offices in the administration. In the Fourth Dynasty a vizier had been regularly one of the royal princes, but during the Fifth Dynasty the high offices of state were being filled increasingly by members of the burgeoning bureaucracy — who wished above all, as one text says, 'to hand over their offices to their children'. The diminution of royal authority was reflected in the burials of these nobles and high officials. At Giza their mastabas had been arranged in orderly rows around the pyramids; as in life, the king was the source of all reward. But from the Fifth Dynasty onwards the mastabas of the elite were neither regimented nor confined to a central site. Provincial administrators, originally royal appointees, enjoyed increasing independence, and, as they established themselves as local hereditary ruling families, were content to be buried where they had lived. Even at Saqqara, which had become sanctified by Djoser's burial there, the emphasis was on the celebration and perpetuation of personal achievement, with mastabas of the Fifth and Sixth Dynasties irregularly distributed as though to appreciate the view – their numerous rooms elaborately decorated with scenes of the good life their owners had attained in this world and fully expected to enjoy in the next.

Unas, the last king of the Fifth Dynasty, did not build sun temples, nor did his two immediate predecessors – though not because the cult of the sun was waning. The reason why is located inside Unas' pyramid at Saqqara. There the walls of his tomb chamber are covered with hieroglyphic inscriptions, the **Pyramid Texts**, which are the earliest extensive mortuary literature in Egypt. The Texts identify the deceased king with **Osiris**, lord of the underworld and originally a god of vegetation and fertility, whose ancient cult had been incorporated by the Heliopolitan priests into their solar theology by the end of the Fifth Dynasty.

Osiris was said to have been born of the sky goddess **Nut**, who in turn was the creation of the sun god. Her naked figure arching across the heavens represented the sun god's vision of an ordered firmament, so that at sundown he would be swallowed by her and then emerge from her vulva at dawn. Nut is described in the Pyramid Texts as 'enfolding the dead pharaoh in her soul', a euphemism for him being placed in his sarcophagus. The practice of burial in stone sarcophagi began with Cheops in the previous dynasty, and subsequently it became common not only for kings but also for lesser mortals to be placed in a sarcophagus whose interior was carved with the naked figure of Nut. The deceased, in being symbolically enclosed by Nut to await rebirth, was therefore associating himself with ancient Egypt's two greatest cults, those of the sun and of Osiris.

But Unas' prayers to Osiris also betray a sense of anxious uncertainty. Previously kings were gods, absolute in their power; later, their authority was shared with Ra, though the sun god was also a guarantor of his royal position. The appearance of Osiris marks another shift in the balance of power. As lord of the underworld, Orisis performed the role of a judge who examined the souls of the dead and condemned those unfit for the afterlife – now even the king must plead his case. With the rise of the cult of Osiris came the notion of a personal god from whom one sought redemption. Socially and theologically Egypt was becoming more egalitarian, but the kingship was less confident than before. The troubled times of the First Intermediate Period were approaching.

MICHAEL HAAG

The first pyramid, built for Djoser by his vizier Imhotep in about 2660 BC, was meant as the king's stairway to the stars

The invention of stone architecture

In the symbolism of its form as a stairway to the stars and in the durability of its material, the **Step Pyramid** was meant to ensure eternal life for Djoser's *ka* (soul). Likewise, its surrounding mortuary complex was an eternal promise in stone that even in the afterlife Djoser would perform the necessary rituals by which Egypt would enjoy continued order and perpetual regeneration.

In the enclosure around the pyramid, Imhotep reproduced a copy of the field of the **Heb Sed**, the jubilee race at Memphis, when a king renewed his claim to the throne by running between two markers representing the limits of Upper and Lower Egypt, thereby demonstrating his continued vitality. Next to this was the Heb Sed court, flanked by chapels – each for the priesthood of a province who, receiving jubilee gifts from the king, would return home under an obligation to recognize his supremacy over their local deities. The original chapels at Memphis would have been tent-like structures supported by poles, cross-supports and other fixtures of wood, reed, papyrus and the like. At Saqqara Imhotep mimicked these shapes in carved columns, capitals, cornices and mouldings. The result was the invention of the language of stone architecture.

Third Dynasty (c.2686–c.2613 BC)

c.2667–c.2648 BC The second king of the new Third Dynasty is **Djoser** (also called **Zoser**), who is thought to have married Khasekhemwy's daughter. He pursues the pyramid concept together with his vizier **Imhotep** – high priest at Heliopolis and responsible for constructing the **Step Pyramid** at Saqqara, the world's first monumental building made entirely of stone.

c.2648–c.2640 BC **Sekhemkhet** begins an even more ambitious stepped pyramid, but it remains uncompleted at his death and construction is abandoned.

c.2640–c.2637 BC **Khaba** also attempts a stepped pyramid, but his reign is too brief to see it through to completion.

EGYPT IN THE ANCIENT WORLD

GREECE

ASIA MINOR

Euphrates

Ugarit

SYRIA

Byblos • • Kadesh

LEBANON

CRETE

CYPRUS

• Damascus

MEDITERRANEAN
SEA

Jerusalem

PALESTINE

CYRENACIA

LOWER
EGYPT

SINAI

ARABIA

Fayyum

Siwa
Oasis

Baħariya Oasis

EASTERN
DESERT

RED
SEA

LIBYA

WESTERN
DESERT

Farafra
Oasis

Kharga
Oasis

• Thebes

Dakhla
Oasis

UPPER EGYPT

Aswan
First
Cataract

N

• Gebel
Uweinat

River Nile

Second Cataract

NUBIA

Third
Cataract

Fourth
Cataract

Fifth
Cataract

Kerma

• Napata

• Meroe

0   200 km

c.2637–c.2613 BC Huni, the fifth and last king of the Third Dynasty, begins a huge stepped pyramid south of Saqqara at **Meidum,** which is nearly complete at his death.

Fourth Dynasty (c.2613–c.2494 BC)

c.2613–c.2589 BC Sneferu, probably the son of Huni by a minor queen, ensures his succession by marrying his half-sister **Hetepheres**, who is in the direct royal line.

Sneferu: conquest, trade and pyramids

Later generations looked back admiringly on **Sneferu** for the prosperity and power he brought to Egypt. He was portrayed as a beneficent ruler, good-humoured and pleasure-loving, who spent idyllic hours in his royal barge being rowed across the palace lake by beautiful girls.

But these were interludes in an exceptionally energetic reign marked by a vigorous foreign policy and the completion of not one, but three, massive pyramids. Sneferu was the founder of Egyptian supremacy in **Sinai**, where he gained control over its turquoise and copper mines; he campaigned against the **Libyans**, who inhabited the coastal region west of the Delta, and brought back a celebrated quantity of booty; and he mounted raids against the **Nubians**, returning with 7000 captives and 200,000 head of cattle. This region south of **Aswan** was also a source of granite, and by establishing his dominance there Sneferu made it possible for his successors to work the quarries for the granite that embellished their pyramids and mortuary temples at Giza. As no timber of any quality was grown in Egypt, he greatly expanded commerce with **Lebanon**, despatching a fleet of forty ships which sailed home laden with cedar logs. He used them not only to build yet more ships and to grace the doors of his royal palace, but also for making the sledges, levers and supports used in building the first true **pyramids** – expressions of the increasingly important Heliopolitan sun cult.

Conquest, trade and the wealth of Egypt put unprecedented resources at his command. Making use of a greater quantity of stone than any other Old Kingdom ruler, he builds the **first true pyramids**.

c.2589–c.2566 BC Cheops (the Greek version of **Khufu**), the son of Sneferu by Hetepheres, comes to the throne in middle age yet survives long enough to build the largest and most perfect of all Egyptian pyramids, the **Great Pyramid** at Giza.

Building the Great Pyramid

The **Great Pyramid** containing the tomb of Cheops is the second most massive structure ever built by man (the stepped pyramid at Cholula in Mexico, built nearly four thousand years later and largely destroyed by the Spaniards, was greater in volume by a fifth). Yet the precision of its construction, observed the Egyptologist Flinders Petrie, was 'equal to an optician's work of the present day'.

In the 5th century BC the Greek historian Herodotus was told by Egyptian priests that Cheops' pyramid had taken 20 years to build with 100,000 men working three-month shifts. These figures may not be far off the mark, though modern calculations suggest that only about 4000 men would have been needed to work on the pyramid itself – more would merely have got in the way – and that these would have been highly skilled stone-cutters, masons, surveyors and so on, employed year-round. Others would have worked in the quarries, but the greatest number would have been unskilled labourers, peasants drawn from the land during the idle months of the inundation, and employed in ancilliary activities such as dragging blocks to the site. In the tradition handed down to Herodotus, Cheops was portrayed as an oppressive tyrant who had compelled his subjects to labour as slaves, but in fact the Egyptian economy was never based on slave labour, and indeed graffiti found at the Great Pyramid expresses the workers' delight in participating in the extraordinary enterprise.

The smooth-sided Pyramid of Chephren, here viewed from atop the yet larger Pyramid of Cheops, symbolized the ascending sun

c.2566–c.2558 BC Cheops' son **Djedefra** is the first to incorporate the name **Ra** into his own, and also to use the epithet 'son of the god Ra'. This perhaps indicates his reliance on the growing priestly power of the sun cult at Heliopolis to ensure his succession to the throne in the face of factionalism within the royal family. He begins a pyramid at **Abu Rawash** to the north of Giza, but dies long before it is completed.

c.2558–c.2532 BC **Chephren** (Greek for **Khafra**), another of Cheops' sons, builds a pyramid that rivals his father's. Within the area of his funerary complex he orders a rocky outcrop to be carved into the **Sphinx**, the largest statue of the ancient world – its body the protective lion of sacred places, its face most likely meant to represent Chephren as the sun god. During his reign and that of his son Mycerinus, **Old Kingdom sculpture** reaches its apogee.

c.2532–c.2503 BC Mycerinus (Greek for **Menkaura**), the son of Chephren, builds a much smaller pyramid on the Giza plateau, covering less than a quarter of the area of the Great Pyramid but making extensive use of **red granite** brought from Aswan, more expensive and enduring than limestone.

MICHAEL HAAG

The falcon god Horus embraces Chephren's head with his wings, granting him divine authority and protection

Egyptian religious belief

An ever-present characteristic of ancient Egyptian religion was its readiness to hold a variety of beliefs simultaneously, though the emphasis might change from period to period. There were deities in wholly animal or human form, others with animal heads and human bodies, while cosmic phenomena such as the stars and sun could be deities also. Moreover they might combine, be elaborated or borrow attributes from one another; they were like energy fields that could operate independently or together. Unlike modern conceptions of an otherworldly god, they manifested themselves in plants, animals, cult objects, statues and in the king himself.

Yet for all their permutations and bewildering variety, religious names and images can be traced from the beginnings of ancient Egyptian history to its end. They were the expression of an unbroken cultural identity whose most fundamental belief was that behind the apparent flux of this world, behind birth, decay and death, there was a changeless essence, an eternal blessedness, for which all Egyptians longed.

Another difference from modern belief systems is that one belief did not exclude the others; the Egyptians spoke of their gods as numbering in the millions and never attempted to catalogue them all. Some were associated with the king and state, their worship guarded from profane eyes by the priesthoods; others were associated with magical medicine and the multitudinous needs of daily life and were venerated by the population at large; and the power of some, like the cult of the ancient fertility god Osiris, ultimately permeated all levels of society.

c.2503–c.2498 BC The brief reign of **Shepseskaf** provides more evidence of factionalism within the royal family. Rejecting the increasing power of the priesthood of Ra, which has been encroaching on the authority and independence of the throne, he does not incorporate Ra in his name, nor does he build a pyramid, but a massive sarcophagus-shaped mastaba at Saqqara. But another brief reign by a king of unknown name terminates the dynasty, ending resistance to the sun cult.

Fifth Dynasty (c.2494–c.2345 BC)

c.2494–c.2487 BC Userkaf, who is most likely descended from Cheops through a secondary line and has been high priest at Heliopolis, **establishes the cult of Ra as the state religion** when he ascends the throne. He builds a small pyramid to serve as his tomb, but more important is his **sun temple**, an innovation adopted by five of his six successors.

c.2421–c.2414 BC Menkauhor, the seventh king of the Fifth Dynasty, is the last to build a sun temple, though the supreme position of Ra remains unaffected. Egypt loses control of Nubia around now, though trade continues.

c.2414–c.2375 BC A trading expedition is sent to Punt (modern Eritrea or perhaps Somalia) during the reign of **Djedkara**, whose vizier is **Ptah-Hotep**.

c.2375–c.2345 BC The **cult of Osiris** intrudes on that of Ra in the **Pyramid Texts** of **Unas**. From now on the belief becomes widespread that by appealing to Osiris the dead can enter the afterlife, corresponding to a lessening of the elite's dependence on the king. Reliefs along the causeway leading to Unas' pyramid show the emaciated victims of famine.

Sixth Dynasty (c.2345–c.2181 BC)

c.2321–c.2287 BC Pepy I, the third king of his dynasty, marries two sisters who are – significantly – not of royal birth but are the daughters of a hereditary official at

> " If you are a wise man, establish a home and love your wife. Fill her belly, clothe her back. Ointment is a good remedy for her limbs. Make her happy as long as you live. She is a good field to her master. "
>
> *The Wisdom Book of Ptah-Hotep*

The worldly wisdom and delights of Ptah-Hotep

Ptah-Hotep, a vizier of the Fifth Dynasty, would be celebrated in ages to come for his **wisdom text**, a set of instructions addressed to his son. These urged him to show obedience and respect for his superiors, to cultivate tolerance towards his inferiors and quickness when dealing with equals, never to shirk endeavour, always to seek learning and above all to master the art of eloquence. The text does not concern itself with spiritual values either as a code for this life or as a means of reaching the next; it is a handbook for seeking worldly advantage issued by a civil servant of one generation to the next.

For a notable like Ptah-Hotep, Egypt was already a paradise, and when he entered the life to come he expected more of the same. His mastaba at Saqqara is covered with exquisitely carved and coloured murals in raised relief (a painstaking technique particularly associated with the Old Kingdom), presenting a complete programme for his *ka*'s enjoyment in the afterlife. An inscription describes Ptah-Hotep 'witnessing all the pleasant activities that take place in the whole country', and there are scenes of children running, wrestling and vaulting over one another, of a cow giving birth assisted by a peasant, of grapes being cultivated and made into wine, of fishing in the marshes. On an adjoining wall Ptah-Hotep is shown preparing for the day-to-day grind – a manicurist at his hands, a pedicurist at his feet, musicians entertaining him, greyhounds beneath his chair and a pet monkey held by his valet. Neither king nor god are depicted, nor are there scenes of judgement or expressions of doubt. It is the tomb of a perfectly contented civil servant.

Abydos. This indicated that it is now important for the Crown to gain the support of the powerful provincial nobility.

For the first time Egypt faces **serious threats from abroad**, with incursions at its northeast frontier requiring several campaigns and a large army to repel.

'Memphis' and 'Egypt'

The Egyptians first called their capital **Ineb-hedj**, meaning 'White Wall', suggesting that it began as a fortress from where Menes controlled the land and water routes between Upper and Lower Egypt; indeed during the Middle Kingdom the city was called **Ankh-tawy**, 'That which Binds the Two Lands'.

Memphis was the later Greek name for the city, derived from the Egyptian 'Mennufer' after a nearby pyramid, **Men-nefru-Mire**, 'The Beauty of King Mire Remains' – 'Mire' being another name of the Sixth Dynasty king Pepy I. Ptah was the god of Memphis, and it is likely that the New Kingdom 'Temple of the Ka of Ptah', **Hikuptah**, which gave its name to a neighbourhood of the city, also supplied the Greeks with their name for the entire country, **Aigyptos**, from which comes our word 'Egypt'.

c.2287–c.2278 BC Relations with Nubia are fruitful during the reign of **Merenra**, a son of Pepy, who has five navigable channels cut in the First Cataract to permit his ships to push as far south as the Second Cataract. This enables the exchange of oil, honey, faience and clothing for incense, ebony, leopard skins, elephant tusks and boomerangs.

c.2278–c.2184 BC **Pepy II**, another son of Pepy I, succeeds his brother at the age of 6 and lives to be 100. Towards the latter part of his reign the authority of kingship

> The wrongdoer is everywhere. There is no man of yesterday. A man goes out to plough with his shield. A man smites his brother, his mother's son. Men sit in the bushes until the benighted traveller comes, in order to plunder his load. The robber is a possessor of riches.
>
> Ipuwer, *Admonitions of a Sage*

is undermined by the Crown's cumulative loss of revenue from temple lands, reverses in trade and the passing of power to hereditary and increasingly autonomous provincial officials. There are **incursions of Asiatics**, disturbances in **Nubia** and a rising sense of insecurity.

c.2184–c.2181 BC A sign that **dynastic infighting** has thrown the succession into confusion is the rare elevation of a queen, **Nitocris** (Greek for **Nitiqret**), to the throne.

Bankruptcy and climate change

For a long time the rulers of the Old Kingdom had been distributing their resources for diminishing returns. Their costly building works and the endowments necessary to service them produced no income for themselves, but they generated an expanded bureaucracy, a proliferation of priesthoods and an increasingly independent nobility which led ultimately to self-interested and regional centres of power.

To ensure loyalty, kings fell into a vicious circle: they were forced to make economic concessions which usually took the form of exempting temples, villages, towns and entire districts from yielding up a share of their produce and labour to the Crown. Pepy II, in one such decree, promised that should ever the exemption be revoked by any royal official in the course of eternity, then he shall be 'cursed with the word "treason"' – a far cry from the days when Djoser commanded the presence and loyalty of his provincial priests at his Heb Sed ceremony. The Crown's monopoly in trade also suffered sudden blows when invaders overran both Byblos and Nubia, sweeping Egypt out of their marketplaces.

Yet it is far from certain that these reasons alone could account for the sudden and complete collapse of central authority that came shortly after Pepy II's death. Climate change may have been the determining factor, a series of low Nile floods ending the long process of desertification across the whole of northern Africa.

c.2181–c.2160 BC The **Seventh** and **Eighth Dynasties** span only 21 years and are crowded with 17 ephemeral kings.

A long series of **low Nile floods** contributes decisively to Egypt's problems. Poverty grows, famine is common, disease is rife and the death rate soars. Finally **central authority collapses** altogether, and a fragmented Egypt subsides into provincial rule.

2: The rise and fall of the Middle Kingdom

c.2160–c.1550 BC

T he **First Intermediate Period**, which followed the collapse of the Old Kingdom, used to be described as a time of anarchy, but more careful investigation has shown that it was a time of remarkable vitality. Indeed the rise of the **Middle Kingdom** gives proof of Egypt's ability to respond to crisis and remake itself, and though many of its monuments have disappeared or have been modified and incorporated into later structures, the great achievement of the Middle Kingdom was the development of a more humanized culture. During the **Second Intermediate Period** Egypt again demonstrated its resilience, this time overcoming disintegration through its vehement rejection of unwanted foreign influence – a recurring theme in Egyptian history.

The First Intermediate Period (Ninth and Tenth Dynasties at Herakleopolis, Eleventh Dynasty at Thebes): c.2160–c.2055 BC

The failure of the Old Kingdom marked the beginning of that trouble-filled century or so known as the First Intermediate Period. Where once there had been an established order in which the king had been a crucial figure, now even the pyramids were robbed, while low Nile floods desiccated the Delta marshlands and brought famine to Upper Egypt. Old certainties were overturned, and the Egyptians' sense of assurance in the cosmic scheme was gone. A vein of pessimism and doubt was introduced into expectations both of this life and the next.

Yet this period of crisis was also a time of resourcefulness and innovation. In the absence of a god-king, a new spirit of self-reliance took hold among ordinary people, as expressed by the phrase that appears in one ancient text: 'He spoke with his own mouth and acted with his own arm.' A vigorous **popular culture** grew up in the provincial towns where something like a mass market emerged, so that technology such as the potter's wheel, although introduced during the Fifth Dynasty, now came into widespread use. Similarly, ethical ideas and religious beliefs reflected the demands and aspirations of a more broadly based society. The **nomarchs** – that is, the governors of regions (nomes) – welded their authority to that of the priesthood and the cults in order to give it moral effect, but they also justified to the populace the practical benefits of their rule while emphasizing justice and allowing that every man had the right to be heard. Though there had been collapse at the centre, and no spectacular monuments were built until the Middle Kingdom, everyday life in provincial Egypt became more culturally complex and in many cases more prosperous.

During the First Intermediate Period, Egypt's provinces were organized around two new dynastic centres: **Herakleopolis**, just south of the Fayyum, and **Thebes** on the east bank of the Nile in Upper Egypt. From about 2160 BC, the Herakleopolitan kings of the Ninth and Tenth Dynasties held sway over the Delta and the lower stretch of the Nile Valley as far upriver as Abydos. They saw themselves as the successors of the Old Kingdom (whose archives, and the literate bureaucracy of Memphis, they had inherited), and from a central geographical position they ruled over the most cultured, populous and productive parts of the country. But the weakness of the Herakleopolitan kingdom was that it was predominantly a confederacy of alliances whose cohesion depended on bonds of friendship, kinship and marriage with provincial aristocrats. Instead, around 2125 BC the nomarchs of what was then the minor provincial town of Thebes transformed themselves into the Eleventh Dynasty, which – after establishing its centralized authority over Upper Egypt – launched the struggle against Herakleopolis that would reunify the entire country and usher in the Middle Kingdom.

c.2160 BC **Khety**, perhaps a hereditary nomarch (governor) under the Old Kingdom, becomes the first king of the **Ninth Dynasty** and makes **Herakleopolis** his royal capital. At first the dynasty claims to rule over the whole of Egypt, but within a few decades a separate line of rulers emerges at Thebes in Upper Egypt. The Herakleopolitans take military action against the Asiatics in the Delta and exert a degree of authority over the Nile Valley as far south as Abydos, but their kingdom and that of their **Tenth Dynasty** successors is more in the nature of a confederation built on provincial alliances and is never highly centralized.

c.2125 BC In the south of the country **Intef the Great**, who combines the positions of nomarch and overseer of priests at Thebes, proclaims himself hereditary prince and overlord of Upper Egypt, though he does not claim to be king. Some generations later, a tradition arises among Intef's descendants that a man they call **Tepy-a**, literally 'the ancestor', and otherwise known as **Mentuhotep I**, rules as king at this time, though in reality he is no more than a posthumous fiction.

A new ethos for a troubled age

All the known literature of the First Intermediate Period springs from the Herakleopolitan kingdom, which inherited the archives and literate elite of Memphis. Comparisons with the Old Kingdom came naturally but were often despairing. One text, the *Song of the Blind Harper*, tells how the old tombs were abandoned by the mortuary priests: 'Their walls are broken apart, and their places are no more, as though they had never been.' For many writers there was a loss of faith, and suicide even became a literary theme. Others turned to hedonism: 'Follow your desire as long as you shall live. Fulfil your needs upon earth after the command of your heart. Behold, it is not given to a man to take his property with him. Behold, there is not one who departs who comes back again!'

Many others held to a belief in an afterlife but adapted the old royal rituals to themselves as commoners – for example inscribing portions of the Pyramid Texts on their coffins so that they too would achieve deification at death by becoming an Osiris. Still others emphasized that anyone could join Osiris by actively pursuing *maat* – truth, justice, righteousness – in the present life. The *Tale of the Eloquent Peasant* instructs: 'Maat lasts unto eternity; it goes down into the necropolis with him who does it. When he is buried and interred, his name is not wiped out upon earth, but he is remembered for goodness. That is a principle of the word of god.' This was a visionary view born out of the perception of fragility and vulnerability that pervaded the First Intermediate Period, but it did not last beyond the Middle Kingdom.

c.2125–c.2112 BC Intef I, later recorded as the son of 'Mentuhotep I', becomes the first king of the **Eleventh Dynasty**. He makes the small town of **Thebes** his capital and initiates the identification of his family's fortunes with a local warrior god, the falcon-headed **Mont**. In this and in other ways he roots his dynasty in local tradition and society. Intef consolidates his authority in Upper Egypt by defeating **Ankhtifi**, the nomarch of Edfu and Hierakonpolis, in battle.

c.2112–c.2063 BC **Intef II**, the brother of Intef I, begins several decades of intermittent war with the Herakleopolitan kings by capturing Abydos, but when he carries his attack further north he is checked at Assiut. He assumes the title 'son of Ra', inaugurates the policy of a royal presence

Ankhtifi and the politics of crisis

Ankhtifi was one of many free-booting provincial magnates loosely in alliance with the Tenth Dynasty kings at Herakleopolis. As overseer of priests and nomarch, he held the top religious and secular positions at Hierakonpolis, from where the kings of a united Egypt had emerged a thousand years before.

Ankhtifi was also invited to take up the same positions at neighbouring Edfu – not by the king of Herakleopolis, however, but by no less a figure than **Horus**, Edfu's resident god. He explains as much in a long autobiographical inscription in his tomb: 'Horus fetched me to the nome of Edfu to re-establish prosperity, health and life.' Tellingly, Ankhtifi mentions King Neferkara only once in his inscription, and then only as if Ankhtifi is invoking a blessing upon him: 'May Horus grant a good Nile flood to his son Neferkara.' This allusion to poor inundations was a common theme during the First Intermediate Period, and Ankhtifi goes on to describe conditions in Upper Egypt: 'The entire south died of hunger, every man devouring his own children.' But this description is an exaggeration, typical of the way rulers justified their necessity by arguing that the common man would be unable to cope with life's hazards if left to his own devices, and that it is in his own interests to bow to authority. As Ankhtifi says, 'On whomever I laid my hand, no harm could approach him, because my reasoning was so expert and my plans were so excellent. But every ignorant person, every wretch who opposed me, I retaliated against him for his deeds.' Ankhtifi exerted his authority as far south as the First Cataract and harried Thebes; in the end, though, it was the Intefs who were more successful in making a necessity of their rule.

> " This land is helter-skelter, and no one knows the result. That which never happened has happened. Men take up weapons of warfare, so that the land lives in confusion. I show you the son as a foe, the brother as an enemy, and a man killing his own father. Every mouth is full of 'Love me!', and everything good has disappeared. Men take a man's property away from him, and it is given to him who is from outside. It is the paupers who eat the offering bread, while the servants jubilate. The land is completely perished, so that no remainder exists. The king has been taken away by poor men. Behold, he who was buried as a divine falcon is now on a mere bier; what the pyramid hid has become empty. "
>
> *Prophecy of Neferti*

at sanctuaries throughout the country by contributing to the temple of Karnak at Thebes and building chapels at Aswan, and he works to impose direct centralized rule throughout his territories. He is succeeded by **Intef III**.

The Middle Kingdom (Eleventh to Fourteenth Dynasties) c.2055–c.1650 BC

The Middle Kingdom is conventionally dated from midway through the Eleventh Dynasty when **Mentuhotep II** ascended the throne at Thebes, but it was another thirty years before he defeated the parallel Tenth Dynasty at Hierakleopolis and reunified Egypt under his rule, then personally led a military campaign to regain control over gold-rich Lower Nubia. Soon Egypt was enjoying renewed prosperity and prestige, and its fleets and caravans were dominating the trade routes of the Near East and the Eastern Mediterranean. Flush with surpluses, Mentuhotep saw to it that the old quarries were reopened, and he inaugurated a new era of great building works. During his reign Egypt belatedly entered the **Bronze Age**, too – though rather than acquire the metallurgical expertise necessary for domestic production, it preferred to buy in from the Near East a ready-made alloy of tin and copper, harder than copper alone.

Outstanding among Mentuhotep's building works was his mausoleum opposite Thebes at **Deir el Bahri**, whose superimposed pyramid harked back to the god-king cult of the Old Kingdom, but which in other features stressed the worship of Osiris – whose cult appealed to the shared humanity of kings and subjects alike. In this, it expressed the poles between which the Middle Kingdom would oscillate: on the one hand the desire to return to the stability, certainty and authority of the Old Kingdom, on the other the emergence of the individual and a sense that all Egyptians, both kings and commoners, shared a view of life that was on a more human scale.

Ammenemes I, the founder of the Twelfth Dynasty, moved his administrative capital from Thebes to a new site in the Fayyum near Lisht and called it 'Amenemhat-itj-tawy' ('Ammenemes is S'izer of the Two Lands'), or, more simply, **Itjtawy**. Near the junction of Upper and Lower Egypt and only twenty miles south of the still thriving city of Memphis, from here he could exert centralized control over the whole of the country in the manner of the Old Kingdom. Indeed one of Ammenemes' names meant 'the Repeating of Births' – that is, 'renaissance' – indicating his intention of marking a new era by recalling old glories. The steady policy of the Twelfth Dynasty rulers was to promote the cult of the king through art and architecture, including the building of pyramids in the Fayyum and at Dahshur, and to limit the independence of the nomarchs whose power they ultimately succeeded in breaking altogether. They also undertook Egypt's first centrally directed **land reclamation** and **irrigation** scheme, developing the Fayyum into one of the most productive regions in the country.

Such was the success of administrative reform that the kings of the Thirteenth Dynasty were hardly more than functionaries and the country was run by a frictionless bureaucracy. Complacency and unresponsiveness to change might well have been the undoing of the Middle Kingdom, though once again there is evidence of serious ecological problems. There seem to have been generally higher Niles, but they were accompanied by wildly erratic annual inundations. The result must have been immensely destructive to agriculture, whose organization was the basis of Egyptian wealth.

MICHAEL HAAG

Ivory from Nubia entered Egypt through Aswan, where an elephant features among the hieroglyphs in this Middle Kingdom tomb

c.2055–c.2004 BC **Mentuhotep II**, probably the son of Intef III, continues the Eleventh Dynasty at Thebes, but by conquering the Herakleopolitan kingdom and reuniting the whole country he inaugurates what Egyptologists call the **Middle Kingdom**. To gain control over Nubia's resources, particularly its gold, he campaigns as far as the Second Cataract. He also sends a trading expedition to Lebanon for cedarwood, revives the caravan route between the Nile Valley and the Red Sea, and reopens the quarries of the Eastern Desert to obtain material for his considerable building works in Thebes and elsewhere in Egypt.

c.2041 BC Mentuhotep II resumes the war against **Herakleopolis**, which with the capture of Assiut enters its final phase.

c.2025 BC **Merykara**, the penultimate king of the Tenth Dynasty at Herakleopolis, dies before Mentuhotep II reaches the city, which falls a few months later and is sacked, though some resistance remains in Lower Egypt.

c.2016 BC Mentuhotep II subdues the whole of Lower Egypt and assumes the title of **'Uniter of the Two Lands'**. But though the nomarchs of Lower Egypt and along the middle stretch of the Nile Valley submit to Mentuhotep, they remain entrenched in their centres of local power. He resurrects the cult of divine king, and to perpetuate his worship builds an impressive terraced **mausoleum** topped by a pyramid on the west bank of the Nile opposite Thebes, where Osiris is also venerated.

c.2004–c.1992 BC **Mentuhotep III** continues with the building, commercial, mining and quarrying projects of his father. His reign is marked by architectural innovations including the first use of temple pylons, and finely worked raised relief sculpture is revived. He sends a trading expedition to the land of Punt to obtain incense, and he attempts to protect Egypt's border against Asiatic incursions by constructing fortifications in the eastern Delta.

> Mentuhotep II's tomb at Deir el Bahri is a fair monument for the Middle Kingdom itself: preserving the most potent symbolism of the past, but transmuting it subtly, with great elegance and sense of form into something new. The pyramid which it is supposed rose above Mentuhotep's burial place links it with the monuments of the Old Kingdom. The immense brick terraced platform on which it stood was a microcosm of Egypt, as much as the space enclosed by the walls of Djoser's monument at Saqqara, yet less assertive, more integrated with the landscape in which it was set.
>
> Michael Rice, *Egypt's Legacy* (1997)

c.1992–c.1985 BC The reign of **Mentuhotep IV** is recorded as a time of disorder throughout Egypt, perhaps accompanied by Bedouin incursions. Civil war breaks out, though the details are not certain.

Twelfth Dynasty (c.1985–c.1773 BC)

c.1985–c.1956 BC The difficulties during the reign of Mentuhotep IV bring his vizier to the throne as **Ammenemes I**. He transfers his administrative capital to a new site called **Itjtawy** in the Fayyum in order to exercise strategic control over both Upper and Lower Egypt, and from where he leads the first **Middle Kingdom campaign** into the Near East to counter the Asiatic threat. Thebes remains important, however: 'Ammenemes' is the Greek version of the Egyptian *Amenemhat*, meaning 'Amun is pre-eminent' – an early reference to the local Theban deity who, in combination with Ra, will become the great imperial god of the New Kingdom.

Previously only kings had identified with Osiris, god of the underworld, but during the First Intermediate Period his cult was adopted by ordinary people

The Murder of Ammenemes

The death of Ammenemes inspired two classic Middle Kingdom literary works that were studied and copied by Egyptian schoolboys for hundreds of years to come. In the ***Instruction of Ammenemes***, the king appears to his son Sesostris in a dream and relates how he was attacked by the palace guard: 'It was after supper when night was come, I took an hour of repose, lying upon my bed. All of a sudden weapons were brandished, and I awoke to fight. But no one is strong at night. No one can fight alone.' With a winning touch of vulnerability, he warns his son of the heavy burdens of kingship, saying: 'No man has adherents on the day of distress.'

In ***The Story of Sinuhe***, the tale is worked out differently. A secret message is sent to Sesostris, who is away campaigning in Libya, telling him of his father's murder and urging his immediate return to Itjtawy. The message is overheard by Sinuhe, a young court official, who flees to the desert and dwells among the Bedouin, fearful that he will be drawn into the intrigues of rival claimants to the throne. After becoming the Bedouins' chieftain, further travels bring Sinuhe to Byblos, where he marries the local prince's daughter, is granted land and becomes extremely wealthy. But in his old age Sinuhe longs to return to Egypt and to be buried there according to the religion of his people. Sesostris welcomes him, clears him of any wrongdoing, and honours Sinuhe with a magnificent tomb.

Quite apart from their appealing drama and adventure, these stories played upon Egyptians' attachment to tradition, while skilfully justifying Sesostris' right to rule and portraying him as a wise and benevolent king.

Using recycled Old Kingdom building blocks, Ammenemes constructs his pyramid in the Fayyum at **Lisht**. His murder is followed by a dispute over the succession of his son **Sesostris**.

c.1956–c.1911 BC An army headed by **Sesostris I** (Greek for Senusret I) turns to **Nubia**, where Egyptian policy changes from sporadic trading and quarrying ventures to a strategy of conquest and colonization. He makes **Lower Nubia** a province of Egypt, so that Buhen just north of the Second Cataract marks Egypt's new southern border. **Upper Nubia** (Kush) is exploited for its gold, copper, granite, turquoise and amethyst, and trade with the Near East is expanded.

Nubia

The ancient land of Nubia extended from the First to the Fourth Cataracts of the Nile, a distance of about 500 miles as the crow flies. The Second Cataract, now the border between Egypt and Sudan, marked the divide between Lower and Upper Nubia. Today, all of **Lower Nubia** lies within Egypt and has been completely submerged beneath the waters of Lake Nasser, which was created by the completion of the High Dam at Aswan in the 1960s. **Upper Nubia**, known to the ancient Egyptians as **Kush**, today lies in Sudan. In recent years, Lake Nasser has also backed up into Sudan – where it has drowned a third of Upper Nubia too.

Effectively Nubia has ceased to exist, but its sacrifice to the larger needs of Egypt is an age-old story: even during the Old Kingdom, Egyptians looked down on the Nubians as their poor relations and regarded the country as theirs to exploit by right. Desert sands and limestone outcrops pressed closely upon the Nile in Nubia, so that it lacked Egypt's almost continuous ribbons of cultivable land, while its population, small and scattered, eked out an existence in fertile pockets. But Nubia was rich in other resources, its name itself deriving from the ancient Egyptian *nbw*, meaning gold. Indeed, it was as a source of gold that Nubia was attractive to the Egyptians; and also for its skilled bowmen and other military recruits; for its minerals, wood, incense, cattle, slaves and hard building stone; and because it was an avenue of African trade. These were the reasons why Middle Kingdom rulers imposed direct military control as far south as the Second Cataract, and why for a thousand years to come their New Kingdom, Ptolemaic and Roman successors would come to Nubia in their turn.

Sesostris dedicates a chapel to Amun at **Karnak**, and he asserts his royal authority and undermines provincial power bases through a prodigious **building programme**, erecting and enlarging temples throughout Egypt, which involves huge quarrying operations in the Eastern Desert and Sinai. His pyramid and funerary complex at **Lisht** are deliberate revivals of Old Kingdom style.

ANCIENT EGYPT PL

The goddess Maat, with her ostrich feather head-dress, symbolized truth, justice and balance – ideals pursued by both individuals and the state

The Fayyum land reclamation and irrigation scheme

Today's Lake Qarun occupies a small portion of the Fayyum, but once it covered a far greater area and was fed, as now, by the Bahr Yusef, which departs from the Nile at Deirut between Minya and Assiut. Before Middle Kingdom times, the lake was probably more like swamp and marshland, abundant in bird and animal life, particularly crocodiles. But though the Fayyum provided a rich hunting ground, the extent of the lake limited its agricultural possibilities and therefore the size of population it could support. The hydrological scheme which Sesostris II initiated – or to which he significantly contributed, if the project began with Ammenemes I as some authorities claim – involved redirecting the waters of the Bahr Yusef into a network of irrigation canals. Denied a direct water supply, the surface area of the lake was reduced by evaporation, while the newly exposed land, irrigated by the canals, increased the cultivable area of the Fayyum by four-and-a-half times, which in turn provided a livelihood for a population six times larger than before.

c.1911–c.1877 BC Ammenemes II extends Egypt's international influence through the peaceful growth in trade with Nubia, Syria, Lebanon, Mesopotamia and the Aegean. One of his names is 'He Who Takes Pleasure in Maat', *maat* meaning justice or truth. This expression of the king's desire to render *maat* to men and gods is a motif that recurs in royal names throughout the Middle Kingdom. He builds his pyramid at **Dahshur**, near those of the Fourth Dynasty king Sneferu.

c.1877–c.1870 BC Continuing the pacific foreign policy of his predecessor, **Sesostris II** concentrates on improving agricultural and economic conditions in Egypt. He inaugurates the **Fayyum land reclamation and irrigation scheme**, the first great hydrological project in Egypt, linking the 'oasis' with the Bahr Yusef, a branch of the Nile, and builds his pyramid nearby at **Lahun**.

c.1870–c.1831 BC Statues of **Sesostris III** show a man with downturned mouth, heavy-lidded eyes and careworn features, perhaps meant to illustrate the burdens of kingship – though because the Middle Kingdom is also a time of naturalistic portraiture, he is immediately recognizable by his large, out-turned ears.

Statues of Sesostris III are among the most realistic royal portraits ever made and probably represent the king's actual features

The king establishes a sizeable **standing army** and campaigns in Palestine, not to conquer but to impress Egyptian influence there, and in Nubia he presses the frontier further south below the Second Cataract.

In Egypt, Sesostris builds a pyramid at **Dahshur** and removes one of the greatest threats to kingly power by curtailing the power of the hereditary provincial nobility as well as abolishing the ancient rights and privileges of the nomarchs. In their place he creates a centralized bureaucracy, which throughout the Middle Kingdom will continue to run the country under its own momentum.

c.1831–c.1786 BC Ammenemes III completes the **Fayyum irrigation scheme**, but it is dependent on the annual level of the Nile's inundations, which fluctuate wildly during his reign. Nevertheless his considerable building, quarrying and mining activity testifies to Egypt's continuing prosperity. Ammenemes builds two pyramids, one at **Dahshur**, the **other** at Hawara in the Fayyum – where the latter's gigantic funerary complex later becomes

> " I have seen this building, and it is beyond my power to describe ... The pyramids, too, are astonishing structures ... but the labyrinth surpasses them ... The underground rooms I can speak of only from report, because the Egyptians in charge refused to let me see them, as they contain the tombs of the kings who built the labyrinth, and also the tombs of the sacred crocodiles. The upper rooms, on the contrary, I did actually see, and it is hard to believe that they are the work of men; the baffling and intricate passages from room to room and from court to court were an endless wonder to me, as we passed from courtyard into rooms, from rooms into galleries, from galleries into more rooms, and thence into yet more courtyards. "
>
> Herodotus, *Histories*, 5th century BC

famous as the **Labyrinth** for its maze of chambers and corridors.

c.1786–c.1777 BC Ammenemes IV proves an ineffectual king, and Egypt's power and prestige suffers abroad.

c.1777–c.1773 BC Named after Sobek, the crocodile god of the Fayyum, **Sobekneferu** adopts the title of king (the first woman to do so), perhaps after ousting her brother-husband Ammenemes IV. She bolsters her position by deifying her father, **Ammenemes III**, whose cult continues in the Fayyum for another 2000 years, and she contributes to his Labyrinth. But the unusual accession of a woman to the throne and her brief reign suggest dynastic feuds, perhaps to do with the continuing erratic levels of the Nile and their disruptive effect on agricultural life.

c.1773–c.1650 BC A number of kings of the **Thirteenth Dynasty** ruling from Itjtawy bear the name 'Sobek', after the crocodile god to whom they are particularly devoted. Possibly succession to the throne is circulated among leading families, for in all there are about seventy kings whose average reign is two years, and in reality Egypt's affairs are run by viziers.

At first the **arts**, particularly literature, flourish, and while grandiose royal building schemes decline there is an increase in **private monuments**, suggesting a sharing of prosperity.

After about 1720 BC central authority weakens: Egypt begins to lose control over **Lower Nubia**, and the eastern Delta is heavily settled by Asiatics whose city of **Avaris** grows increasingly rich and powerful.

The records for this time are confusing, so that some Egyptologists think that contemporary with the Thirteenth Dynasty there is also a **Fourteenth Dynasty** with its capital at **Xois** in the central Delta, while some place it at Avaris – and others dispute its very existence. But certainly by about 1650 BC centralized rule from Itjtawy entirely **breaks down**, and the Middle Kingdom comes to an end.

The Second Intermediate Period (Fifteenth to Seventeenth Dynasties) c.1650–c.1550 BC

The traditional Egyptian explanation for the collapse of the Middle Kingdom, at least as expressed by Manetho 1400 years later, was the invasion by a foreign people, the **Hyksos**, who established their capital at Avaris in the Delta, and whose subjugation of the country and demands for tribute were frequently remembered as a national humiliation.

Though long accepted by Egyptologists, Manetho's story is now seen as an exaggeration – to say the least – and has been overturned by recent research. In fact the inhabitants of Avaris, whom the Egyptians called *Aamu*, their term for Near Eastern peoples and whom Egyptologists refer to as 'Asiatics', were probably never an invading force but instead had settled peacefully in the Delta over time. Some were captives brought back from foreign campaigns, while others were traders and merchants who saw opportunities in developing commercial links between Egypt and the Levant. Indeed the archeological evidence at Avaris suggests that the population was basically Egyptian but received influxes of immigrants from Palestine, Lebanon, Syria and Cyprus, whose prosperous elite married local women.

Who, then, were the Hyksos? The name derives from the Egyptian *hekau khasut*, 'rulers of foreign (literally, "mountainous") countries', and was applied only to the rulers of the Asiatics. In other words a ruling caste from the hill country of the Near East imposed itself on the Aamu and others of Avaris, but they did not come to Egypt as conquerors. Rather, as central rule from Itjtawy collapsed for internal or ecological reasons, Avaris simply filled the power vacuum. For the most part Hyksos rule was pacific; neither the

Hyksos kings nor the Asiatics of Avaris and elsewhere in the Delta were much interested in Upper Egypt (from which they were content to receive tribute), and instead they preferred to look outwards to their ancestral lands in the Levant.

Hyksos contact with the Near East and the Eastern Mediterranean brought many innovations to Egypt, among them the vertical loom and an improved potter's wheel, new vegetable and fruit crops and also hump-backed cattle (*zebu*), new musical instruments and dances, the composite bow, the horse and chariot, and metallurgical expertise which allowed bronze to be manufactured locally rather than having to rely on ready-alloyed imports. By the end of the Second Intermediate Period and thanks to the Hyksos, Egypt was on a technological par with the wider world.

The Hyksos kingdom included the entire Delta and also the lower Nile Valley as far south as present-day Mallawi, and it also maintained communications and trade with its ally Nubia, now entirely in the hands of the kings of Kush, via routes through the Western Desert oases. Contemporaneous with the Hyksos **Fifteenth Dynasty** at Avaris were the **Sixteenth** and **Seventeenth Dynasty** rulers at Thebes. What had formerly been under the central rule of Itjtawy was divided in three. But after nearly a century of peace Thebes resumed the now familiar historical role of Upper Egypt by launching the long struggle that once again would bring unity to the country.

c.1650–c.1550 BC From **Avaris**, their walled capital in the eastern Delta, the **Hyksos** kings of the **Fifteenth Dynasty** assert their claim to Upper and Lower Egypt, but in reality their border lies just north of **Assiut**. Further south, they tolerate local kings by whom they are paid a tribute and who recognize the Hyksos as the pre-eminent rulers throughout the whole of Egypt. The wealth of Avaris derives from **trade** with Palestine, Lebanon, Syria and Cyprus, and its military power from the introduction of the horse and chariot and its superiority in bronze weaponry.

c.1650–c.1580 BC The **Sixteenth Dynasty**, a line of local rulers at **Thebes**, maintains its independence at the price of paying tribute to the Hyksos king in the north.

c.1580–c.1550 BC From **Thebes** the **Seventeenth Dynasty** extends its control over Upper Egypt from the First Cataract to the Hyksos border near Assiut while continuing to pay tribute to the northern kingdom.

Lower Nubia is conquered by peoples from Kerma above the Third Cataract in Upper Nubia (Kush), where they control its quarries, its gold and copper mines, and its control of the desert and river trading routes.

c.1560 BC The Hyksos period reaches its apogee during the reign of **Apepi**, who revives scribal traditions – enabling him to establish an effective bureaucracy to govern his territories from Avaris in the Egyptian mode.

According to a **traditional tale**, Apepi sends an insulting message to the Theban king **Sekenenra**, complaining that the noise from his hippopotamus pool is disturbing his

ANCIENT EGYPT

MEDITERRANEAN SEA

Alexandria • • Xois
Naucratis • • Tanis
Lake Sais • • Pelusium
Mareotis • Bubastis
(Mariut) LOWER EGYPT
Necho's Canal Avaris/
Wadi Bubastis • Pi-Ramesse
Natrun
Heliopolis
Giza • • Babylon SINAI
Saqqara • • Memphis
Dahshur • Lisht •
Lake Qarun Itjtawy •
Fayyum • Meidum Gulf
Hawara • of
• Lahun Suez
Herakleopolis •

Bahariya
Oasis

• Beni Hasan RED
SEA

• Amarna
(Akhetaten)
• El Badari
Farafra
Oasis River Nile
• Akhmin

UPPER EGYPT
Dakhla Abydos • • Coptos
Oasis Naqada •
Hibis • • Thebes
Esna •
Heirakonpolis •
Kharga Edfu •
Oasis
• Kom Ombo

0   100 km Aswan •
First Cataract

N

sleep at Avaris (400 miles away). If Sekenenra offers a pithy reply it has been lost, for at this point the papyrus is torn, but history records that Sekenenra begins the thirty-year struggle to drive the Hyksos kings and their Asiatic followers out of Egypt.

c.1555 BC Sekenenra dies violently from an axe wound to the forehead and a dagger blow to the back of the neck, probably in the heat of battle against the Hyksos.

> For the Second Intermediate Period we lack information about mummification techniques, very few bodies having been preserved. One famous mummy of the late Seventeenth Dynasty, now in the Cairo Museum, is that of King Sekenenra, which exhibits fearful damage to the head inflicted by blows from an axe and other weapons. These combined injuries must have been fatal, although it has been suggested that they were received in two separate attacks, and the assumption has been made that the king died in battle against the Hyksos invaders. While this may well be the correct interpretation, we must bear in mind that the facts tell us only that King Sekenenra died as the result of wounds received from a battle-axe of Asian type. Probably as a consequence of the circumstances of the king's death, the embalming of the corpse seems to have been somewhat hastily carried out. The viscera had been extracted through a cut in the left side of the abdomen and the cavity was filled with linen, but no treatment of the badly damaged head was attempted, the brain having been left in place. Most of the flesh has disappeared from the mummy, leaving a skeleton within a covering of decaying skin.

A.J. Spencer, *Death in Ancient Egypt* (1982)

c.1555–c.1550 BC During the reign of **Kamose**, Sekenenra's successor, Thebes launches campaigns against the Nubians and the Hyksos who are in alliance.

c.1553 BC Kamose **campaigns in Nubia** as far south as the Second Cataract, capturing Buhen from the king of Kerma, before turning his attention northwards to **Avaris**.

c.1551 BC Kamose moves north from Thebes with his army and battle fleet, and to 'prevent there being any enemies in

ANCIENT EGYPT PL

The Hyksos, who originated in the Near East, brought many innovations to Egypt, among them the horse and chariot

my rear' he sends soldiers to **Bahariya oasis** in the Western Desert to cut the lines of communication between the Hyksos and the Nubians. He blockades **Avaris** with his fleet, but Apepi refuses to come out and engage him.

Kamose **dies** the following year and Apepi some time after, and the final phase of the war against the Hyksos will not begin until nearly two decades pass.

3: The New Kingdom

c.1550–c.1069 BC

T he whole of the New Kingdom was marked by constant contact with the peoples of Asia – whether Egypt advanced as conqueror or as a trading power. The rapid increase of wealth that came from Egypt's exploitation of its empire in the Near East and Nubia was accompanied by a rapidly increasing taste for luxury, an architecture of gigantic scale and a culture pervaded by an atmosphere of opulence. When people think of ancient Egypt, they are for the most part thinking of the New Kingdom: it was during this age of unparalleled confidence and prosperity that nearly every familiar great monument of Egyptian antiquity – the Pyramids excepted – was built. This unusually outward-looking era found its spiritual expression in **Amun-Ra**, an increasingly universal deity that absorbed lesser gods into itself and tended towards a kind of solar monotheism. The climax of the New Kingdom came when the religious revolutionary Akhenaten developed an autocratic variation on the solar theology, which when it collapsed also broke the divine mystique of kingship.

The rise to empire and the age of opulence (early Eighteenth Dynasty) c.1550–c.1352 BC

The war against the Hyksos, begun by Sekenenra and carried forward by Kamose, was brought to victory when **Amosis I** captured the Hyksos capital at Avaris. His swift follow-up campaign against Palestine and Syria and his southern campaign into Nubia laid the foundations for the Egyptian empire.

The aim of Egypt's foreign conquests, which reached their greatest extent under the warrior kings **Tuthmosis I** and **Tuthmosis III**, was to gain command over the routes of trade and the sources of raw materials – agriculture, trade and Nubian gold were the basis of Egypt's wealth and power. By the close of **Amenophis III**'s reign, two centuries after the expulsion of the Hyksos, Egypt was wealthier and more powerful than it had ever been. It was also at peace with its neighbours and no longer saw the world beyond its borders as hostile. The country became cosmopolitan in atmosphere, open to foreigners and their cultures. Though Memphis was the seat of government throughout the early Eighteenth Dynasty, its kings had originated at Thebes – a city that they embellished with great monuments and transformed into the most opulent and important in the ancient world.

But if the driving force in this success was the discipline and determination of the royal family, two other institutions became major beneficiaries of the imperial system: the **army** and the **priesthood** of Amun. The empire required a standing army, which if not on active service was kept employed in other ways (on major construction works, for example), while army men and former officers increasingly filled many of the most important positions in the administration. Amun, the local god of Thebes, had grown in prominence with the rising fortunes of the town during the Middle Kingdom, and by the New Kingdom he was grafted onto the solar Ra as Amun-Ra, king of the gods. *Amun* means 'hidden', and being an unseen god he became immanent everywhere – a suitably embracing and universal quality for a cosmopolitan and imperial age. The military conquests in Nubia and the Near East provided endowed lands for supporting Amun's priesthood and for building, enlarging and

> The other priesthoods, desirous of securing for their own perhaps purely local deity a share of the sun god's glory, gradually discovered that their god was but a form and name of Ra; and some of them went so far that their theologizing found practical expression in the god's name. Thus Amun, hitherto an obscure local god of Thebes, who had attained some prominence by the political rise of the city, was from now on a solar god, and was commonly called by his priests Amun-Ra. There were in this movement the beginnings of a tendency towards a pantheistic solar monotheism, which we shall yet trace to its remarkable culmination.
>
> James Henry Breasted, *A History of Egypt* (1905)

maintaining his temples in Egypt. Such, then, was the triumvirate of the early Eighteenth Dynasty – the priesthood, the army and the kingship, each reinforcing one another.

Eighteenth Dynasty (c.1550–c.1295 BC)

c.1550–c.1525 BC The rebirth of Egypt's fortunes under **Amosis I** (Greek for the Egyptian Ahmose I) explains why tradition marks his accession as the start of a new dynasty, though there is no break in the family line. His mother is **Ahhotep** and his father probably Sekenenra or possibly Kamose – all three of whom are full or half-siblings. During the early years of Amosis' reign, while he is still in his minority, real power is in the hands of his mother, who puts down a **rebellion** in Upper Egypt.

c.1532 BC Amosis begins the **final campaign against the Hyksos**, sailing downriver from Thebes during the late summer inundation, bypassing Memphis but capturing **Heliopolis**. In October when the Nile falls and chariots can be deployed, he lays siege to **Avaris** from both land and water. The city surrenders and the Hyksos are driven out of Egypt.

During the following years Amosis asserts Egyptian authority in **Palestine** and **Nubia**.

c.1530–c.1525 BC Amosis devotes the last five years of his reign to a massive **building programme** at the great cult centres of Heliopolis, Memphis, Abydos and Thebes. In particular he ensures closer ties between the royal family and Amun by adding to the temple at **Karnak** and putting

The formidable royal women of Thebes

Brother-sister marriage in ancient Egypt preserved the divine royal blood from contamination, kept wealth and power in the family and cut down the number of potential pretenders to the throne. But the sister-wives of the Eighteenth Dynasty were especially remarkable for their formidable characters and the various ways in which they each advanced the fortunes of their line.

Ahhotep, the sister-wife of Sekenenra, claims the credit for urging him to wage war against the Hyksos. She also held the country together during the minority of their son Amosis, who later hailed her as 'One who cares for Egypt; she has looked after its soldiers; she has pacified Upper Egypt and expelled its rebels.' Amosis then married **Ahmose-Nefertari**, who was probably his mother's daughter and his own full sister, and linked his family more closely to Amun by creating a new priesthood of the god at Karnak and placing her in charge as God's Wife – an inheritable position that carried considerable religious and economic power. Ahmose-Nefertari outlived her brother-husband and continued as God's Wife throughout the reign of their son, Amenophis I; when he died without a male heir, it was most likely Ahmose-Nefertari who ensured the smooth succession of the non-royal Tuthmosis I by marrying him to **Ahmose**, who was probably her own daughter and, again, a sister of Amenophis. Tuthmosis and Ahmose also had a daughter who in turn became the god Amun's wife, probably inheriting the position from her grandmother Ahmose-Nefertari. The daughter's name was **Hatshepsut**, and she proved the most assertive of Theban women – so much so that she became king of Egypt.

> **❝** The Nubian bowmen fall by the sword and are thrown aside on their lands; their stench floods their valleys ... The pieces cut from them are too much for the birds carrying off the prey to another place. **❞**
>
> Inscription left by Tuthmosis I at the Third Cataract

his wife **Ahmose-Nefertari** in charge of a newly created second priesthood of the god.

c.1525–c.1504 BC Under the guidance of Ahmose-Nefertari, his powerful mother, **Amenophis I** (Greek for Amenhotep I) continues the policies of his father Amosis. In particular he emphasises his dynastic links with Amun by extensive building works at **Karnak**, which he finances by extending Egyptian power further south into Nubia.

c.1504–c.1492 BC As Amenophis I is not survived by any offspring, the throne passes to **Tuthmosis I** (Greek for the Egyptian Thutmose I) who is married to the late king's sister Princess Ahmose, herself the daughter of Amosis I and Ahmose-Nefertari. Keenly aware of this break in the dynastic line, Tuthmosis claims divine descent from Osiris, introducing a new element to the royal ideology of the Eighteenth Dynasty.

c.1503–1502 BC At the end of a ruthless military campaign during which he sacks the Kushite capital at **Kerma** and advances as far south as the Fourth Cataract, Tuthmosis I makes all Nubia an **Egyptian colony**, subject to a viceroy.

c.1500 BC Tuthmosis I opens up new military, diplomatic and trade horizons for Egypt when he leads a **campaign into Syria**. He enjoys some success in bringing petty local princes under his sway, but when he advances to the Euphrates he meets resistance from the expanding Mesopotamian kingdom of **Mitanni**, a new power in the region.

c.1499–c.1492 BC On the west bank of the Nile opposite Thebes, Tuthmosis founds **Deir el Medina** – a community of craftsmen and necropolis workers who will continue to build and decorate royal tombs throughout the New

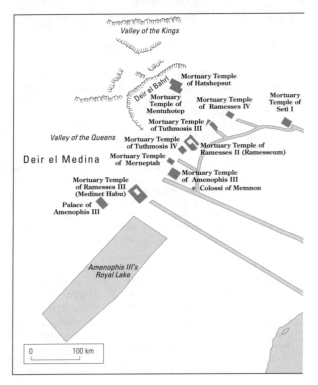

Kingdom. He builds his own funerary temple nearby, but for protection against grave robbers he puts his tomb in a remote and secret place – in fact his is the first to be cut from the rock in the **Valley of the Kings**.

c.1492–c.1479 BC **Tuthmosis II**, the son of Tuthmosis I

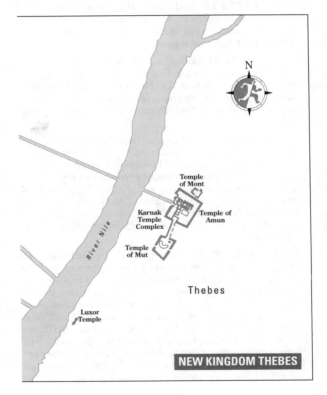

Temple of Mont

Karnak Temple Complex

Temple of Amun

Temple of Mut

N

River Nile

Thebes

Luxor Temple

NEW KINGDOM THEBES

by a minor non-royal wife, marries his half-sister **Hatshep-sut**, who is the God's Wife and the late king's daughter by his royal wife Ahmose. But Hatshepsut fails to bear her husband a son, and before his premature death Tuthmosis names his son by a concubine as his heir.

c.1479–c.1473 BC **Tuthmosis III** will bear the title of king for 54 years (to c.1425 BC), but he is only a child when he comes to the throne, and for the first six years **Hatshepsut rules as regent**.

c.1473–c.1458 BC Having a royal lineage superior to that of her late husband or her stepson, and with the support of the priests of Amun-Ra, **Hatshepsut declares herself king**, and for the remaining fifteen years of her life she entirely overshadows Tuthmosis III, her nominal co-ruler.

There is almost no military activity during Hatshepsut's reign, and many of the gains made by her father in Palestine and Syria disappear. Hatshepsut instead focuses on Egypt itself: she promotes **trading ventures** (most notably a fabled expedition to Punt) and initiates Egypt's **artistic revival**, restoring temples neglected by the Hyksos, raising obelisks at Karnak and building her mortuary temple at Deir el Bahri, one of the finest architectural achievements of all time.

c.1458–c.1425 BC At Hatshepsut's death **Tuthmosis III** launches Egypt into its **imperial age,** beginning with the defeat of a coalition of Syrian princes at Megiddo, also known as **Armaggedon,** whose name becomes a byword for cataclysmic events. Over the course of seventeen annual campaigns against **Mitanni** and its vassals, he establishes Egyptian dominance in Palestine and southern Syria, and even crosses the Euphrates to drive the Mitannians back into their Mesopotamian heartland. He conquers the petty states of the Near East, gains their loyalty by educating and acculturating their young princes to Egyptian ways and

An obelisk at Karnak shows Hatshepsut kneeling to receive the blessing of Amun, whom she claimed as her divine father

makes Egypt yet more prosperous from their tribute and from his direct control of the overland and maritime trading routes of the Levant.

Hatshepsut's story in stone

Hatshepsut built her funerary temple next to Mentuhotep II's mausoleum at **Deir el Bahri**, where she incorporated the looming cliff face with its tapering pyramidal peak into her architectural conception, as though taming the wild mountainside with the elegance of her gleaming white limestone terraces. Here Hatshepsut told the story of her reign, but her funerary temple also reveals what came after – and, intriguingly, it reveals a story she never meant to tell.

Reliefs on one colonnade celebrate the expedition to Punt, after Amun asked Hatshepsut 'to establish a Punt in this house'. There had been voyages before to procure the precious myrrh burnt as incense at temple services, but for the first time Hatshepsut's expedition returned with myrrh trees themselves, which she planted on her temple terraces. Hatshepsut, she declared, was the god Amun's wife and in this way she pleased him; and she proclaimed herself as his divine daughter too – points she made in the face of Tuthmosis III's faction, warning that 'he who shall do me homage shall live, he who shall speak evil in blasphemy of her Majesty shall die'. Meanwhile, the acquiescent Tuthmosis III and his stepmother were depicted together at Deir el Bahri, Hatshepsut's slender frame dressed in the robes of a king. But Tuthmosis eventually took control: following Hatshepsut's death, he ordered her face to be gouged out from the temple walls.

Yet it was not Tuthmosis who attacked all memory of **Senenmut**, a commoner who rose to high office under Hatshepsut and was most likely her architect and lover. Taking advantage of his position, Senenmut had introduced reliefs of himself in concealed places in her funerary temple and planned secretly to be buried with his mistress there. But his images and sarcophagus were smashed, apparently by Hatshepsut herself. She was not prepared to extend their intimacy into the life beyond.

Reliefs of Hatshepsut with Amun on the walls of her mortuary temple at Deir el Bahri were defaced by her successor Tuthmosis III

As Egypt is increasingly awakened to the benefits of **trade**, especially in luxury goods, Tuthmosis seeks to regularize relations with the region by **marrying three Asiatic princesses** and shows interest in achieving peace with Mitanni.

Late in his reign, Tuthmosis **campaigns in Nubia** and establishes **Napata** as a provincial capital near the Fourth Cataract.

> " [Tuthmosis III] built the first real empire, and is thus the first character possessed of universal aspects, the first world-hero. From the fastness of Asia Minor, the marshes of the upper Euphrates, the islands of the sea, the swamps of Babylonia, the distant shores of Libya, the oases of the Sahara, the terraces of the Somali coast and the upper cataracts of the Nile, the princes of his time rendered their tribute to his greatness. He thus made not only a worldwide impression upon his age, but an impression of a new order. "
>
> James Henry Breasted, *A History of Egypt* (1905)

c.1433–c.1425 BC In the last years of his reign Tuthmosis III **desecrates Hatshepsut's monuments**, smashing her statues and gouging her images from reliefs. He replaces them with his own and those of her two predecessors, and even walls up her towering obelisks at Karnak. He also builds more monuments in Nubia and Egypt than any king previously, lavishing the proceeds from his conquests most of all on **Karnak**, where he erects inscribed annals giving full accounts of his Syrian campaigns and the portion of tributes due to Amun. The temple of Amun now **possesses huge wealth**: 81,000 slaves and their families, 240,000 head of cattle and 83 ships, and it receives from 65 cities and towns a vast annual tribute in gold, silver, copper and precious stones.

Taking no chances with the succession, the ageing Tuthmosis has his son **Amenophis II** join him as co-regent.

The war of the obelisks

The obelisk, like the pyramid, derived its shape and significance from the *benben*, the original solar symbol at Heliopolis. Its form was deliberately spectacular: a monolithic granite shaft tapered to a pyramidium, which was sheathed either in gold or the even more precious **electrum** (an alloy of gold and still-rarer silver), designed to catch the rays of the rising sun.

At **Karnak**, Hatshepsut had her architect Senenmut raise two gigantic obelisks, each towering 97 feet high, and covered with electrum not only at the top but continuing halfway down their sides. As her inscription says, 'Hatshepsut made as her monument for her father Amun two great obelisks of enduring granite from the south, their upper parts, being of electrum of the best of all lands, seen on the two sides of the river. Their rays flood the two lands when the sun-disc rises between them at its appearance on the horizon of heaven.' The imposing size of Hatshepsut's obelisks and her claim to be the daughter of Amun incensed Tuthmosis III and his son Amenophis II, who resorted to the absurdity of hiding them behind high sandstone walls. Then, to outdo Hatshepsut, Tuthmosis erected a 101-foot tall obelisk nearby, but this has since been lugged to Rome, while another of his obelisks once at Karnak stands today in Istanbul. Two smaller obelisks raised by Tuthmosis at **Heliopolis** were taken by the Romans to Alexandria where they mistakenly acquired the name 'Cleopatra's Needles' before they went travelling again in the nineteenth century – one to London's Thames Embankment, the other to New York's Central Park. In fact, all Tuthmosis III's obelisks have either disappeared or, as perhaps befits a conqueror of foreign lands, have gone abroad. And Tuthmosis's walls, once meant to silence Hatshepsut, have been taken away: her assertion that she is the daughter of Amun can again be seen in the god's temple at Karnak, inscribed on the largest obelisk still standing in Egypt today.

> **"** His Majesty returned joyful of heart to his father Amun when he had slain with his own club the seven chieftains who had been in the district of Takhsy [in Syria], they being placed head downwards at the prow of His Majesty's ship. Then six of these enemies were hanged on the face of the enclosure wall of Thebes, the hands likewise, and the other enemy was shipped up to Nubia and hanged upon the enclosure wall of Napata in order to cause to be seen the victorious might of His Majesty for ever and ever. **"**
>
> Amenophis II, described on a stele erected at Amada in Nubia

c.1427–c.1400 BC During the two years of their co-regency, **Amenophis II** joins his father in desecrating Hatshepsut's monuments, and perhaps in reaction to the power attained by Hatshepsut and other royal women, he admits to having no wife other than his mother, who serves him as Great Royal Wife.

c.1420–c.1418 BC Amenophis II **campaigns** ruthlessly in Syria, Nubia and again in Syria.

c.1418–1400 BC After his second Syrian campaign Amenophis announces that Egypt is at peace with Mitanni, which is followed by a period in which emphasis on military pursuits is replaced by a growing interest in cultural refinement.

c.1400–c.1390 BC The reign of **Tuthmosis IV** begins with a brief show of force in Syria. The renewal of peace with Mitanni is sealed by Tuthmosis' marriage to a Mitannian princess. His chief wife, however, is Mutemwiya, an Egyptian-born commoner, who becomes the mother of the next king, Amenophis III.

c.1390–c.1352 BC During the reign of **Amenophis III**, the New Kingdom reaches its apogee of opulence. Not more

MICHAEL HAAG

Looking up towards the knees and head of a gigantic seated statue of
Amenophis III at Thebes, one of a pair known as the Colossi of Memnon

than twelve when he comes to the throne, Amenophis is still young when he marries a commoner, **Tiye**, who becomes the most influential figure in his life and bears the title of Great Royal Wife. He also marries a Babylonian and two Mitannian princesses, sealing Egypt's peaceful relations with the great powers of the Near East, and vastly expands trading relations with Crete and the Greek mainland.

Amenophis builds most of the temple of **Luxor**, which he dedicates to Amun, and he lays out the great processional way lined with sphinxes that connects it with Amun's great temple

Queen Tiye

Another of the remarkable women of the Eighteenth Dynasty was Queen Tiye, the wife of Amenophis III. Though born a commoner, she was clearly a woman of great influence, judging from how frequently and prominently she appears alongside her husband in statues, reliefs and inscriptions.

Tiye's parents, **Yuya** and **Tuyu**, were royal dignitaries from Akhmim, between Thebes and Assiut, who were accorded burial in the Valley of the Kings – an exceptional occurrence. Tiye's son, who appointed her a close adviser, was the religious revolutionary **Akhenaten**; her brother may have been **Ay**, who succeeded Tutankhamun as king; while **Nefertiti**, the beautiful wife of Akhenaten, may have been Ay's daughter and Tiye's niece.

Tiye stands, therefore, in the middle of what has been called 'perhaps the single most important event in Egypt's religious and cultural history', the suppression of Amun and the elevation of the sun-disc **Aten** to supreme deity by her son Akhenaten. It is not possible to say what role she or her family played (if any) in introducing the new religion, but certainly she was its enthusiast through three generations. Tiye was there at the beginning, when she and her husband would sail across the pleasure lake he had dug for her in a barge called 'Aten Gleams', and the memory of her was there at the end, when Tiye's grandson Tutankhamun took a lock of her auburn hair to his grave.

> **"** Amun has given [Amenophis III] the southerners as
> well as the northerners; the westerners and easterners hand
> over to him. They offer him personally their children; they
> come so that he may give them the breath of life. **"**
>
> Inscription from reign of Amenophis III

at Karnak. He also creates a new **royal area** across the Nile,
including a palace, an enormous artificial lake and his own
funerary temple guarded by gigantic statues of himself,
known to future generations as the **Colossi of Memnon**.

Egypt attracts numerous **foreign visitors** and is a flourishing centre of cosmopolitan fashions, ideas and gods, all
under the benevolent rule of Amun-Ra.

Religious revolution and reaction (late Eighteenth Dynasty) c.1352–c.1295 BC

Amenophis III identified himself with Ra and sometimes
with the sun-disc Aten, as when he called himself in one
inscription 'the dazzling Aten'. But he never lost sight of the
various other gods of Egypt, which he saw as aspects of the
sun god. In particular he honoured **Osiris**, whom he saw as
complementary to Ra; death and the darkness of the underworld were positive and necessary states in the cycle of
regeneration. For all that Amenophis tended towards a
notion of divine unity, he took care to preserve the traditional tolerance of plurality.

But Amenophis III's son by Tiye, who took the throne as
Amenophis IV, was soon representing the sun god as a disembodied sun-disc, the Aten, whose rays reached out to the

king and his chief wife Nefertiti and their children, offering them the *ankh*, the sign of life. Significantly, no priesthood intervened; the king was now the intercessor between mankind and the god. Possibly Amenophis IV felt that royal authority was being challenged by the growing power of the Amun establishment at Karnak, which was a major beneficiary of imperial wealth, and he soon began diverting revenues from the priesthood of Amun to the cult of Aten. But his programme went far beyond bringing the priesthood to heel, and must largely have been driven by a genuine and impassioned vision of the divine.

In about the fifth year of his reign, Amenophis changed his name to **Akhenaten** – from 'Amun is Content' to the 'Creative Manifestation of Aten'. Abandoning Thebes, he built a new religious capital, **Akhetaten**, 200 miles to the north (though whether Memphis remained the seat of government is unclear). Here, in temples open to the sun, Aten was worshipped to the exclusion of all other gods, the king himself composing a new *Hymn to the Sun* in which the Aten lovingly pervades all creation. Four years later, Akhenaten closed the temples of all the other gods throughout the land. The name Amun was hacked out everywhere, and sometimes too the word 'gods' in plural – a vast undertaking which probably required the army's help.

As the creative manifestation of the Aten, the king 'made' his people, especially the elite, who now denied their family backgrounds (however eminent) and claimed they owed everything to the king. Piety towards the Aten was identical with absolute loyalty to Akhenaten. The king even ensured life after death, for Osiris too had been proscribed and no longer sat in judgement on Egyptian souls. From being a representative theocracy in which Amun had acted through the king, during the late Eighteenth Dynasty the country became a direct **theocracy**, with the king as the sole manifestation of Aten in everyday life and the afterlife.

But it is unlikely that these changes enjoyed wide popular support, and there are signs that exclusive devotion to Aten was collapsing even before Akhenaten's death. How and why this came about is not known, but it is easy to imagine that a king who so completely dominated spiritual and worldly realms alike would suffer from discontent when anything went wrong. The army had supported Akhenaten against the priesthood at the start, but – most probably after military reversals in the Near East – it was the army that turned against him.

Akhenaten left two great defining legacies. One was that his failure irreparably weakened the independent authority of the kingship. The second was his contribution to **Egyptian art**. He himself claimed to have instructed his craftsmen in what Egyptologists call the **Amarna style** (Amarna, or Tell el Amarna, being the name of the village standing on the site of ancient Akhetaten). This could involve the distortion of the human figure, especially Akhenaten's, to create a startling bisexual appearance, but could also render its subjects elegantly and – in the case of Akhenaten's wife **Nefertiti** – with exquisite beauty. Intimate representations of the king and queen and their six daughters kissing and embracing under the beneficent rays of the Aten, too, are charming and delightful. Something of this expressiveness would continue in Egyptian art for centuries to come.

c.1352–c.1336 BC Once again a king of the Eighteenth Dynasty pays homage to Amun by ascending the throne as **Amenophis IV** (Greek for the Egyptian Amenhotep, meaning 'Amun is content'). He starts his reign, in accordance with tradition, by giving himself the title of 'high priest of the sun god', but soon embarks on a revolutionary interpretation of the solar religion. He builds extensively just to the east of the existing Amun temple at Karnak, closer to the rising sun. Here he first represents

Rays from the Aten, the divine solar disc, reach down protectively towards the revolutionary king Akhenaten and his queen Nefertiti

the sun god in a new way, no longer as a falcon (Horus) but as a disembodied abstraction, the sun-disc, called the **Aten**, which is shown with its rays ending in hands that hold out the hieroglyph for life to the king and his chief wife **Nefertiti**.

c.1348 BC In about the fifth year of his reign Amenophis IV changes his name to **Akhenaten**, meaning the 'Creative Manifestation of the Aten'. Abandoning both the cult city of Thebes and the administrative capital of Memphis, he founds a new city (at the site of the present-day village of Tell el Amarna, or Amarna) which he calls **Akhetaten**, meaning 'Horizon of the Aten'. This marks the beginning of the **Amarna period**, during which there is a complete break with the religious and artistic conventions of ancient Egypt.

> **❝** Here is a Pharaoh who ostensibly broke with the sacrosanct traditions of a millennium and a half, and showed himself as a human being in the intimate circle of his family, dandling his infant daughters, kissing his wife or taking her on his knee, or leading his mother by the hand. Here is a ruler who does not appear as the all-conquering hero of gigantic size slaughtering the foes of Egypt, or as the aloof divine king greeting one of the many deities as an equal. Here was a poet who is credited with having written hymns to his God which anticipate the Psalms of David, and who introduced a new and vital art style of his own conception in which to express his novel ideas. Above all, here is a courageous innovator who abandoned the worship of the multifarious gods of Ancient Egypt in their human and animal forms and substituted for them an austere monotheism with an abstract symbol by which to represent it. **❞**
>
> Cyril Aldred, *Akhenaten: Pharaoh of Egypt* (1968)

c.1344 BC Akhenaten now **bans all other gods** but Aten and sets out to remove their names and images throughout the country – a massive programme which probably requires the help and support of the army.

c.1341 BC Akhenaten holds a great **ceremony** to receive tribute from 'all foreign countries gathered together as one'. But the balance of power in the Near East is upset when the **Hittites**, from their heartland in Anatolia, inflict defeat on Mitanni. The Egyptian army suffers reversals and begins to **lose control** over the vassal states in Syria. The feeling grows that the gods have abandoned Egypt and no longer answer to prayers.

Nefertiti becomes Akhenaten's co-regent under the name **Neferneferuaten**.

c.1338–c.1336 BC At Akhenaten's death **Smenkhkara** comes to the throne. His origins and identity are unclear; he may be a younger brother of Akhenaten or his son by a secondary wife, but 'he' may be Nefertiti in male guise, for the new king also bears Nefertiti's co-regency name, Neferneferuaten.

> **"** Now when His Majesty appeared as King, the temples from one end of the land to the other had fallen into ruin; their shrines were desolate and had become wildernesses overgrown with weeds; their sanctuaries were as though they had never been; their precincts were trodden paths. The land was in confusion for the gods had forsaken this land. If an army was sent to Asia to widen the frontiers of Egypt, it met with no success. If one prayed to a god to ask things of him, he did not come. If one supplicated a goddess, likewise she did not come either. Their hearts were enfeebled because what had been made was destroyed. **"**
>
> Tutankhamun's Restoration Stele

A Hittite prince was sent from central Anatolia to marry Ankhesenamun, but the prospect of power going to a foreigner alarmed Egypt's entrenched court and military elite, and the prince was promptly murdered en route. Instead, the kingship went to Tutankhamun's vizier, **Ay**, who offered the best chance of salvaging the careers of other one-time followers of Akhenaten – he was probably a relative of Queen Tiye, the wife of Amenophis III, and was therefore a link with the pre-revolutionary past. The only alternative was **Horemheb**, commander-in-chief of the army, who as his subsequent career would show was more radically opposed to Atenism and all those associated with the Amarna period.

One theory suggests that Tutankhamun himself was murdered; if this was so then the finger points to Ay, if only because he reaped the immediate fruits of Tutankhamun's death. Perhaps he also struck pre-emptively, realizing that if he didn't then Horemheb would.

But perhaps the last word should go to Howard Carter, who discovered Tutankhamun's tomb: 'We shall probably be safe in assuming that it was Ay who was largely responsible for establishing the boy king upon the throne. Quite possibly he had designs upon it himself already ... It is interesting to speculate, and when we remember that Ay in his turn was supplanted by another of the leading officials of Akhenaten's reign, the General Horemheb, and that neither of them had any real claim to the throne, we can be reasonably sure that in this little by-way of history ... there was a well-set stage for dramatic happenings. However, as self-respecting historians, let us put aside the tempting "might have beens" and "probablys" and come back to the cold hard facts of history.'

c.1336–c.1327 BC **Tutankhaten**, who is Akhenaten's son by a secondary wife, becomes king at about the age of eight. Under the guidance of his vizier **Ay** and of **Horemheb**, commander of the army (both of whom had served Akhenaten), the young king abandons Akhetaten and **returns to Memphis**. There he rejects the exclusive worship of Aten, begins the restoration of the old cults and comes to an accommodation with the priesthood of Amun, changing his name to **Tutankhamun**.

c.1327 BC At Tutankhamun's sudden death at about the age of nineteen, his young widow **Ankhesenamun**, formerly Ankhesenpaaten, a daughter of Akhenaten and Nefertiti, finds herself the only surviving member of the dynasty founded by Amosis over two centuries before. In the tradition of the royal women of her line she does not want to marry a non-royal personage, and so she puts an offer to the Hittite king. Her letter says: 'My husband has died and I have no son. They say concerning you that you have many sons. You might give me one of your sons and he might become my husband. I would not want to take one of my servants. I am loath to make him my husband.' The king consents, but his son is **murdered** en route to Egypt.

c.1327–c.1323 BC To legitimize his position as king, Ay possibly **marries** Tutankhamun's widow Ankhesenamun – though whether she serves his purpose in this way or not, she too now swiftly disappears from the record. He fails to assuage Hittite outrage over the murder of their prince, however, and for decades to come Egypt meets with intensified **Hittite hostility** in the Near East.

c.1323–c.1295 BC At Ay's death **Horemheb** becomes king, instituting what is effectively a military dictatorship, appointing soldiers to priestly positions with instructions to extirpate the remnants of Atenism and fully restore the worship of Amun. He **dismantles** Akhenaten's temples at Karnak and begins the great **Hypostyle Hall** there which will become the most spectacular feature of the temple of Amun.

Being childless, Horemheb names his vizier **Peramessu** as his heir – an old army general from the Delta who has the attraction of a son and a grandson in line to succeed him.

The Ramessids: glory and gathering crisis (Nineteenth and Twentieth Dynasties) c.1295–c.1069 BC

With the death of Tutankhamun and the disappearance of his widow Ankhesenamun, the royal line was completely exhausted. Egypt was now to experience a run of commoner kings – **Ay** and **Horemheb**, who concluded the Eighteenth Dynasty, and **Rameses I**, the founder of the Nineteenth Dynasty, whose son **Seti I** and grandson **Rameses II** were both born before he was even made king. The first three Ramessids were acutely aware of their origins, so that even the bombastic Rameses II waited some years into his reign before reviving the Eighteenth Dynasty practice of legitimizing his rule by claiming divine descent from Amun. Even then the degree of his divinity was compromised by the vivid memory of Akhenaten, after whose death the kingship lost many divine attributes. Amun-Ra, the universal god, became the true king, while kings became more human. At the **battle of Kadesh**, Rameses II even called out to Amun to save him – demonstrating that the king was no longer the god on earth but, like the three million other human beings in Egypt, was subservient to him.

Seti I continued Horemheb's work of restoring the old temples, and he also began the active persecution of Akhenaten's memory, removing his name and those of his three successors from the records. He further distanced himself from the Amarna period by reverting to Old Kingdom artistic canons, decorating his works at Abydos and Thebes with finely cut and delicately coloured raised reliefs of exquisite – if orthodox – taste. Seti I and his son Rameses II also attempted to restore royal prestige by means of their

Asian campaigns, whose spoils ensured the loyalty of the Amun priesthood – though in the longer term the effect was to create a priesthood of such power and wealth that it rivalled the kings of the succeeding Twentieth Dynasty. This priestly dynasty would ultimately secure control over Upper Egypt.

Wider changes in Egyptian society were also underway. One of the most significant items in Tutankhamun's gold-filled tomb was a small dagger with an iron blade; it was included because iron was still a rare and precious metal in Egypt, though it was becoming more common in the Near East – as Rameses II would discover to his cost while fighting the Hittites. During the Twentieth Dynasty (the 12th century BC), Egypt finally entered the **Iron Age**. This proved a mixed blessing for the Twentieth Dynasty. Because Egypt could only obtain supplies in western Asia, the country was short on iron weaponry and its hold on the Near East began to slip. And Egypt had to pay for iron with gold; one reason why tomb-robbing became so common during the Twentieth Dynasty and afterwards was the need to obtain gold – gold that the country could no longer afford to leave buried with its dead.

But again, as towards the end of the Old Kingdom, Egypt's greatest difficulties may have been caused by a change in the climate. Drought and famine throughout the lands surrounding the Eastern Mediterranean caused huge migrations of people, some of whom – in the form of the **'Sea Peoples'** (see p.96) – made repeated attempts to invade Egypt. Though the Sea Peoples were successfully repelled, the havoc caused by these mass population movements transformed the world beyond Egypt as empires foundered and trade was disrupted. Within Egypt itself, a new epoch of low Niles began, reducing agricultural productivity for hundreds of years to come, and delivering a final blow to the New Kingdom.

The shaduf

For all the remarkable construction activities of the Old, the Middle and the New Kingdoms, the means of irrigation remained primitively simple. Apart from relying on the annual inundation, fields were irrigated by carrying water from the Nile in pairs of buckets attached to either end of a yoke which the farmer carried on his back. The evidence from tomb scenes is that the first mechanical device was introduced only towards the end of the Eighteenth Dynasty. This was the **shaduf**, still familiar in Egypt today, which is simply a form of lever. By pressing down at one end of a pivoted pole, a bucket of water suspended from the opposite end of the pole is raised. The pole can then be swung round to allow the water to be tipped into an irrigation channel. This time-consuming process was next to useless for increasing the productivity of main-crop agriculture, which because it depended on the Nile's annual flood meant only one harvest a year, and was instead used to maintain a family's supply of kitchen garden crops throughout the seasons.

The shaduf, the earliest mechanical device for lifting water from the Nile, was introduced only in the New Kingdom

Nineteenth Dynasty (c.1295–c.1186 BC)

c.1295–c.1294 BC Paramessu, an aged general from Avaris who has served as Horemheb's vizier, comes to the throne as **Rameses I**. He is a commoner without royal connections, and his reign lasts barely more than a year, but as father of Seti I and grandfather of Rameses II, he is the **founder of the Nineteenth Dynasty**.

c.1294–c.1279 BC **Seti I** becomes king after holding both military and religious offices under his father and probably under Horemheb too. His aim is to restore Egypt to its former power and glory, and in choosing '**Repeater of Births**' as one of his names he indicates that his reign will inaugurate a new era. A formidable warrior, he reclaims some Egyptian possessions from the Hittites, including for a time the important fortress town of **Kadesh** on the Orontes. Seti also repels incursions by Libyans, and to further his task of restoring and embellishing the old cult centres he raids **Nubia** for gold and also for captives to use as cheap temple-building labour.

Seti continues work on the **Hypostyle Hall** begun by Horemheb at Karnak, erects a magnificent temple at Abydos and cuts the finest tomb in the Valley of the Kings. He also reverts to Old Kingdom artistic tastes, producing coloured raised reliefs of exquisite taste – most notably at **Abydos**, the cult centre of Osiris, where also he lists his version of the legitimate kings of Egypt from Menes to himself, leaving out Akhenaten, Smenkhkara, Tutankhamun and Ay, the kings associated with the Amarna period.

c.1279–c.1213 BC Aged about 25 when he comes to the throne, **Rameses II** will reign for 66 years, longer than any monarch since Pepy II of the Sixth Dynasty. By his two principal wives, his chief queen **Nefertari** and his associate queen **Istnofret**, and by secondary wives and other women of his harem, he will have about 85 children, many of whom he will outlive.

The great temple of Amun at Karnak, here viewed across the sacred lake, was added to by king after king; the building work continued for 1300 years

A prodigious builder, Rameses adds to the temples at Luxor and Karnak, and builds the **Ramesseum**, his gigantic mortuary temple, but his finest work is at **Abu Simbel**. In all he is responsible for more buildings and colossal statues than any other king, though he also has his name carved or reliefs cut on many older monuments to further increase his fame. In fact Rameses' building works impress more by their size and quantity than by their quality: the delicate and time-consuming raised relief favoured by Seti I is abandoned early in his reign, with shoddy building techniques, inferior materials and poor carving becoming increasingly common. Nor, though his reliefs and inscriptions broadcast his role in the battle of Kadesh (which he claims as a famous victory), does he match the military achievements of his father.

A party of 19th-century tourists visits the Ramesseum, where the fallen statue of Rameses II inspired Shelley to write his mocking poem "Ozymandias"

> His pride was evidently boundless. Every temple which he erected was a monument to his own glory; every colossus was a trophy; every inscription a paean of self-praise ... There are even instances in which he is depicted under the twofold aspect of royalty and divinity – Rameses the Pharaoh burning incense before Rameses the Deity.
>
> Rameses II, described by Amelia Edwards in *A Thousand Miles up the Nile*
> (1877)

c.1279 BC On his accession Rameses II decides to make Avaris, long the residence of his family, the new capital of Egypt. As **Pi-Ramesse** (Domain of Rameses) it soon becomes the most important international trade and military base in the country, so that Egypt's strategic and economic centre of gravity shifts to the Delta.

> **"** His Majesty has built himself a residence whose name is Great of Victories. It lies between Syria and Egypt, full of food and provisions. It follows the model of Upper Egyptian Thebes, its duration like that of Memphis. The sun arises in its horizon, and even sets within it. Everyone has left his own town and settles in its neighbourhood. **"**
>
> Rameses II, on founding Pi-Ramesse

c.1275 BC Rameses II heroically extricates himself from a Hittite trap during the **battle of Kadesh** in Syria. But their possession of iron weaponry makes the Hittites especially formidable; the Egyptians have only bronze. Rameses agrees a truce, then returns to Egypt where he repels a **Libyan incursion** and builds defensive works at **Alamein** and elsewhere along the coastal road to the west.

Rameses also begins two rock-cut temples at **Abu Simbel** in Nubia, where he vividly illustrates his 'victory' at Kadesh, and he continues work on the temple of **Luxor**, adding a colonnaded court and a massive entrance pylon on which he again advertises his exploits at Kadesh.

> **"** When Menna my shield-bearer saw the vast number of enemy chariots hemming me in, he blanched and fear gripped him. He cried out to My Majesty, 'My good Lord, Mighty Prince, we stand alone amidst the foe. See, the infantry and chariotry have deserted us! Why do you stay to save them? Let's get clear!' Then said His Majesty to his shield-bearer, 'Stand firm, steady yourself, my shield-bearer! I shall go for them like the pounce of a falcon, killing, slaughtering and felling them to the ground!' **"**
>
> Rameses II, inscription describing the battle of Kadesh

Rameses II was often depicted with his wife Nefertari, but his sense of his own greatness demanded that she only come up to his knees

The temples of Abu Simbel

The larger of Rameses' two rock-cut temples at Abu Simbel was dedicated to **Ra-Herakhte**, who is Horus as the sun god rising on the horizon. The smaller was dedicated to **Hathor**, the Lady of the Sky, who is the daughter of the sun god Ra and the symbolic mother of the king. Colossal statues of Rameses form part of the facade of the Ra-Herakhte temple (with whom the king identified himself at Abu Simbel), while statues of Nefertari set in the facade of the second temple identify the queen with Hathor. Within the inner sanctuary of his temple Rameses carries his message further, for here four seated figures are carved out of the wall: **Ptah** the god of Memphis, **Amun** the god of Thebes, Re-Herakhte the god of Heliopolis and the divinized Rameses himself.

But if here he gives the appearance of being among equals, that is certainly not the way he understands his relationship with Amun, on whom he is dependent. This is clear from scenes within his temple giving a full account of the Battle of Kadesh. When all looks lost, Rameses desperately beseeches Amun: 'What ails you, my father Amun? Is it a father's part to ignore his son? Have I done anything without you, do I not walk and halt at your bidding? I have not disobeyed any course commanded by you … What does your heart care, O Amun, for these Asiatics so vile and ignorant of God? – What will men say if even a little thing befalls him who bends himself to your counsel?'

c.1259 BC Egypt and the Hittite empire sign a formal **peace treaty** in which Rameses has to accept the permanent loss of Kadesh and control over the Orontes valley and the coast of Syria to the west. But the treaty opens the borders to the Euphrates, the Black Sea and the eastern Aegean, permitting trade to flourish again as it has not done since the reign of Amenophis III. Peace in the Near East also frees Rameses to turn once more against the **Libyans**, a persistent and ever increasing threat.

> **66** Rameses II, he has made a temple, excavated in the mountain, of eternal workmanship, for the Chief Queen Nefertari Beloved of Mut, in Nubia, forever and ever, Nefertari for whose sake the very sun does shine! **99**
>
> Rameses II, inscription at Abu Simbel

c.1256 BC Rameses inaugurates the rock-cut temples at **Abu Simbel**. For once eschewing personal bombast, he poignantly dedicates one of the temples to Nefertari – who is too ill to attend and is probably already dying.

c.1255 BC Rameses' chief queen, Nefertari, dies.

c.1249 BC An **earthquake** at Abu Simbel causes the head of one of the colossal statues of Rameses to fall.

c.1246 BC **Istnofret** dies; Rameses marries a Hittite princess.

c.1239 BC Rameses marries another Hittite princess.

MARK EVANS PL

When Rameses II's temples at Abu Simbel were rediscovered in the 19th century, they were half-hidden behind mountains of sand

c.1228 BC Following the death of several of Rameses' older sons and heirs, **Khaemwaset**, one of Rameses' sons by Istnofret, becomes crown prince. Khaemwaset is high priest of Ptah at Memphis and a magician and scholar with antiquarian interests; he is an admirer of Old Kingdom tomb reliefs (which he copies for his own monuments), and he restores several Old Kingdom pyramids.

The Exodus myth

In a stele dated to the reign of Rameses, mention is made of a people called the **Apiru** who are employed as labourers in the building of Pi-Ramesse. There used to be speculation that Apiru (or Habiru/Hapiru) referred to the **Hebrews** – whom the Old Testament describes as engaged in building works immediately before the Exodus. The current scholarly view, however, is that 'Apiru' does not describe an ethnic group but was a term used in both Syria and Mesopotamia to describe mercenaries, raiders, bandits, outcasts and the like; while in Egypt the term 'Apiru', from the verb *hpr*, meaning 'to bind' or 'to make captive', probably referred to the Asiatic prisoners employed in state building and quarrying projects. In fact, the only non-biblical reference to Israel at this time is located in a stele dating to the reign of Merneptah, which commemorates the king's campaign of 1209 BC and deals mostly with the Libyans. A brief entry reads: 'Israel is laid waste, his seed is not', but instead of referring to a place it describes Merneptah's successful follow-up campaign in Palestine against a tribe.

Nothing in these Egyptian records, then, supports the story of an Exodus, which in any case was only written down some time between the 9th and 5th centuries BC. Indeed, the broadly accepted view is that there was no Exodus from Egypt at all – though a few Israelites who were also *apiru* may have escaped to Canaan, where their account added drama to a more pedestrian reality. It seems most likely that the Israelites were a disruptive outsider caste of mercenaries or bandits, already living in the mountainous parts of Canaan, who gradually took over the whole of what they called their 'Promised Land'.

This relief on the side of Rameses III's mortuary temple at Medinet Habu shows the king's giant figure repelling the invasion of the Sea Peoples

c.1225 BC Crown prince Khaemwaset **dies**. By now Rameses' twelve eldest sons have died, and his new heir is **Merneptah**, his fourth son by Istnofret.

c.1213–c.1203 BC Merneptah inherits a stable and peaceful kingdom from his father, but **climate change** is causing drought and widespread crop failure beyond Egypt; early in his reign Merneptah sends shipments of **grain** to his Hittite allies, who are suffering from famine.

c.1209 BC Changing climatic conditions all around the Eastern Mediterranean are setting in motion vast **population migration**. The Mycenaean centres in Greece are already destroyed, the Hittite empire is beginning to disintegrate, and now large numbers of **'Sea Peoples'** from across the Mediterranean land in Libya. There they join up with the local tribes and march with their families and their cattle into Egypt. In their tens of thousands they advance on **Heliopolis** and **Memphis**, but they are checked and defeated by Merneptah, who sends those who survive to military colonies, mostly in the Delta. The descendants of these and later captives, known as **Meshwesh**, will become an important political force in Egypt during the Third Intermediate Period.

c.1203–c.1194 BC At Merneptah's death, the kingship is usurped by **Amenmesse**, viceroy of Nubia and a member of the royal family, who gains control over the south of the country. However, Merneptah's son and rightful heir **Seti II** establishes himself on the throne around 1200 BC.

c.1194–c.1188 BC The succession is again thrown into question when Seti II is predeceased by his intended heir, his son by his principal queen, **Tausret**. **Septah**, Seti's young son by a Syrian concubine, becomes king under the regency of Tausret – who in turn is under the thumb of **Bay**, also a Syrian, who holds the all-important post of chancellor of the entire land.

c.1188–c.1186 BC Tausret **declares herself king**, but her reign soon founders amid a **civil war** that is probably linked to Bay's ambitions. With her death, the line of Rameses I ceases to rule Egypt.

Twentieth Dynasty (c.1186–c.1069 BC)

c.1186–c.1184 BC **Sethnakht** emerges as king from the civil war that broke out during Tausret's reign. Nothing is known of his origins nor of how he acquired the throne beyond his announcement on a stele that he has put the rebels to flight. But quite possibly the 'rebel' is the former chancellor Bay.

c.1184–c.1153 BC Sethnakht leaves a peaceful and stable Egypt to his son **Rameses III**, who models himself on his hero Rameses II. His funerary temple is a close copy of the nearby Ramesseum. On its walls he depicts famous victories of his own, and indeed Rameses III proves to be the last great warrior king of Egypt, though his battles are mostly defensive. The most dramatic of these is his repulse of the Sea Peoples' invasion during the eighth year of his reign.

However, **economic problems** begin to dominate later.

These arise from Rameses' early attempts to counter the turmoil preceding his accession by making huge donations of land to the great cult temples at Heliopolis and Memphis, and especially to the temple of Amun at Thebes – which by the end of his reign owns about a quarter of all cultivable land in Egypt. Grain prices rise, state officials and workers go unpaid and corruption increases as the king loses control over resources and finances.

c.1183 BC Rameses III begins work on his **funerary temple** at Medinet Habu, across the Nile from Thebes.

c.1180 BC Libyans penetrate the **western Delta**, where they attempt to establish their own rule, but Rameses III brings them under Egyptian control.

c.1177 BC A combined land and sea attack on the Delta by the **Sea Peoples** is anticipated by Rameses, who beats the invaders back.

The Sea Peoples

A coalition of barbarian northerners driven from their homelands by famine, or perhaps by other migrants, the 'Sea Peoples' included Sardinians, Etruscans, Cretans, Lycians, Philistines and others (though as yet they were en route to their eventual homelands), not all of whom have been identified. Having overwhelmed the Mycenaean and Hittite worlds, they advanced on Egypt by sea and overland in ox-carts with their women and children, bent on permanent settlement in the rich Delta pasturelands. One group, whom the Egyptians called the *Danu* – the 'Danaoi' of the *Iliad* – here emerged into history for the first time. Though successfully repulsed by Merneptah and again by Rameses III, some groups within the Sea Peoples managed to establish themselves nearby, establishing what became Phoenician culture along the coast of the Near East.

> ❝ A net was prepared for them to ensnare them, those who entered into the river mouths being confined and fallen within it, pinioned in their places, butchered and their corpses hacked up. ❞
>
> Rameses III's description at Medinet Habu of his victory over the Sea Peoples

c.1174 BC Rameses fights a **second campaign** against the Libyans.

c.1173 BC Rameses completes his **funerary temple** at Medinet Habu and records on an outer wall his victory over the Sea Peoples.

c.1156 BC A sign of growing economic difficulties is the world's first recorded **strike** as tomb workers at Deir el Medina protest at arrears in pay.

c.1155 BC A **conspiracy to assassinate Rameses III** is uncovered in the harem. The judges hear how a secondary wife attempted to put her son on the throne with the support of some officials and a military commander related to one of the harem women. The more socially prominent of the convicted conspirators are permitted to take their own lives, and the rest are put to death.

c.1153–c.1147 BC Rameses III's successors all adopt the famous Rameses name on their accession, beginning with his son **Rameses IV**. But during his reign power passes increasingly from the kingship to the **priesthood of Amun**, which now becomes at least partly responsible for paying the wages of the necropolis workers, while the office of the high priest becomes hereditary and almost entirely independent of royal control.

Rameses IV continues work on his father's last great project, the **temple of Khons** at Karnak. But this will also be

MICHAEL HAAG

The goddess Nut, who promises life after death by swallowing the sun at night but giving birth to it each morning, adorns the ceiling of Rameses VI's tomb

the last major building work of the New Kingdom, and it will not be completed until the Ptolemaic period, nearly a thousand years later.

c.1126–c.1108 BC On reliefs at Karnak the **high priest of Amun** has himself depicted on the same scale as **Rameses IX**, whose authority at Thebes is now no more than nominal. Amid increasing social and economic instability in Upper Egypt, necropolis workers at Deir el Medina turn to robbing tombs.

c.1099–c.1069 BC **Rameses XI** is king, but during the last ten years or so of his reign authority over Upper Egypt passes to **Herihor**, high priest of Amun at Thebes and commander in chief of the army, and then to Herihor's son **Piankh**. The palaces, temples and tombs at Thebes are robbed as it suffers from famine and from marauding bands of Libyans.

> **"** We opened their sarcophagi and their coffins, finding the noble mummy of this king equipped with a scimitar; many golden amulets and jewels lay about his neck, and his golden mask was upon him. The noble mummy of this king was completely bedecked with gold, and his coffins adorned with gold and silver inside and out and inlaid with all kinds of precious stones. We gathered the gold we found on the noble mummy of this god, together with his amulets ... Finding the queen to be similarly adorned, we gathered all that we found and set fire to the coffins. We also took all the offerings of gold, silver and bronze and divided them among ourselves. And we made eight portions from the gold ... coming from these two gods, leaving twenty *deben* for each of us. **"**
>
> Confession of tomb robbers during the reign of Rameses IX, describing their despoiling of the mummies of the Seventeenth Dynasty king Sobekemsaf II and his wife

At Pi-Ramesse the king delegates executive authority over Lower Egypt to **Smendes**, his son-in-law and commander of the army in the north.

Egypt begins to descend into a loose-knit and almost feudal society where king, priests, generals and settler groups compete for control over various parts of the country. But **the political and economic breakdown** that marks the end of the New Kingdom may, above all, be owed to a failure of the Nile.

4: The Third Intermediate Period and the Late Period

c.1069–332 BC

With the disintegration of the New Kingdom, Egypt lost control over Nubia and surrendered its military and commercial influence in the Near East. The reduction in revenues from abroad hurt the Egyptian economy, which had also been suffering from the fall in agricultural production after a period of low Niles. Yet despite these initial setbacks, and though the country gradually became more politically fragmented than at any time since Menes two thousand years before, Egypt during the **Third Intermediate Period** would come to enjoy a considerable degree of internal peace, prosperity and stability.

This was all the more surprising given that Egypt was adjusting to large-scale influxes of **Libyans** and **Nubians**, whose presence permanently changed the demographic nature of the country. The old divide between Lower and Upper Egypt was now reinforced by a new ethnic division: the north of the country became predominantly Libyan, while Egyptians predominated in the south – albeit with a Nubian contingent there too. Political control of Egypt would pass between Egyptians, Libyans and Nubians over the coming four hundred years, but the prevailing culture would remain Egyptian throughout. Ultimately the Nubians imposed a brief unity on the country during the Twenty-fifth Dynasty (c.720 BC), but their assertion of Egyptian power in the Near East brought them face to face with

Assyria, the rising superpower of the time, and an Assyrian occupation of Egypt followed.

The **Late Period** began with a new Delta dynasty, again Libyan in origin, which drove out the Assyrians. This was accomplished with the help of the **Greeks** – a new people on the international scene, who now began to play a decisive role in Egyptian history. The importance of the Greeks as mercenaries and traders continued to grow even during the two Persian occupations of Egypt, and when the Persians were driven from the country by **Alexander the Great**, Egypt was orientated once more towards the Mediterranean world.

The Third Intermediate Period (Twenty-first to Twenty-fifth Dynasties): c.1069–664 BC

Egypt's changing racial makeup is revealed by the fact that the Egyptian army may have been almost entirely composed of Libyan mercenaries by the end of the New Kingdom, while throughout the first century of the Third Intermediate Period there was continued heavy settlement by **Meshwesh** (see p.94), who established numerous local chiefdoms. Meshwesh communities settled in the oases of the Western Desert and along the Nile between Memphis and Herakleopolis, but by far the greatest number settled in the **western Delta** – which until now had been a neglected area, thinly inhabited and used largely for grazing. The rising economic and strategic importance of the Delta had already been confirmed when Rameses II built his capital of Pi-Ramesse in its eastern part; now peoples of Libyan descent would found dynasties in both the eastern and western Delta, and by the end of the Third Intermediate Period the predominance of Lower Egypt would be established. Upper Egypt would decline into provincial status, a situation that has continued to the present day.

At the beginning of the Third Intermediate Period the fiction of a united Egypt was still maintained, but in reality the country was divided between the kings of the Twenty-first Dynasty ruling at **Tanis** in the northeastern Delta and a succession of military commanders at **Thebes**, who also held the post of high priest of Amun. During this time Egypt became a theocracy and was governed supposedly by the god Amun, who uttered oracular commands that were followed at Thebes and Tanis alike. The theocratic nature of government diminished, however, as the Libyans who comprised the succeeding Delta dynasties confidently asserted their kingly powers.

In the vacuum left by the collapse of the New Kingdom, the **Nubians** had made incursions as far north as the First Cataract at Aswan and, during the 8th century BC, came to regard the whole of Upper Egypt as within their sphere of influence. When, towards the end of the century, the autonomy of Thebes and its satellite territories looked threatened by the expansionist policy of Libyan dynasts in the Delta, the Nubians marched northwards and, from about 712 BC, they ruled over a united Egypt from Memphis for half a century.

The Nubians had already become somewhat Egyptianized in Nubia (where they already worshipped Amun), and now in their eagerness to be recognized as authentic kings of Egypt they showed special respect for Egyptian traditions, particularly those rooted in the Old Kingdom. Their art, literature and religion were all strongly marked by archaizing tendencies, while they took advantage of centralized rule to undertake impressive building schemes at **Karnak** and elsewhere. They also found the wherewithal to mount a major military expedition in the Near East, in which they clashed with the Assyrians – the new power in the region. But this military involvement ushered in the end of Nubian domination: two Assyrian invasions of Egypt followed and the Nubians were driven out. Amid the fighting, great destruction was done to the country, provoking a new Egyptian effort towards unification which would usher in the Late Period.

c.1069–c.1043 BC When Rameses XI dies childless, **Smendes**, his son-in-law and northern army commander, becomes king and establishes the **Twenty-first Dynasty** (c.1069–c.945 BC). He rules over Lower Egypt as far south as the Fayyum from his capital at **Tanis**, a new town he begins building in the northeastern Delta, though much of his administration may be based at Memphis. Intermarriage between the extended families of Smendes and the high priests of Amun at Thebes ensure a degree of accord between Lower and Upper Egypt.

c.1039–c.991 BC The kingship passes to **Psusennes I**, the son of Pinudjem, the high priest and military commander at Thebes. In an unprecedented step for a king, Psusennes assumes the title of **high priest of Amun**, underlining the degree to which Egypt has become a theocracy where it is as important to be high priest as it is to be king. His sister-wife becomes Amun's high priestess, and they build a temple to the god at Tanis to provide an alternative site to Thebes for his worship.

Because stone is scarce in the alluvial Delta, Psusennes is **buried** within two Nineteenth Dynasty granite sarcophagi taken from Thebes, one of them Merneptah's, while as a further economy measure some of Psusennes' burial ornaments are taken from the tombs of New Kingdom kings.

The gold burial mask of Psusennes I, who assumed the titles of king and high priest of Amun and ruled over Lower Egypt from his capital at Tanis

c.978–c.959 BC Siamun advances the fortunes of his capital **Tanis**, an important merchant city trading with the ports of the Levant, by engaging in limited **military action** in Palestine against Egypt's commercial rivals, the Canaanites. According to the Old Testament (I Kings 9:16) he marries off one of his daughters to his new ally king **Solomon** of Israel, presumably to consolidate Egypt's position in the region. There is no mention of this event, however, in Egyptian records.

c.959–c.945 BC Psusennes II, the high priest of Amun at Thebes, ascends the throne at Tanis, so that for a while Upper and Lower Egypt are **united** in his person – if not as an integrated political unit.

Priestly deeds at Thebes

The Twenty-first Dynasty marked a low point in royal authority, with kings at Tanis barely more important than the high priests at Thebes – whose official residence was **Medinet Habu**, the funerary temple of Rameses III, which they had fortified during the troubled final years of the New Kingdom. Supreme power supposedly lay with **Amun**, who made oracular pronouncements at Karnak. This procedure often involved the high priest putting forward alternative proposals on two tablets, the god giving the nod to one.

Probably it was to have a hand in this wire-pulling act that king **Psusennes I** took the unprecedented step of becoming **high priest of Amun**. In other ways too Psusennes knew how things worked at Thebes – where, rather than being left to the anarchy of grave robbers, New Kingdom royal tombs were now systematically emptied by the priests themselves. Psusennes obtained the sarcophagi and ornaments for his own burial from the Theban priests, presumably at a knockdown price.

This recycling of royal graves provided a much-needed income for the high priests, while for the kings of the Twenty-first Dynasty it was a helpful economy measure. The tombs and even the mummies of some of the greatest kings of the Seventeenth to Twentieth dynasties were systematically stripped bare by the priests, their ornaments sold, their gold melted down, their coffins reused, and their bodies tagged and removed to a secret cliff-face cache at Deir el Bahri. It was here that they were discovered nearly 3000 years later, in 1881 AD, and taken to the Cairo Museum.

Libyans settled in Lower Egypt are gaining in influence, among them the future king **Sheshonk**, who is both commander of the Egyptian army and chief of the Meshwesh at Bubastis in the Delta. Members of his family marry into the families of the high priests of Ptah at Memphis, and his eldest son marries the daughter of Psusennes.

c.945–c.924 BC On the death of Psusennes, **Sheshonk I** ascends the throne at Tanis, establishing the **Twenty-second Dynasty** (c.945–c.715 BC) which sets about restoring royal authority. During his reign, which marks the high point of the Third Intermediate Period, the dynasty of high priests at Thebes dies out, and Sheshonk installs his younger son, whom he also makes commander of the army, as high priest of Amun, a practice continued by his successors. Amun still utters oracular remarks but the god's role in royal policy is consultative only.

Having brought unity and stability to Egypt's internal affairs, Sheshonk looks abroad. Making a show of strength in Lower Nubia, he opens up **trade relations** with Upper Nubia further to the south, while in the Near East he revives commercial relations with the port of **Byblos**.

According to the Old Testament, Sheshonk gives asylum to **Jeroboam**, a pretender to the throne at Jerusalem, for Solomon's kingdom of Israel is now at odds with itself.

Meanwhile Egypt's **increased prosperity** is reflected in Sheshonk's ambitious building programme, especially at **Karnak**, where he lays out the great court which serves as a monumental anteroom to Horemheb's Hypostyle Hall in the temple of Amun.

c.931 BC At the death of Solomon, according to the biblical story, Jeroboam is **recalled to Israel** by his supporters to challenge **Rehoboam**, Solomon's son and heir.

c.930 BC With the support of ten of the twelve Hebrew tribes, Jeroboam becomes **king of Israel**, but two tribes support Rehoboam and these form the **kingdom of Judah** to the south, which includes Jerusalem.

c.925 BC Sheshonk campaigns in Palestine in support of Jeroboam, where 'Shishak', as the Jewish chroniclers call him, loots **Jerusalem**.

Libyans became important as soldiers, settlers and eventually as dynastic rulers during the Third Intermediate Period

> **❝** And he took away the treasures of the house of the Lord, and the treasures of the king's house; he even took away all: and he took away all the shields of gold which Solomon had made. **❞**
>
> The Bible, I Kings 14:26

c.924 BC Sheshonk commemorates his **Palestinian campaign** in reliefs in the temple of Amun at Karnak – but though he mentions 150 places, Jerusalem is not among them, nor is there any hint that he touched Judah at all.

c.874–c.850 BC **Osorkon II** fails to make his son high priest of Amun at Thebes and quickly learns the cost: the high priest **Harsiese** assumes royal titles and has to be removed; he is then replaced by Osorkon's son. Osorkon is a great builder at Tanis and Bubastis, using recycled stone from Pi-Ramesse.

c.850–c.825 BC **Takelot II** follows tradition by appointing his son and intended heir Osorkon high priest of Amun, but he is rejected by the Thebans and **civil war** suddenly erupts, lasting for a decade or more. The outward forms of accord between king and priests now vanish and Upper and Lower Egypt quite evidently go separate ways. This marks the beginning of a century when Egypt becomes increasingly **fragmented** and is ruled by numbers of autonomous royal princes and Libyan chiefs.

c.825–c.773 BC Following the death of his father and taking advantage of the debacle at Thebes involving his older brother, Prince Osorkon, **Sheshonk III** usurps the throne at Tanis. Elsewhere in the Delta rival claimants are accepted locally as kings, so that the later Twenty-second Dynasty at Tanis is overlapped by a Twenty-third Dynasty at Leontopolis and a Twenty-fourth Dynasty at Sais. The process of fragmentation is only halted by yet another overlapping dynasty, the Twenty-fifth, which arises out of Nubia and eventually asserts itself over the entire country.

c.818–c.715 BC Libyans at **Leontopolis** in the southeastern Delta establish the **Twenty-third Dynasty**, which for a century is simultaneous with the Twenty-second Dynasty at Tanis.

c.727–c.715 BC With dynasties still active at Leontopolis and Tanis, the vigorous **Twenty-fourth Dynasty** is established by Libyans at **Sais** in the western Delta. Its ambition to reunite the country brings it into conflict with the Nubian kingdom based at Napata, which exercises control over Upper Egypt as the Twenty-fifth Dynasty.

c.727–c.720 BC Tefnakht (c.726–c.720) of the Twenty-fourth Dynasty takes over all of the western Delta and Memphis, and then begins to expand into the northern

ANCIENT EGYPT PL

Jewellery such as this from the tombs of Tanis kings was often recycled from looted New Kingdom tombs as an economy measure

territories of Upper Egypt, where he is opposed by Nubian garrisons.

c.720 BC On reports that Tefnakht is advancing south, the Nubian king **Piankhi** (c.747–c.716 BC), also known as Piy, marches north into Egypt from his capital at Napata near the Fourth Cataract. After **Thebes** opens its gates to Piankhi's troops and **Memphis** is taken by storm, Piankhi accepts the submission of the local Delta rulers. The **Twenty-fifth Dynasty** (c.747–c.656 BC) – which is dated from Piankhi's accession to the throne in Nubia, when Nubian hegemony was accepted at Thebes – now becomes the dominant ruling house in Egypt, though Piankhi himself retires to Napata.

c.720–c.715 BC The Twenty-fourth Dynasty at Sais again attempts to **expand southwards** towards Thebes, this time under **Bakenrenef**, provoking Piankhi's successor **Shabaka** to lead the Nubian army back into Egypt.

c.716–c.702 BC Shabaka, Piankhi's brother and successor, defeats and kills Bakenrenef, the king of Sais, in c.715 BC. He **unites Egypt** with Nubia and from his capital at Memphis brings the whole of his kingdom under firm centralized rule.

c.690–c.664 BC The early years of **Taharka**'s reign are marked by peace, good fortune and prosperity. Reunification stimulates the **Egyptian economy**, while **plentiful rainfall** in Nubia and high Nile floods in Egypt bring especially abundant harvests. Taharka builds widely, including at Karnak – where he adds a colonnade and kiosk to the great court of Sheshonk I at the temple of Amun and begins work on the huge **first pylon**.

c.674 BC Angry at Egyptian interference in Palestine and Syria, which Assyria regards as lying within its own sphere of influence, the **Assyrians attempt to invade** but are repulsed by Taharka.

> **❝** I fought daily very bloody battles against Taharka, king of Egypt and Nubia, the one accursed by all the great gods. Five times I hit him with the point of my arrows inflicting wounds, and then I laid siege to Memphis, his royal residence; I destroyed it, tore down its walls, and burnt it down. ... All Nubians I deported from Egypt, leaving not even one to do homage to me. Everywhere in Egypt I appointed new kings, governors, officers, harbour overseers, officials, and administrative personnel. **❞**
>
> Cuneiform inscription of the Assyrian king Esarhaddon

c.671 BC Again the Assyrians **attack Egypt**, this time led in person by their king **Esarhaddon**; he succeeds in capturing Memphis, and Taharka flees south to Nubia. Assyrian policy is to rule Egypt through local princes, who are made to pay tribute.

c.667 BC Taharka returns to Egypt and **retakes Memphis**, leading to an invasion by the new Assyrian king **Ashurbanipal**, son and successor of Esarhaddon. Taharka once more flees to Nubia.

c.664 BC At Taharka's death his successor **Tanutamani** (c.664–c.656 BC) promptly **invades Egypt** and defeats Assyria's vassals in the Delta.

c.663 BC Ashurbanipal replies with a powerful retaliatory force and **sacks Thebes**. The temple of Amun is looted and a massive amount of booty is carried back to the Assyrian capital Nineveh. The Nubians are permanently expelled from Egypt, and Tanutamani lives out his days at Napata. The wars fought over Egypt between the Nubians and Assyrians **devastate Egypt**; agricultural production suffers and the impoverished population declines in numbers.

Taharka, a Nubian, gave Egypt peace and prosperity but was eventually driven from the throne by an Assyrian invasion

The Late Period (Twenty-sixth to Thirty-first Dynasties): 664–332 BC

Egypt during the Late Period alternated between local and Persian rule, yet the country seems to have remained prosperous throughout. Little physical evidence remains, however – most of the country's wealth and the considerable building works undertaken by its kings were concentrated in the Delta, where they have since been buried under silt or their limestone blocks recycled as fertilizer by peasant farmers, the fellahin. But though the archeological record is meagre, the past can be reconstructed from the increasing quantity of **written material** – much of it from outside sources, especially the vivid accounts of Greeks. These sources also help to pin down chronology more accurately, so that from now on it is usually possible to give exact dates.

The Late Period began with the expulsion of the Assyrians by Libyans, whose capital was Sais in the western Delta. This Saite or Twenty-Sixth Dynasty was not Meshwesh in origin, however, but made up of latecomers to Egypt, the **Libu** (whence the name Libya). Their ruler **Psammetichus** saw that Assyria was overstretched and ejected its occupying forces with the help of Greek and other foreign mercenaries, mercenaries who also formed a counterbalance to the mainly Meshwesh Libyan military caste within Egypt. When not trying to emulate New Kingdom conquests in Palestine and Syria, the Saites sought to maintain the balance of power in the Near East by supporting the rivals of whomever was the dominant power of the moment.

The Saite rulers brought a period of revived splendour to Egypt. Culturally they harked back to the Old and Middle kingdoms, capturing not only the form but the vigour of original tomb reliefs, pyramid texts and architectural details. Ironically, perhaps, it was engagement with other Mediterranean communities that made this possible: encouraged by the Saite kings, large numbers of Greeks were pouring into Egypt, at once a consequence and a cause of Egyptian prosperity. **Greek settlements** sprang up around the country, most importantly at Naucratis in the western Delta, where for a time its Greek merchants enjoyed a monopoly on the Egyptian import and export trade. Hardly surprisingly, Egyptian influence makes itself felt in Greek art of this time.

For the increasingly powerful **Persian empire**, Egypt was a vital strategic cornerstone to its ambitions in the west and also a much-needed source of corn and gold. But it was the Greeks, whose writings provide the fullest contemporary account of Egyptian history, who became indispensable for their trading and military skills even as the Persians occupied the country. In little more than a century, the Greeks would overturn the Persian empire and make themselves masters of Egypt.

664–610 BC Psammetichus I is a Libyan of the Libu group whose father, Necho I, ruled as prince of Sais. With the Assyrians still campaigning against the Nubians in Upper Egypt, Necho dies and Psammetichus, founder of the **Twenty-sixth Dynasty** (664–525 BC) begins strengthening his family's power base in the Delta.

660 BC Psammetichus gains control over the entire Delta and improves his economic position by developing **trading links** with Phoenicians and Greeks.

656 BC Backed by **foreign mercenaries** – mostly Greeks and Carians, but also Phoenicians, Jews and Bedouin – Psammetichus establishes his authority over the whole of Egypt and has his daughter made heir to the God's Wife of Amun to secure the loyalty of Thebes. He makes Egypt

independent of Assyria, and in the Near East he supports Lydia and Babylon against the Assyrians.

c.630 BC Greeks from the island of Thera found their colony of **Cyrenaica** and its capital **Cyrene** on the coast of North Africa, adjacent to Egypt.

A passage round Africa

It was probably to improve Egypt's trade with the worlds of the Mediterranean and the Indian Ocean that Necho II conceived his plan for a **canal**. Unlike the modern-day Suez Canal, which cuts straight through from the Red Sea to the Mediterranean, Necho's plan was to reduce the labour required by making use of existing waterways. From the Red Sea a channel was cut up to the Bitter Lakes in the isthmus of Suez, that narrow neck of land which is all that joins Africa to Asia, and from there a second channel was dug westwards towards Bubastis in the Delta and so into a now-vanished arm of the Nile, which flowed northeastwards into the Mediterranean. According to Herodotus, 120,000 lives were lost before construction was halted on the advice of an oracle, who said that the beneficiaries of the canal would be the barbarians – that is, those who did not speak the Egyptian tongue. Sure enough, the scheme was completed a century later by the Persians.

By that time it was known that Africa was entirely encircled by water, except where it joined Asia at the isthmus of Suez. The man responsible for this information was, again, the pioneering Necho – after calling off construction of his canal, he sent out a fleet manned by a Phoenician crew with orders to **circumnavigate Africa**. The plan was to begin from the Red Sea and return via the Strait of Gibraltar, and so through the Mediterranean and back to Egypt. The voyage took two years, the Phoenicians reporting on their return that as they sailed westwards round southern Africa they had the sun on their right, to the north – a statement Herodotus flatly disbelieved, but clear proof that they had crossed the equator. The next occasion such a feat was achieved, this time from west to east, was more than two thousand years later, by Vasco da Gama.

620 BC Psammetichus begins to **side with the Assyrians** as their empire declines in the face of the growing power of Babylonia and Persia.

616 BC Travelling further afield than even in the days of Tuthmosis I and Tuthmosis III, Egyptian forces operate inside **Mesopotamia** as allies of the Assyrians against the Babylonians.

612 BC The Babylonians **sack Nineveh**, the Assyrian capital, as Babylonia and Persia conquer and divide Assyria. Now Babylonia becomes the greatest threat to Egypt.

610–595 BC **Necho II** works to **increase trade and commerce** and to increase Egyptian influence abroad. He encourages the Greeks to found their trading port of **Naucratis** in the Delta, he begins a **canal** linking the Red Sea and the Mediterranean, and he sends an expedition to **circumnavigate Africa**. He also fits out the Egyptian navy in the Mediterranean and Red Sea with **trireme** galleys, but his military adventures in the Near East bring him into conflict with the Babylonians.

c.610 BC **Naucratis**, the chief trading port in Egypt, is founded not far from Sais in the western Delta by Greeks from Miletus in Asia Minor. Other Greeks soon follow.

> " In old days Naucratis was the only trading port in Egypt, and anyone who brought a ship into any of the other mouths of the Nile was bound to state on oath that he did so of necessity and then proceed to the Canopic mouth; should contrary winds prevent him from doing so, he had to carry his freight to Naucratis in barges all round the Delta, which shows the exclusive privilege the port enjoyed. "
>
> Herodotus, writing about 160 years later, in the *Histories*, II, 179

610–605 BC Necho campaigns in **Palestine** and **Syria**. He defeats Judah in 609 BC at **Megiddo** and stations Egyptian forces on the Euphrates.

605 BC The Egyptian army on the Euphrates frontier is forced to withdraw all the way to the eastern border of Egypt, after suffering a crushing defeat at **Carchemish** at the hands of the Babylonians.

601 BC **Nebuchadnezzar II**, the Babylonian king, leads his army against Egypt but is repulsed by Necho, who inflicts heavy losses on the invaders.

597 BC **Jerusalem** is captured by Nebuchadnezzar. He takes the Jewish elite to Babylon, where they remain for fifty to sixty years.

593 BC During the reign of **Psammetichus II** (r. 595–589 BC), Greeks are particularly important as mercenaries and are put in charge of the Egyptian fleet. To forestall a Nubian attack on Egypt, Psammetichus launches an expedition southwards that reaches as far as **Napata**, near the Fourth Cataract. Greek mercenaries record their passage in **graffiti** at Abu Simbel and Buhen.

589 BC **Apries** (r. 589–570 BC) succeeds to the throne and continues the policy of his predecessors in working against Babylonian power in Palestine and Syria.

> **❝** When King Psammetichus came to Elephantine, this was written by those who sailed with Psammetichus the son of Theocles, and they came beyond Kerkis as far as the river permits. Those who spoke foreign tongues were led by Potasimto, the Egyptians by Amasis. **❞**
>
> Greek inscription carved on the leg of one of the colossi of Rameses II at Abu Simbel

586 BC After a Jewish rebellion against the Babylonians, Nebuchadnezzar again seizes **Jerusalem**, this time razing it to the ground and deporting many of its inhabitants to Babylonia. Others seek refuge in Egypt, among them the biblical prophet **Jeremiah**.

571–570 BC The Libyan ruler appeals to Apries for help in driving the Greek colonists out of **Cyrenaica**, but the Egyptian army is defeated and **mutinies**. The mutiny originates among the Meshwesh military caste and is a backlash against what they feel is the favouritism shown by the king towards Carians and Greeks in the military establishment. **Amasis**, the same general mentioned in the Greek graffiti during the Nubian campaign, is sent to quell the mutiny but joins it, overthrows Apries and **takes the throne**.

c.570 BC Amasis (r. 570–526 BC), or Ahmose in Egyptian, confines all Greek trading activities to Naucratis and garrisons all mercenaries at Memphis, so restricting contact and reducing tension between foreigners and Egyptians.

567 BC Amasis forms an **alliance** with Greek Cyrenaica against Babylonia.

562 BC Nebuchadnezzar II dies.

559 BC Cyrus II, 'the great', ascends the throne of Persia. In the face of ever-rising Persian power, Egypt, Babylonia, Lydia and Sparta enter into an **alliance**.

546–545 BC Cyrus **defeats Lydia**, the keystone in the alliance against him, in 546 BC, and by the following year the Greeks of Asia Minor are in his thrall.

538 BC Cyrus **takes Babylon**, leaving Amasis with no major allies in the Near East. Instead Amasis forms closer relations with the Greeks to ward off the Persian threat.

529 BC Cyrus dies and is succeeded to the throne of Persia by his son, **Cambyses**.

526 BC Amasis dies and his son **Psammetichus III** (r. 526–525 BC) succeeds him.

526–525 BC At Pelusium on the eastern edge of the Nile Delta, Psammetichus puts up stiff resistance against Cambyses, but eventually the Egyptians are forced to withdraw to Memphis. After a prolonged siege the city surrenders and **the Persians occupy the whole of Egypt**. This First Persian Period is listed by the Egyptian historian Manetho as the **Twenty-seventh Dynasty** (525–404 BC).

525–522 BC **Cambyses** is the first ruler of Egypt whose primary interest is not in that country. But though Herodotus is later very critical of him in the *Histories*, Egyptian records of the time show that Cambyses is **eager to accommodate local feeling**. He assumes the forms of Egyptian kingship, Egyptians fill important posts in his administration, and he shows respect for Egyptian religion. When he attempts to

> **"** The force which was sent against the Ammonians started from Thebes with guides, and can be traced as far as the town of Oasis, which belongs to Samians supposed to be of the Aeschrionian tribe, and is seven days' journey across the sand from Thebes. The place is known in Greek as the Islands of the Blessed. General report has it that the army got as far as this, but of its subsequent fate there is no news whatever. It never reached the Ammonians and it never returned to Egypt. There is, however, a story told by the Ammonians themselves and by others who heard it from them, that when the men had left Oasis, and in their march across the desert had reached a point about mid-way between the town and the Ammonian border, a southerly wind of extreme violence drove the sand over them in heaps as they were taking their mid-day meal, so that they disappeared for ever. **"**
>
> Herodotus, *Histories*, III, 26

reduce the incomes of the politically influential temples, however, he causes much resentment. He also betrays arrogance (or foolhardiness) in the **campaigns** he launches across the desert, one against **Nubia**, the other against the **Ammonians** at the Siwa oasis, home to the oracle of Ammon; the first fails for lack of water and provisions, while the army sent across the Western Desert to Siwa is lost.

Cambyses **returns to Persia** to deal with a pretender to his throne and dies there, at which the Egyptians rise in revolt.

522 BC Cambyses is succeeded by **Darius I** (r. 522–486 BC), who spends the first two years of his reign absorbed in suppressing revolts within Persia.

519 BC The Persian army regains control over Egypt.

c.518 BC Darius visits Egypt where he codifies the law and reforms the administration; he also **completes Necho II's canal** between the Mediterranean and the Red Sea with an eye on improving communications and trade between Egypt and Persia, which is part of his larger scheme for integrating Egypt into the Persian empire. In an effort to be more conciliatory towards religious sensibilities, he commissions numerous **temple buildings**, among them the temple of Amun at **Hibis** in the Kharga oasis.

The Persians introduce the **camel** to Egypt, making desert travel easier and increasing the importance of the oases of the Western Desert.

499 BC The Greeks of Asia Minor revolt against Persian domination and receive help from mainland Greece.

490 BC The Persians send a punitive expedition to Greece under the command of Darius' nephew, but it is defeated at the **battle of Marathon**.

486 BC The repercussions of the Persian defeat in Greece are felt in Egypt where **resistance to Persian rule** is renewed on news of the death of Darius. The western Delta is the centre of resistance, from where grain is exported to Greek states in return for military aid. The Persians, however, dominate the Nile Valley, where they can now supply themselves from Persia via the Red Sea and the canal.

485–484 BC Darius' son **Xerxes** (r. 486–465 BC) crushes the Egyptian revolt. His rule is harsh and he shows little concern for Egyptian sensitivities. Egypt becomes **impoverished** under Xerxes' rule and that of his successors, and a mood of insecurity and hatred grows.

480 BC Xerxes **invades Greece**, where his fleet is defeated at the **battle of Salamis**.

479 BC The Persian army is defeated at the **battle of Plataea** in central Greece. The Greeks of Asia Minor free themselves from Persian rule.

465 BC At the death of Xerxes, who is succeeded by **Artaxerxes I** (r. 465-424 BC), there is a **new uprising** in the Delta, led by **Inarus**, a local prince who is probably a descendant of the Saite royal family. Egyptians gain control of most of the Delta.

459 BC Inarus receives help from the Greeks, and the Egyptian rebels **capture Memphis**, but not the inner citadel, into which the Persian forces withdraw.

454 BC The Persians **counterattack**; Inarus is captured, taken to Persia and killed, while the Greeks are all but wiped out.

c.447 BC The Greek historian **Herodotus** visits Egypt, where foreigners are welcome now that the country is at peace. The Greeks have long been fascinated by Egypt, and Herodotus gives it a considerable amount of space in his *Histories*.

Naucratis loses its monopolistic trading position and its special importance around this time – but only because there are so many Greeks in Egypt carrying out such wide-ranging commerce in so many different parts of the country.

424 BC Artaxerxes I dies and is succeeded by **Darius II** (r. 424–405 BC).

405 BC Darius II dies and is succeeded by **Artaxerxes II** (r. 405–359 BC), who almost immediately faces a rapidly growing **rebellion** in the Delta, which soon brings to an end the first Persian occupation of Egypt.

404 BC Amyrtaios (r. 404–399 BC), who is probably descended from the former Saite royal family, is listed by Manetho as the sole king of the **Twenty-eighth Dynasty** based at Sais. He frees the Delta from Persian rule.

400 BC By now the **Persians are ejected from the whole of Egypt**, and the country is in Amyrtaios' hands. But his personal success is shortlived: his throne is usurped by the founder of the Twenty-ninth Dynasty.

399–380 BC The brief **Twenty-ninth Dynasty** consists of three kings whose capital is **Mendes** in the eastern Delta. Their domestic policy is one of generosity towards the temple priesthoods, while their foreign policy is to preserve Egyptian independence with Greek help against the Persian empire – which persists in seeing Egypt as a rebellious province.

386–383 BC An attempt by **Artaxerxes II**, who is still on the Persian throne, to regain Egypt is repulsed by **King Achoris** (r. 393–380 BC), Hakor in Egyptian, with the help of the Athenian general **Chabrias**.

380 BC The **Thirtieth Dynasty** (380–343 BC), the last dynasty of an independent Egypt, is inaugurated by **Nectanebo I** (r. 380–362 BC), a general from a military family who almost certainly comes to power by a coup. His reign is a period of **great prosperity** during which he undertakes considerable building works throughout the country. He builds the oldest parts of the temple of Isis on the island of **Philae**, and he donates much of the land for the temple of Horus at **Edfu**.

373 BC Nectanebo I defeats a Persian invasion with help from the Nile's annual flood which inundates much of the Delta as the Persians attempt to advance towards Memphis.

362–360 BC Teos (sometimes known as Tachos) succeeds his father, but does not last long. While leading an attack on **Phoenicia**, dissension breaks out among his forces, the operation turns into a fiasco and Teos goes into exile in Persia. His cousin **Nectanebo**, a commander in the army, returns to Egypt as king.

360 BC **Nectanebo II** (r. 360–343 BC), like his namesake, is a patron of the arts and major builder; he begins the enormous temple of Isis at **Bahbeit el Hagar** in the Delta.

350 BC Nectanebo II withstands an attempted **Persian invasion**.

343 BC Led by their new king **Artaxerxes III** (r. 343–338 BC), and this time waiting until after the annual inundation, **the Persians successfully invade Egypt**, inaugurating the **Thirty-first Dynasty** (343-332 BC), also known as the Second Persian Period. Nectanebo flees to Nubia and is never heard of again.

339–338 BC The Persians are faced with an armed rebellion led by **Khababash** (a figure of whom next to nothing is known), who for a year or two is recognized as king in both Upper and Lower Egypt.

338 BC Philip II, king of Macedon, defeats the Greeks at the **battle of Chaeronea**.

336 BC Philip is murdered and is succeeded as king of Macedon by his son **Alexander**.

334 BC Alexander begins his campaign against the Persians, crossing into **Asia Minor**.

333 BC The Persian king **Darius III** (r. 338–330 BC) is defeated by Alexander at the **battle of Issus** in northern Syria.

332 BC **Alexander the Great** enters Egypt and is welcomed by the Egyptians as a deliverer.

5: The Ptolemaic Period

331–30 BC

T he Egypt encountered by **Alexander the Great** was as it had always been – a land inhabited by millions of fellahin, their lives rooted in their fields, a peasantry taxed and dominated for at least three thousand years by the Egyptian elite, and more recently by the Persians. But though Alexander was the conqueror of the country, he knew that he could not rule without being accepted by the priests, who were powerful, articulate, and the chief repositories and exponents of Egypt's ancient culture and traditions.

This lesson was not lost on Alexander's general **Ptolemy**, the founder of the dynasty that was to rule Egypt for 300 years from the newly built city of **Alexandria**. Though Alexandria, like the dynasty, was culturally Greek, Ptolemy and his successors took care to root themselves in Egyptian concerns, in particular honouring Egypt's gods and maintaining its temples and its priesthoods. Priests, especially the high priests of Memphis, enjoyed political influence as the Ptolemies saw them as a way of gaining the acquiescence of the Egyptian population.

The Ptolemies' ultimate interest lay in the financial management of their kingdom. All the land was the king's, and nothing that grew upon it belonged to the fellahin until the king had received his quota. The Crown commanded what amount should be grown, it set the price for the harvested produce, and it lent the seed for the new season's planting. In particular, it was the vast flow of wheat from the hinterlands of Egypt to the king's granary at Alexandria that accounted for much of the wealth of the Ptolemies. Mining, quarrying, manufacturing and foreign commerce were also closely controlled and taxed by the state. In fact, almost every article in daily use was manufactured either in royal factories or under royal licences, with the king having the outright monopoly in wool, salt, cloth, scent, the manufacture of papyrus and the production of vegetable oils.

On the back of this wealth from the land, and from the control of manufacture and trade, the Ptolemies built up Alexandria on the edge of the Mediterranean, so linking Egypt to the Greek lands across the sea. Alexandria as a beacon of Hellenism also served to dim the lustre and nationalistic appeal of Memphis, the ancient religious and political centre, and helped make a strange land familiar to the large number of **immigrants** now pouring into Egypt from all over the Greek world.

There was some intermarriage between Greeks and Egyptians, and this increased as time went on, especially at a distance from Alexandria – for example, in Upper Egypt and in the Fayyum. How far this went, however, is uncertain. Likewise, it is not clear how great the cultural exchange between Greeks and Egyptians actually was. Greeks, it seems, rarely troubled to learn Egyptian, leaving it to socially ambitious Egyptians to become bilingual. Indeed, the first Ptolemaic ruler to speak Egyptian was also the last: the famous **Cleopatra**. On the other hand, the Olympian gods lost ground as ordinary Greeks turned to the worship of Egyptian gods, especially Isis, while the Ptolemies went a long way towards blending Greek and Egyptian artistic canons, which resulted in some of the most handsome temples and sensuous sculpture in Egyptian history.

Certainly there was no attempt to submerge Egyptian culture, and though the Ptolemies exposed Egypt to Hellenism and turned it towards the Mediterranean, they allowed political, economic and social change to occur fairly gradually. In a very real sense, pharaonic civilization was still alive in Ptolemaic Egypt – and continued into Roman times.

The golden age of the Ptolemies: 331–221 BC

Throughout most of the 3rd century BC, the Ptolemies controlled an empire that included the ancient centres of Greek culture in and around the Aegean, and it was from these areas that settlers came to Egypt in search of land and opportunity. This was a period of development for Egypt, fostered by royal monopolies in manufacturing and trade, by agricultural innovations, and by the royal policy of settling Greek and other foreign soldiers on Crown land in exchange for military service. Greek settlements grew up throughout the country, especially in the Fayyum – where the Ptolemies greatly increased the amount of cultivable land. The invention of the **saqiya**, an improved water-lifting device, revolutionized irrigation throughout the country, and together with close management of the land, resulted in an expansion of agricultural productivity that would not be matched again until the 19th century AD.

Wheat production, for example, was raised to new levels of quality and abundance by introducing Syrian and Greek varieties and developing new methods of irrigation. Already at the start of the 3rd century BC, and in spite of the expenses of transportation, Egyptian wheat sold in Greece for a fifth less than locally produced Greek wheat. Soon Egypt overtook Sicily, Tunisia, and the Crimea in wheat production and became the largest grain producer in the entire Mediterranean area.

Immigration and **foreign trade** turned Egypt's face towards the Mediterranean, and for the first time its northern coast and sea harbours became important, confirming Lower Egypt as the demographic and political centre of the country. The Ptolemies' greatest achievement was their Mediterranean capital, **Alexandria**, which in the lifetime of the dynasty grew to perhaps a million people and was the largest and wealthiest city in the known world. Under the patronage of the first three Ptolemies, the city became the resort of artists, poets and scholars, and was particularly outstanding in its scientists and mathematicians. Indeed, it is no exaggeration to say that, within half a century of its founding, Alexandria became the cultural and intellectual capital of Western civilization.

But if the Ptolemies brought to Egypt progressive Greek ideas, they entirely went against Greek practice by routinely engaging in marriage between full brothers and sisters, and by furthermore not hesitating to declare themselves divine. In claiming descent from **Zeus**, each Ptolemaic king was claiming a spiritual relationship with Alexander the Great himself, the conqueror of Egypt, who was widely seen as the god's son. Brother-sister marriage was also meant to reinforce the dynasty by preventing royal sisters from marrying outside the family and creating new power bases – or, as one historian has put it, it was a way of 'keeping the business in the family by keeping the family in the business'.

> **"** A stern verdict was passed on the two hundred years of Persian 'misrule and neglect' by priests who exaggerated Persian sacrilege beyond all recognition; Artaxerxes III, who had reconquered Egypt eleven years earlier, was known to the priests as the Sword and was accused of killing the sacred bull of the god Apis, eating it roast and substituting that accursed animal the donkey in its place. Under Persian rule the temples may have had their presents and privileges reduced, but these legends of atrocity went far beyond the truth. However, they suited the purpose of Alexander, the acclaimed avenger of Persian impiety. **"**
>
> Robin Lane Fox, *Alexander the Great* (1973)

332 BC At the head of an army of 40,000 Macedonians and Greeks, **Alexander the Great** arrives in Pelusium at the northeast edge of the Delta, where the Persian satrap surrenders Egypt to him without resistance. Continuing on to **Memphis**, Alexander wins over the high priests by sacrificing to the Egyptian gods and especially to the god Ptah in the form of the Apis bull. In return, Alexander is crowned **king of Egypt** in the temple of Ptah. He is 24 years old.

331 BC Early in the year, Alexander sails northwards through the Delta seeking a suitable place to build a city open to Greek maritime trade and from which to govern Egypt. Just west of the Delta on the edge of the desert and between Lake Mareotis and the Mediterranean he founds **Alexandria**. From there, with a few of his companions, he makes the long journey westwards to the border of **Cyrenaica** to receive pledges of friendship and alliance from its leaders. Then he turns inland across the Western Desert to the remote oasis of **Siwa** to consult the oracle at the temple of Ammon, the Libyan version of Amun, where he is told he is the son of Zeus.

Alexander returns to **Memphis** and organizes the administration of Egypt. He appoints **Cleomenes**, a Greek of Naucratis, to levy taxes for the building of Alexandria and to maintain Greek garrisons and a naval force in the country. The position makes Cleomenes effective master of the country, soon formalized when Alexander appoints him **satrap** ('governor' in Persian) of Egypt.

In May, Alexander leaves Egypt to pursue the war against **Darius** and the Persian empire.

323 BC After conquering Persia, marching as far as India and making himself master of the largest empire the world has seen, in June Alexander dies at **Babylon** in Mesopotamia at the age of 32. His vizier Perdiccas delegates rule over provinces of the empire to Alexander's generals, with Egypt going to **Ptolemy**.

Alexander at Alexandria

Alexander himself laid down the plan for the great city that was to bear his name. He indicated where the agora should be constructed, how many temples there should be – to the gods of both the Greeks and the Egyptians – and he marked out the course of the city's perimeter wall. But no chalk could be found for marking his design on the ground, and so Alexander used grains of barley for the task, which was taken as a good omen, auguring the future prosperity of the city. According to some accounts, huge flocks of birds suddenly appeared and gobbled up all the grain, causing Alexander great dismay. But his diviners urged him to take heart, interpreting the occurrence as a sign that the city would not only have abundant resources of its own but that it would be the nurse of men of innumerable nations.

The foundation of his city would prove to be Alexander's greatest contribution to civilization – yet he did not stay long enough to see a single building rise. After his death eight years later, his body was returned to Alexandria for burial by his general Ptolemy, then moved to a monumental tomb, the **Soma**, built by Ptolemy IV Philopator, where it was last reported to have been seen by the Roman emperor Caracalla in AD 215. By the late 4th century AD the mystery of the tomb's whereabouts had become proverbial; possibly it was destroyed in city riots in the late 3rd century AD or by the great earthquake of AD 335. The latest idea to gain currency is that the so-called Alabaster Tomb in the city's Latin Cemetery is in fact part of the Soma.

In November, **Ptolemy arrives in Egypt**, where he has Cleomenes put to death and assumes the powers of satrap (in which position he will remain until 305 BC). Ptolemy brings **Alexander's body** with him, which after a time at Memphis is buried at Alexandria.

322 BC Ptolemy gains control of **Cyrenaica**.

321 BC Perdiccas, who is trying to maintain the unity of Alexander's empire, **attacks Egypt** but his army fails in its attempt to cross the Nile, many of his soldiers are devoured by crocodiles and he is assassinated by his own men. This marks the opening phase of the **Wars of Alexander's Successors**, which will last forty years.

Alexander the Great was 25 when he conquered Egypt and founded Alexandria, which became the cultural capital of the Mediterranean world

305 BC Ptolemy I Soter I (r. 305–282 BC) is crowned king of Egypt on 7 November. He regards himself as the regenerator of the country and takes the name **Soter** – that is, 'Saviour'. He builds and restores Egyptian temples and introduces the worship of **Serapis**, an amalgam of Greek and Egyptian gods. In Alexandria he founds the **Museion** and the **Great Library** and perhaps begins construction of the **Pharos**. In Upper Egypt near Abydos, he establishes **Ptolemais**, a new Greek city, which grows to the size of Memphis.

The emergence of the Ptolemaic empire

After Alexander's death at Babylon in 323 BC, his vizier **Perdiccas**, acting as regent, promoted the joint recognition of Alexander's mentally deficient half-brother **Philip Arrhidaeus** (r. 323–317 BC) and Alexander's infant son **Alexander IV** (r. 317–310 BC). Through this legitimate – if unpromising – line of the Macedonian royal house, Perdiccas attempted to maintain the unity of the empire.

The first challenge came when **Ptolemy** diverted the body of Alexander from its homeward journey to Macedonia, saying it ought to be buried at Siwa instead. But so potent a symbol of power and legitimacy served Ptolemy better at Alexandria, where a tomb was built and a cult established to honour the city's founder. Perdiccas' attempt to bring Ptolemy to heel in 321 BC was only the first in a long series of **wars** between Alexander's generals, which culminated in about 280 BC in the emergence of three dynastic successors to Alexander's empire: the **Seleucids**, based in Mesopotamia, Syria and parts of Asia Minor; the **Antigonids**, who ruled in Macedonia; and the **Ptolemies** in Egypt, where already in 305 BC the first Ptolemy had declared himself king. From Alexandria, their capital city, the Ptolemies looked outwards on the Mediterranean, and throughout most of the 3rd century BC, despite intermittent warfare with the Antigonids and the Seleucids, they ruled over Cyprus, the southwest coast of Asia Minor and the islands of the Aegean, as well as Palestine and Cyrenaica. Unlike their pharaonic forebears, however, Nubia held no interest for the Ptolemies, who hardly ventured beyond the First Cataract.

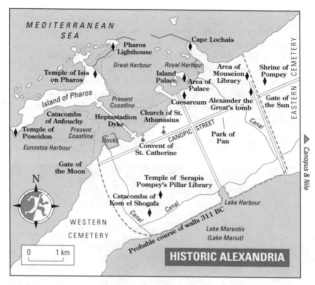

HISTORIC ALEXANDRIA

MEDITERRANEAN SEA

Pharos Lighthouse
Cape Lochais
Great Harbour
Royal Harbour
Temple of Isis on Pharos
Island Palace
Area of Palace
Area of Mouseion Library
Shrine of Pompey
Island of Pharos
Present Coastline
Caesareum
Alexander the Great's tomb
Gate of the Sun
EASTERN CEMETERY
Catacombs of Anfouchy
Heptastadion Dyke
Church of St. Athanasius
Temple of Poseidon
Present Coastline
CANOPIC STREET
Park of Pan
Canal
Eunostos Harbour
Docks
Convent of St. Catherine
Gate of the Moon
N
Temple of Serapis
Pompey's Pillar Library
Catacombs of Kom el Shogafa
Canal
Canal
Lake Harbour
WESTERN CEMETERY
Probable course of walls 311 BC
Lake Mareotis (Lake Mariut)
0   1 km
Campus & Nile

0   1 km

285 BC Ptolemy I associates his son with him as co-regent; in his lifetime he is known as 'Ptolemy, the son of Ptolemy',

> " In Egypt they have everything that exists or is made anywhere in the wide world: wealth, sports, power, excellent climate, fame, sights, philosophers, gold, young men, a shrine of the sibling gods, an enlightened king, the Museion, wine ... And women! more women, by Hades' Persephone, than the sky boasts stars. And looks! like the goddesses who once incited Paris to judge their beauty. "
>
> Herondas, *Mimes*, I, 23–6, c.270 BC

> One can understand how the Greeks of that extraordinary time came to think of Fortune as an incalculable deity who might play the strangest game in human affairs, when some one who in boyhood had anticipated probably no other life than that which a Macedonian country gentleman might naturally lead amongst his native fields and hills found himself, at the age of sixty-four, Pharaoh in the land of Egypt!

Edwyn Bevan, *A History of Egypt under the Ptolemaic Dynasty* (1927)

The god Serapis, a Ptolemaic invention combining Greek with Egyptian beliefs, was variously depicted as a jolly-looking Zeus or as an Apis bull

though in history he is known as **Ptolemy II Philadelphus** (r. 285–246 BC).

282 BC Ptolemy I dies, and Ptolemy II Philadelphus begins **sole rule**. Unlike his father he is no general, but he is a strong and ambitious ruler, highly educated, an able diplomat and a masterful organizer. During his reign, Ptolemaic Egypt reaches the zenith of its power and wealth. He extends state control over every aspect of the economy through a system of royal monopolies, shareholdings and licences. To facilitate trade and communication between the Nile and the Red Sea he restores the **canal** begun by Necho II and improves the caravan route from **Coptos** (modern Qift) across the Eastern Desert. He lowers the level of the lake in the **Fayyum** to greatly extend the area of cultivation, and turns the region into an area of large-scale Greek settlement.

The saqiya

Ptolemaic technology improved considerably on the **shaduf**, the primitive bucket-and-pole irrigation device introduced during the New Kingdom (see p.85). The Ptolemies' principal innovation was the **saqiya**, a vertical waterwheel for raising water from a well, which was linked by a drive shaft to a horizontal wheel turned by a buffalo, a camel or a donkey. Compared to the shaduf, the saqiya could lift more water, could lift it higher, and could distribute it in a continuous stream, permitting perennial irrigation of the fields and the harvesting of two or even three crops a year. The effect of the saqiya was most felt in the **Fayyum**, where the Ptolemies added to the achievements of the Middle Kingdom by extending the canal system and lowering the level of the lake further – thereby trebling the cultivable area and quadrupling the population of the region. Indeed, by about 150 BC the population of Egypt as a whole rose to what would be its maximum in ancient times, thought to be about five million – though, according to some estimates, as high as eight million.

279 BC Numerous spectacular games and processions are introduced by Ptolemy II – among them the **Ptolemaieia**, a four-yearly celebration inaugurated at Alexandria in honour of the deified Ptolemy Soter and meant to rival the Olympics. This establishes the Ptolemaic tradition of deifying kings at their death. At the same time, Ptolemy brings Alexandria to its height of brilliance and magnificence by dedicating the **Pharos**, the towering lighthouse that becomes the seventh wonder of the world, and also completing the **Great Library**. Attracted by Ptolemy's patronage, the most outstanding minds in literature, science and mathematics come to Alexandria. With his encouragement, the **Pentateuch** is translated from Hebrew, by now a dead language, into the Greek spoken by the city's large Jewish population, and **Manetho**, a Hellenized Egyptian priest, writes the *Aegyptiaca,* his account of 3000 years of Egypt's history divided into **dynasties** – the system used to the modern day.

c.270 BC The **Seleucid** and **Macedonian** kingdoms form an alliance against Ptolemaic Egypt which lasts throughout the 3rd century BC.

> " The sensation it caused was tremendous. It appealed both to the sense of beauty and to the taste for science – an appeal typical of the age. Poets and engineers combined to praise it. Just as the Parthenon had been identified with Athens and St Peter's was to be identified with Rome, so, to the imagination of contemporaries, the Pharos became Alexandria and Alexandria became the Pharos. Never, in the history of architecture, has a secular building been thus worshipped and taken on a spiritual life of its own. It beaconed to the imagination, not only to ships at sea, and long after its light was extinguished memories of it glowed in the minds of men. "
>
> The Pharos lighthouse, described by E.M. Forster

The Museion and Library at Alexandria

Ptolemy I founded the **Mouseion** – literally, a place for the cultivation and worship of the Muses – in the palace quarter of Alexandria, to which he and the next two Ptolemies attracted some of the greatest scientific and mathematical minds of the age. Among these were **Euclid** (fl. c.300 BC) who in his theories of numbers and plane and solid geometry demonstrated how knowledge can be derived from rational methods alone; **Eratosthenes** (c.276–194 BC), the mathematician and geographer who determined the earth's circumference; the astronomer **Aristarchus of Samos** (fl. 280–264 BC) who, anticipating Copernicus by 1800 years, declared that the earth went round the sun; and **Erasistratus** (304–245 BC), who came close to discovering the circulation of blood and was the first to make the distinction between sensory and motor nerves. The Museion included laboratories, an observatory, a dining hall, a park and a zoo; it was like a university, except that the scholars it supported were under no obligation to teach.

Linked to the Museion was the famous **Library** of 700,000 papyrus rolls, the world's first great collection of written works. Among the outstanding figures associated with the institution were the poets **Theocritus** (c.320–250 BC), the creator of the pastoral style of poetry, and **Callimachus** (c.310–240 BC), composer of some of the finest elegies in the Greek language; while **Zenodotus** (c.310–245), a literary scholar, dedicated his life to producing a critical edition of Homer which preserved the *Iliad* and the *Odyssey* for posterity.

276 BC Ptolemy II's full sister **Arsinoë**, an intelligent, resolute and ambitious woman, makes her brother marry her, accounting for his name **Philadelphus** (which means 'sister-lover'). Henceforth, it is Arsinoë who directs Egyptian foreign policy.

273 BC Ptolemy and Arsinoë initiate an *amicitia*, a friendship, with **Rome**, which amounts to establishing diplomatic relations, and is an indication that the Roman Republic is gaining recognition as one of the great powers in the Mediterranean.

Serapis, Isis and Horus

Three gods are particularly associated with Ptolemaic Egypt: Horus and his mother Isis, both ancient Egyptian deities; and Serapis, a god invented by Ptolemy I.

Already, by 3000 BC, **Horus** was identified with the king, and so the Ptolemies were eager to identify with the god. His father was Osiris, who had been murdered by his brother Seth, but **Isis** was able to sufficiently arouse the dead Osiris to have intercourse with him. She therefore played the vital role in transmitting the kingship from the dead Osiris-king to the living Horus-king, and for this reason Isis too was important to the Ptolemies, who made a special point of celebrating her – as at the Ptolemaic temple of Isis on the island of **Philae** near Aswan, where she is shown suckling her vulnerable infant son Horus, who is a Ptolemaic king. Through her suffering over the death of Osiris and her joy at the birth of Horus, Isis became an emotionally powerful and all-embracing figure in whom both Egyptians and Greeks could find solace, so that in time she would become identified with all other goddesses of the Mediterranean and so absorb them. Not surprisingly, Ptolemaic queens sought to identify themselves with Isis, particularly **Arsinoë**, the wife of Ptolemy II, and also the last **Cleopatra**.

Ptolemy I Soter I had anticipated this absorbing of gods when he invented **Serapis** with the intention of uniting Greeks and Egyptians in a common worship. At Memphis, the Egyptian priests kept a sacred bull, the **Apis**, which in life represented the god Ptah and in death became identified with Osiris. Ptolemy combined the Apis with the Greek Dionysus and had him sculpted as a Zeus-like figure, but softened and benign – more a healer than an autocrat – and with a basket on his head to show that he was a harvest god. A huge temple, the **Serapeum**, was built for him at Alexandria, from where his worship, like that of Isis, spread throughout the Mediterranean world.

This relief at Philae shows Isis suckling the infant Horus. Her face was gouged out by early Christians, who reinvented her as the Virgin Mary

270 BC Arsinoë dies – but not before having the satisfaction of being **deified** along with her husband, setting a precedent for the dynasty that is to follow.

246 BC **Ptolemy III Euergetes I** (r. 246–221 BC) comes to the throne at his father's death. He makes significant contributions (as 'Euergetes', meaning 'benefactor', attests) to temples and cults, especially of the Apis bull at Memphis and Saqqara. His other works include a gateway to the temple complex at **Karnak**, and at Alexandria he builds the **Serapeum**, a temple for the worship of Serapis, which includes a 'Daughter' Library to the great 'Mother' Library.

237 BC Ptolemy begins the **temple of Horus** at Edfu, though it will not be completed until 57 BC.

The Ptolemies and Rome:
221–30 BC

Ptolemy IV Philopator inherited a strong and tightly knit realm, but through slackness, self-indulgence and an indifference to the quality of people in his government he left Egypt enfeebled, never to recover. Military defeats abroad meant the gradual erosion of its overseas empire, which contributed to an economic decline at home. This period also saw the beginnings of **civil strife**, with outbreaks of mob violence in Alexandria and native uprisings in Upper Egypt. Matters were made worse by dynastic infighting which now became a byword for Ptolemaic rule. None of this was conducive to the nurturing of cultural or scientific activity, so that the brightness of Alexandria dimmed during the 2nd century BC, only reviving somewhat during the reign of the last Ptolemy, **Cleopatra VII**.

But behind everything was the growing power of **Rome**. In the face of a united Greek front, it is unlikely that the Romans would have been able, or even have wanted, to advance eastwards. In fact, the problem was least with Egypt, which in 273 BC signed a treaty of friendship with Rome and renewed it a century later; rather, Rome first stepped into Eastern affairs to counter the aggressive ambitions of the Greek dynasties ruling **Macedonia** and **Syria**, who had both allied themselves with **Hannibal of Carthage** – Rome's most dangerous enemy, even after his defeat in 202 BC. During the 2nd century BC, the chronic dissensions of the Hellenistic kings of Ptolemaic Egypt, Seleucid Syria and Antigonid Macedonia invited and even demanded Roman interference in the Eastern Mediterranean.

A collapse in Greek immigration from about 200 BC was perhaps a consequence of the Ptolemies' loss to the Seleucids of their territories in **Asia Minor** and the **Aegean islands**, but also a judgement on the growing lack of security in Egypt in the face of native insurrections. These became serious after the **battle of Raphia** in 217 BC when a shortage of Greek troops obliged Ptolemy IV to field an army, half of which was native Egyptian. From now on, the Egyptian national consciousness was armed. But any chance that the Greeks would be overthrown – or would be submerged into the Egyptian population through intermixing – was countered by the rising power of Rome. **Ptolemy XII** understood that Rome had come to stay in the Eastern Mediterranean and the Near East; the only real surprise is that his daughter, Cleopatra VII, was able to maintain Egyptian independence for so long.

Cleopatra was not exceptionally beautiful, says Plutarch, the 1st-century AD Greek historian, but she was extraordinarily amusing, vital and attractive. And she took intelligent advantage of the Roman **civil wars**, first between Pompey and Julius Caesar, then between Octavian and Mark Antony. The later Ptolemies might submit to necessity, but they never gave up their dreams of power beyond Egypt. And so it was with Cleopatra, whose ambition it was to use Mark Antony to restore the glory days of Ptolemaic rule – which she very nearly succeeded in doing.

221 BC The 25-year-old **Ptolemy IV Philopator** (r. 221–205 BC) ascends the throne at the death of his father. He is a self-indulgent aesthete, but ruthless in preserving his hold on power. Fearing rivals within his family, he has his uncle put to death, his mother **Queen Berenice** poisoned, and his younger brother **Magas**, the idol of the army, killed by having boiling water poured over him in his bath. He builds the **Soma**, the great mausoleum in Alexandria to which the body of Alexander is transferred and where the Ptolemaic kings are buried.

217 BC The Seleucid king **Antiochus III** attempts to invade Egypt but is defeated by Ptolemy at the **battle of Raphia** on 22 June. The most significant aspect of the battle, however, is that Ptolemy's victorious army, instead of being almost entirely Greek, is half comprised of Egyptian troops.

After reasserting Egyptian control over **Palestine**, Ptolemy returns to Egypt and marries his sister **Arsinoë III** in the autumn.

211/10 BC With **Hannibal of Carthage** marching on Rome and much of the Italian countryside laid waste by the contending armies, a Roman embassy visits Alexandria to request **grain supplies** from Egypt. From now on, the arrival of Alexandrian grain ships is to be vital to the economy of Rome.

208–186 BC Native **revolts** flare up against Ptolemaic rule, first in the swamps of the Delta and then in Upper Egypt. With the support of Nubian troops and the Amun priesthood, two Egyptian kings, **Haronnophris** and **Chaonnophris**, reign in succession at Thebes. This marks the beginning of Egyptian **nationalist literature** directed against the Greeks and their city, Alexandria.

205 BC Ptolemy IV dies in October/November, but the news is concealed until the following September, and the government continues to be run by a court cabal.

204 BC The 5-year-old **Ptolemy V Epiphanes** (r. 204–180 BC) is placed on the throne in September by court intriguers who have murdered his mother, Arsinoë III.

> ❝ The Egyptians were so elated that there was a revolt of the native population, which continued for some years. When the revolt was finally suppressed the Egyptian element in the country had established their power and could no longer be ignored. ❞
>
> Polybius, *History*, v, 107 (2nd century BC)

> *Since King Ptolemy has founded temples and shrines and altars, and has repaired those requiring it, having the spirit of a beneficent god in matters pertaining to religion, and finding out the most honourable of the temples, did renew them during his sovereignty, as was becoming ... it seemed good to the priests of all the temples in the land to increase greatly the existing honours of king Ptolemy, the Everliving, the Beloved of Ptah, the God Epiphanes Eucharistos.*
>
> Decree of 27 March, 196 BC, inscribed on the Rosetta Stone in Greek, Egyptian demotic and hieroglyphics

202 BC The Roman general **Scipio Africanus** defeats Hannibal at the **battle of Zama** in North Africa; Carthage is humbled and Rome emerges as the paramount power in the Western Mediterranean.

197 BC The Romans defeat Philip V of Macedon at the **battle of Cynocephalae** in Greece.

196 BC Rome declares all **Greece** free from Macedonian rule.

A decree of 27 March inscribed on what later will be known as the **Rosetta Stone** (discovered in 1799 AD and deciphered by Jean-François Champollion in 1822) shows Ptolemy V ingratiating himself with the Egyptian priesthood to assure himself of their loyalty during these times of native discontent.

195 BC Hannibal arrives at the court of the Seleucid king **Antiochus III** amid rumours that he plans another invasion of **Italy** at the head of a Seleucid army.

189 BC A Roman army commanded by Scipio Africanus defeats Antiochus III at the **battle of Magnesia** in Asia Minor as Hannibal looks on.

> **"** The peace of Apamea altered the face of the Hellenistic east; Rome was now the predominant power ... The naval disarmament clauses of the three great peace treaties of 202, 196 and 188 had made the Mediterranean a Roman lake. The time that followed was one of constant Roman interference; every weaker disputant, every person aggrieved, appealed to Rome, and Roman commissioners were perpetually travelling eastward. **"**
>
> W.W. Tarn and G.T. Griffith, *Hellenistic Civilisation* (1952)

188 BC At the **peace of Apamea**, Rome makes Antiochus III surrender Asia Minor, give up his fleet and pay a large indemnity. Rome also demands Hannibal, but he escapes.

186 BC The uprising in **Thebes** is suppressed.

180 BC For the second time in 24 years, the dynasty falls into the hands of court intriguers. **Ptolemy VI Philometor** (r. 180–145 BC) is only about 7 years old when he comes to the throne following his father's premature death.

173 BC Rome and Egypt renew their agreement of friendship (*amicitia*) on its hundredth anniversary.

c.170–160 BC Many **Jews** leave Palestine during the Maccabean risings against the Seleucids and settle in the Delta, in the military settlements of the **Fayyum** and in **Alexandria**, where they join its already substantial Hellenized Jewish population. According to the Greek historian **Polybius**, the administration of the entire country and the control of the armed forces during the reign of Ptolemy VI was entrusted to two Jews, **Dositheus** and **Onias IV**, the latter the son of the hereditary high priest at Jerusalem.

170 BC Ptolemy VI is led into a disastrous war against the Seleucid king Antiochus IV by his regents, a pair of palace courtiers, formerly Asian slaves. After making rabble-rousing speeches to the Alexandrian mob, they march the Egyptian army towards **Palestine**, but Antiochus counterattacks and invades **Egypt**. Now the Alexandrian mob overthrows the regents of Ptolemy VI and puts his younger brother on the throne as **Ptolemy the Brother** (the future Ptolemy VIII Euergetes II).

169 BC Antiochus establishes a **protectorate** over Ptolemy VI, who is at Memphis – which is placed under the control of a Seleucid governor. Meanwhile Ptolemy the Brother is king at Alexandria, and the country is divided against itself, which entirely suits Antiochus as he leaves Egypt.

169 BC Cleopatra II, the sister-wife of Ptolemy VI, arranges that her brothers should rule jointly, thus upsetting Antiochus' divisive scheme.

168 BC Antiochus IV again invades Egypt and besieges **Alexandria**, but the Romans now intervene and their ambassador **Popillius Laenas** hands Antiochus the Senate's decree that he must withdraw from Egypt immediately, then draws a line in the sand.

164 BC Ptolemy VIII wins popularity with the Alexandrian mob and drives his older brother out of Egypt. But Ptolemy VI pleads before the Roman Senate, which rules that he is to have **Egypt** and **Cyprus** while Ptolemy VIII is to have **Cyrenaica**.

> **❝** And then the Guardian Spirit will desert the city [Alexandria] which they founded and will go to god-bearing Memphis and their city will be deserted. That will be the end of our evils when Egypt shall see the foreigners fall like leaves from the branch. The city by the sea will be a drying-place for the fishermen's catch and passers-by will say, 'This was the all-nurturing city in which all the races of mankind lived.' **❞**
>
> *Oracle of the Potter* (3rd century BC)

> **"** Popilius did something which seemed insolent and arrogant to the highest degree. With a vine stick which he had in his hand he drew a circle around Antiochus and told him to give his reply to the message before he stepped out of the circle. The king was taken aback by this high-handed action, but after hesitating a little he said he would do everything required of him by the Romans. **"**
>
> Polybius, *History*, xxix, 27 (2nd century BC)

163 BC The Alexandrian mob tires of Ptolemy VIII and rises against him. His life is saved by a Roman embassy which enacts the Senate's decree and despatches Ptolemy the Brother to **Cyrene**. Henceforth **Ptolemy VI** is the sole king of Egypt and remains so until the end of his life.

147 BC **Macedonia** becomes a Roman province.

146 BC The total destruction of **Carthage** concludes the **Third Punic War**, which began in 149 BC. North Africa becomes a Roman province.

145 BC Ptolemy VI's young son becomes co-ruler as **Ptolemy VII Neos Philopator**. But when Ptolemy VI dies while campaigning in Palestine, Ptolemy the Brother returns to Alexandria from Cyrene and ascends the throne as **Ptolemy VIII Euergetes II** (r. 145–116 BC) – being exceptionally fat, the Alexandrians call him 'Physcon' (potbelly). One of his first acts is to marry Ptolemy VI's wife **Cleopatra II** and to murder her son, Ptolemy VII. In reprisal for being thrown out of the city in 163 BC, he viciously persecutes everyone he suspects of disloyalty, ordering confiscations, banishments, executions and even massacres of the Greek citizens of Alexandria by his hired soldiers. Intellectuals are a special target, with many artists and scientists abandoning the Library and the Museion, and fleeing to Greece. Life in Alexandria is brutalized by his rule, and Greek culture is impoverished for generations to come. Egyptians and Jews play a greater role in the administration from now on, while the Greek household troops and the garrison are replaced by Cretans, Gauls, Cilicians, Egyptians and others.

142 BC Ptolemy VIII formally dedicates the **temple of Horus** at Edfu, 95 years after its foundation stone was laid by Ptolemy III, and he builds elsewhere round the country – notably at **Philae** and **Kom Ombo**. Around this time, he marries his sister-wife's daughter, **Cleopatra III**. Ptolemy and the two Cleopatras are all officially styled as sovereigns of Egypt.

131–130 BC Cleopatra II is the focus of a rebellion against Ptolemy VIII, who flees to **Cyprus** with their son and also with Cleopatra III and his children by her. Once abroad, Ptolemy kills his son by Cleopatra II, has the body chopped up and sends the pieces in a box to Alexandria as a birthday present to the boy's mother. Meanwhile Ptolemy VIII's illegitimate son **Ptolemy Apion** becomes king of Cyrenaica.

129 BC Ptolemy regains **Alexandria** by military force as Cleopatra II flees abroad to Antioch, but factional violence continues in Egypt.

> " The growth of Egyptian nationalism, with the accompanying menace of riots by the urban population, the threat and even the reality of foreign invasion, and – after the earlier part of the reign of Philometor – dynastic strife, which very soon and increasingly involved the Alexandrian urban mob in its continuous struggle, did not offer an attractive background for creative activity of any sort. "
>
> P.M. Fraser, *Ptolemaic Alexandria* (1972)

124 BC Cleopatra II agrees a **reconciliation** with Ptolemy and returns to Alexandria, while throughout Egypt the violence between their supporters gradually diminishes.

118 BC Dynastic infighting is finally brought to an end when a **decree** is issued by Ptolemy VIII, Cleopatra II and Cleopatra III which settles the differences between their partisans and grants a universal amnesty.

116–107 BC When Ptolemy VIII dies peacefully in his bed, Cleopatra III rules jointly with their son, **Ptolemy IX Soter II**. He is popularly known as 'Lathyrus' (chickpea),

Animal cults

With the old order confronted by foreign influences, Egyptians of the Late and Ptolemaic periods increasingly clung to tangible shreds of belief, so that animal cults came to enjoy an astonishing popularity. At Saqqara the priests had long been giving magnificent burials to the Apis bulls, but now new and vast underground chambers were established – the **Anubieion**, sacred to Anubis, with a gallery for dogs; the **Bubasteion**, sacred to Bastet, filled with mummified cats; the temple of **Thoth**, its subterranean galleries piled high with thousands of baboons and millions of mummified ibises and falcons; and the **Isieion**, the temple of Isis, with underground galleries containing the sarcophagi of the sacred cows that had given birth to the Apis bulls. These uncountable numbers of mummified creatures were brought over hundreds of years by pilgrims as offerings to a favoured god, or as supplication by those seeking a cure.

For the Egyptians, animals carried within them the quality of the eternal; animal cults provided a reassurance that Egypt was at one with the sacred, and that things would remain fundamentally unchanged. The intensity of Egyptians' feelings in the matter can be gauged from the incident witnessed in the first century BC by the Greek historian **Diodorus Siculus** in Alexandria, when a Roman diplomat accidentally killed a cat and was immediately lynched by the mob.

though the point of this Alexandrian joke has been lost.

107 BC Cleopatra III stirs up the Alexandrian mob against her son Ptolemy IX, who flees abroad and is replaced by his mother's favoured younger son, **Ptolemy X Alexander I** (r. 107–88 BC), with whom she now rules jointly.

101 BC Cleopatra III dies – some say murdered by Ptolemy X, who now rules with **Cleopatra Berenice III**, the daughter of his brother Ptolemy IX.

96 BC Ptolemy Apion dies and leaves **Cyrenaica** to Rome.

89 BC The army turns against Ptolemy X, who flees to **Syria** – where he raises a mercenary force and re-enters Alexandria. To pay his troops, he melts down the golden sarcophagus of Alexander the Great.

88 BC The population of **Alexandria** rises against Ptolemy X, who is killed while fleeing to Cyprus. **Ptolemy IX Soter II** (second reign 88–80 BC) is restored to the throne.

Mithridates, the king of Pontus on the southern shore of the Black Sea, overruns Asia Minor and massacres its Roman residents.

88–86 BC **Thebes** is severely punished and left in ruin after a native rebellion there is put down.

80 BC At the death of Ptolemy IX, **Cleopatra Berenice III** rules alone for six months, then in association with **Ptolemy XI Alexander II**, who is almost immediately assassinated by the Alexandrian mob. The Romans allege that he leaves Egypt to them in his will. **Ptolemy XII Neos Dionysos** (r. 80–51 BC), popularly known as 'Auletes' (flute-player), ascends the throne, but Rome refuses to recognize him.

74 BC **Cyrenaica** is formally made a Roman province.

c.70–69 BC Ptolemy XII and (probably) his sister-wife Cleopatra V Tryphaena have a daughter, **Cleopatra VII**.

66 BC The Roman general **Gnaeus Pompey** is given the command against Mithridates, who is finally defeated.

65 BC In Rome, **Julius Caesar** and his political ally, the plutocrat **Marcus Licinius Crassus**, show an interest in annexing Egypt for its riches.

64 BC Pompey enters **Syria** and puts an end to the Seleucid monarchy.

62 BC Pompey annexes Syria, which becomes a Roman province.

60 BC Rome is governed by Caesar, Pompey and Crassus, who form the **First Triumvirate**.

59 BC Caesar pursues his scheme for the annexation of Egypt, but Ptolemy XII buys him off with a gigantic bribe – in return for which the Senate recognizes Ptolemy as **king of Egypt** and Caesar and Pompey recognize him as 'Ally and Friend of the Roman People'.

58 BC Rome makes **Cyprus** a province, and its king, a brother of Ptolemy XII, commits suicide. The Alexandrian mob is outraged at Ptolemy's failure to protect the island, and he goes to Rome to seek military support.

57 BC Ptolemy's eldest daughter **Berenice IV** and his wife **Cleopatra V Tryphaena** rule in his absence, though his wife dies in the same year and his daughter, with the support of the Alexandrian mob, usurps the throne. The temple to Horus at **Edfu**, second in size only to the temple of Amun at Karnak, is completed on 5 December, after 180 years.

55 BC After paying an enormous bribe to Pompey's friend **Aulus Gabinius**, the proconsul of Syria, Ptolemy XII is restored to his throne. His first act is to have his treacherous daughter **Berenice IV** killed. A Roman garrison is left behind at **Alexandria**.

51 BC The 9-year-old **Ptolemy XIII** (r. 51–47 BC) and his sister-wife the 17-year-old **Cleopatra VII Philopator** (r. 51–30 BC) rule jointly with their father, who dies the same year. From now on, Cleopatra is effectively sole ruler of Egypt.

> **"** Destiny had determined that the fortune of the house of Ptolemy, before going out, should blaze up in a manner dramatic and astonishing. The reign of the last sovereign would be the reign which men afterwards would remember more than any other. When everything seemed lost, the heirs of the house of Ptolemy would suddenly have almost put within their grasp a dominion stretching not only over the lost ancestral lands, but over wider territories than Ptolemy I or Ptolemy II or Ptolemy III had ever dreamed of. Those kings, being men, had based their dominion on the power of their arms; but now, when the military power of Egypt had become contemptible beside that of Rome, the sovereign of Egypt would bring to the contest power of a wholly different kind – the power of a fascinating woman. The strength of Rome was so great that no king of Egypt could hope to save the falling kingdom by any power a king could command, but a queen of Egypt, with this power of a different order, might actually convert the very strength of Rome to be the instrument of her purposes. At no other moment of history do we see the attraction exercised by woman upon man made so definitely a determining force in the political and military field, used so deliberately by a woman amid the clash of great armies to achieve the ends of her own imperialist ambition. And Cleopatra came very near ultimate success. **"**
>
> Edwyn Bevan, *A History of Egypt under the Ptolemaic Dynasty* (1927)

50 BC Caesar crosses the Rubicon, marking the beginning of the **civil war** with Pompey.

49 BC Supposedly in accordance with Ptolemy XII's will, Pompey is appointed by the Senate as **legal guardian** of Ptolemy XIII after Cleopatra is driven from Alexandria by palace supporters of her brother, assisted by the mob.

48 BC The Roman civil war ends with Caesar's defeat of Pompey at **Pharsalus**. With Caesar at his heels, Pompey flees to Egypt, arriving in the camp of Ptolemy XIII at **Pelusium**, where Cleopatra, at the head of a Bedouin army, is invading Egypt from the Sinai desert. But Ptolemy betrays Pompey and has him murdered. Though Pompey has been Caesar's rival, Caesar determines to avenge the death of his fellow Roman and makes common cause with Cleopatra against her brother **Ptolemy XIII**. During the fighting in Alexandria, a quantity of books in a harbour warehouse are burnt, giving rise to the false belief that Caesar destroyed the Library.

47 BC Ptolemy XIII is defeated and drowned. Caesar grants the Egyptian throne to Cleopatra and her yet younger brother **Ptolemy XIV**, whom she marries, and also gives them **Cyprus**. Caesar and the pregnant Cleopatra enjoy a sightseeing voyage up the Nile. Leaving a substantial Roman garrison behind him, Caesar leaves Egypt before Cleopatra gives birth to their son **Caesarion**.

46 BC Cleopatra, Caesarion and Ptolemy XIV arrive in **Rome**. The government, wholly in the hands of the dictator Caesar reaffirms with Cleopatra the **treaty** of alliance and friendship agreed with her father in 59 BC.

44 BC Caesar is **assassinated** on 15 March, and Cleopatra leaves for Egypt soon afterwards. No later than September Ptolemy XIV is dead, possibly murdered on Cleopatra's orders.

Cleopatra and the modern calendar

The calendar in use throughout the world today can be traced back to Cleopatra's relationship with Caesar – for among her entourage when she came to Rome was the Alexandrian astronomer **Sosigenes**. Various forms of solar calendar had been tried in Egypt since about 3000 BC, and further research had been done at the Ptolemies' Musieon in Alexandria before arriving at a 365-day calendar with a leap day every four years. In Caesar's time, the less exact Roman solar calendar was completely out of phase with the seasons, but during Cleopatra's visit Caesar introduced the **Alexandrian calendar** to Rome, though to bring the old reckoning into line with the new he had to extend the year 46 BC to 445 days. Thereafter the new calendar was applied throughout the Roman Empire and so passed into the modern world.

After Octavian had defeated Cleopatra and Antony and had renamed himself **Augustus**, he celebrated his career by renaming the two months of high summer. He called one 'July' after his adoptive father Julius Caesar, and the other 'August' after himself – and because it was in this month that he entered Alexandria, the month in which Cleopatra committed suicide.

43 BC Caesar's chief assistants **Mark Antony** and **Lepidus**, together with Caesar's adopted son **Octavian**, form the Second Triumvirate.

42 BC Antony and Octavian defeat Caesar's assassins Brutus and Cassius at **Philippi** in northern Greece. Antony takes over the eastern provinces as his share of the Roman world.

41 BC Summoned by Antony to meet him at **Tarsus** on the Mediterranean coast of Asia Minor, Cleopatra arrives aboard her yacht in the guise of a goddess making her appearance before a god.

41–40 BC Antony winters with Cleopatra at Alexandria.

> **"** She came sailing up the river Cydnus in a barge with a poop of gold, its purple sails billowing in the wind, while her rowers caressed the water with oars of silver which dipped in time to the music of the flute, accompanied by pipes and lutes. Cleopatra herself reclined beneath a canopy of cloth of gold, dressed in the character of Venus, as we see her in paintings, while on either side to complete the picture stood boys costumed as Cupids, who cooled her with their fans. Instead of a crew the barge was lined with the most beautiful of her waiting-women attired as Nereids and Graces, some at the rudders, others at the tackle of the sails and all the while an indescribably rich perfume, exhaled from innumerable censers, was wafted from the vessel to the river-banks ... The word spread on every side that Venus had come to revel with Bacchus for the happiness of Asia. **"**

Plutarch, *Life of Mark Antony*

40 BC Cleopatra gives birth to twins by Antony, **Alexander Helios** (Sun) and **Cleopatra Selene** (Moon). The two chief partners of the Second Triumvirate supplement their political pact by a dynastic alliance when Antony marries Octavian's sister **Octavia**.

37 BC Antony rejects Octavia and **marries Cleopatra**, to whom he grants large extensions of territory from Roman conquests in the East.

36 BC Antony launches an expedition against **Parthia**, but it fails, depleting his war funds and making him more reliant on Cleopatra and the resources of Egypt. Cleopatra gives birth to another son by Antony, **Ptolemy Philadelphus**, and begins joint rule with Caesarion, her son by Caesar.

35 BC Octavian begins a five-year propaganda war against Cleopatra and Antony, depicting him as an un-Roman drunkard and libertine caught in the toils of a scheming oriental queen.

Cleopatra and Caesarion, her son by Julius Caesar, are carved in traditional Egyptian form at the temple of Hathor at Dendera in Upper Egypt

Cleopatra's dream of a Graeco-Roman partnership

The **Donations of Alexandria** were the centrepiece of a great festival arranged by Cleopatra and Antony at which their children were proclaimed kings of Armenia, Media, Parthia, Cilicia, Syria and Phoenicia, and where her eldest, Caesarion, her son and heir by Julius Caesar, was proclaimed 'King of Kings'. Cleopatra herself, dressed as the goddess Isis, was proclaimed 'Queen of Kings' as she and Antony distributed these kingships among her brood.

Theatrical as the occasion was, the Donations were neither empty words nor meaningless pomp; they were part of Cleopatra's and Antony's realizable – if ambitiously far-reaching – design for a **Romano-Hellenic empire** based on Alexandria. All the same, things did not work out that way: in 30 BC the victorious Octavian, addressing the same throng in the same stadium, promised the Alexandrians leniency because their city was so splendid, because Alexander was its founder – and then had Caesarion put to death, Octavian's companion remarking that 'it is bad to have too many Caesars'. The entire Greek world was now under Roman rule, yet hardly more than 300 years later Cleopatra's dream of a Graeco-Roman empire was in fact realized; its capital was not Alexandria but Constantinople.

34 BC Antony and Cleopatra stage the spectacular **Donations of Alexandria**, which promise the restoration of the old Ptolemaic empire and more. Roman lands in the East – and even lands yet to be conquered – are parcelled out among Cleopatra and her children.

32 BC Italian public opinion turns decisively against Antony when he divorces Octavia, and when Octavian broadcasts the contents of **Antony's will**, which declares Caesarion the legitimate heir of Caesar (thus undermining Octavian's adoption by Caesar) and expresses Antony's wish to be buried alongside Cleopatra. The will feeds rumours that Antony intends to transfer the seat of Roman government to Alexandria. Octavian **declares war** on Cleopatra.

31 BC Antony and Cleopatra base their fleet and army at Actium on the western coast of Greece, but they are hemmed in by Octavian's legions, which have crossed from Italy, and by the Roman fleet under Octavian's admiral **Agrippa**. At the **battle of Actium** Cleopatra's fleet is more successful at breaking out than Antony's and creates the impression that she has fled to Egypt with Antony in her wake, demoralizing his forces in Greece, who soon surrender to Octavian.

30 BC During the summer, Octavian enters Egypt and defeats Antony outside the walls of **Alexandria**. Antony commits suicide. On 1 August, Octavian enters the city.

> ❝ Her death was very sodain. For those whom Caesar sent unto her ran thither in all haste possible, and found the soldiers standing at the gate, mistrusting nothing, nor understanding of her death. But when they had opened the doors, they found Cleopatra stark dead, laid upon a bed of gold, attired and arrayed in her royal robes, and one of her two women, which was called Iras, dead at her feet: and her other woman called Charmian half dead, and trembling, trimming the diadem which Cleopatra wore upon her head. One of the soldiers seeing her, angrily said to her: Is that well done, Charmian? Very well said she again, and meet for a princess descended of so many royal kings. She said no more, but fell down dead hard by the bed. ❞
>
> Plutarch, *Life of Mark Antony* (trans. Sir Thomas North (1579), the version used by Shakespeare in *Antony and Cleopatra* and his other Roman plays)

Three years later, when he renames himself 'Augustus', he will give his name to this month. Rather than be taken back to Rome captive, Cleopatra commits suicide on 12 August – possibly poisoned by the bite of an asp (though no one is sure). Octavian has Caesarion, her son by Julius Caesar, killed at about the same time.

6: The Roman and Christian periods

30 BC–640 AD

At first, little changed in Egypt as a result of the **Roman occupation**. Like the Ptolemaic kings before them, the Roman emperors were now carved on the walls of temples in traditional pharaonic guise and were shown receiving the approbation of the old divinities of the land. Egyptian religion continued to function as before, with the Romans building temples in the ancient style and the priesthood propagating the timeless beliefs and rituals. Indeed, the popularity of Egyptian cults throughout the Mediterranean, which had already begun in Ptolemaic times, continued to grow apace under the Roman Empire.

The chief aim of the Romans, as it had been for the Ptolemies or indeed for Egyptian kings going back to the Old Kingdom, was to reap the surplus of Egypt's agricultural harvest. They also opened granite and porphyry quarries in the Eastern Desert, where for the first time they mined and smelted iron ore in quantity. But the fine grey granite from Mons Claudianus was exported exclusively to Rome where it was used extensively in the forum; the porphyry cut at Mons Porphyrites was likewise shipped across the Mediterranean where it was valued for its imperial connotation; while the primary importance of the Egyptian wheat crop was that it provided Rome with sufficient grain to supply the needs of the entire city for four months of every year. Where the Ptolemies exploited Egypt for the ultimate benefit of Egypt, the Romans exploited Egypt for the benefit of Rome.

Egypt was squeezed in every possible way. All the money extracted from the country, like all the grain sent to Rome (and later to Constantinople) was sheer loss – going out without any return – so that the fellahin were driven into a miserable condition. The consequences were already apparent by the end of the 1st century AD when the **population** began to fall sharply – from five million to about three million at the time of the Arab conquests in the seventh century. Though Alexandrian prosperity was enhanced by its control of trade with **India**, which passed between the Red Sea and the Mediterranean, the countryside entered a period of prolonged **economic decline**. The over-taxation of Egyptians led to the abandonment of marginal land and a fall in agricultural productivity, with further ruin caused by Rome's failure to maintain critical irrigation systems, by religious strife and civil war, by epidemics and by the devastations of **Nubian** and **Bedouin incursions**.

Significantly, very few Egyptian temples were built after the 1st century AD. The financial burden and the mismanagement of Roman rule meant the crippling of temple funding and the marginalization of the social role of the priesthood. Under these conditions, Egypt's ancient religion was undermined, while **Christianity** offered a simpler, less expensive form of worship – as well as the rejection of earthly bonds.

Roman Egypt: 30 BC–313 AD

Octavian made Egypt a province of the Roman Empire, but instead of placing it under the authority of the Senate, he took Egypt as his personal estate and forbade any senator or member of the nobility to set foot in it without his permission. Antony and Cleopatra had used the resources of Egypt to challenge the power of Rome, and Octavian was determined not to risk that happening again. In particular, he wanted to keep the Egyptian **wheat supply** in his hands and thereby control Rome's hungry populace. Octavian appointed a prefect who administered the country on his behalf, an arrangement followed by every Roman emperor for the next six centuries.

The **Greeks of Egypt**, who had been its governing class, were denied all administrative powers and made to feel they were a conquered people. Their sense of humiliation and resentment was compounded when Octavian – or **Augustus** as he styled himself after 27 BC – renewed the rights and privileges that the Jews had enjoyed under the Ptolemies, which included regulating their own affairs through a community leader and a council of elders. The rivalry and tension between Greeks, Jews and Romans would often explode into violence. As for the native Egyptians, the Romans did nothing for them at all except burden them with oppressive levels of taxation. In later Ptolemaic times intermarriage between Greeks and Egyptians had become more common, but the Romans put an end to it with harsh decrees of social separation.

Alexandria under the early Ptolemies had enjoyed a brilliant intellectual life, though conspicuously one that did not encourage **philosophy** – the Ptolemies were autocrats and wanted no questions asked. But now that Alexandria was merely a provincial capital far from the centre of Roman power, philosophy flourished, and the city became the birthplace of **Neo-Platonism** – developing Plato's idea that we live in an imperfect copy of an ideal world, to which they added a powerful mystic dimension. The greatest of the Alexandrian Neo-Platonists was **Plotinus** (205–70). Unlike his Christian contemporaries, who promised that each person could see God, Plotinus taught that the way to discover God was by developing one's inward vision, because each individual is God. Yet it was typical of the relaxed and fluid intellectual and spiritual atmosphere in Alexandria at this time that **Ammonius Saccas**, the founder of Neo-Platonism, was a convert to paganism from Christianity and counted among his students not only the pagan Plotinus but the great Christian theologian **Origen**. There was toleration between pagans and Christians, while Christianity itself had not yet hardened into dogma. For the time being persecution came from outside Egypt, in the form of Roman emperors claiming divinity the better to impose their authority – ironically, a trick they had learnt from the Ptolemies and from the god-kings of ancient Egypt.

Despite ferocious **persecution**, the worst anywhere in the Roman Empire, Christianity spread from the Greek and Jewish environment of the cities to the native Egyptian countryside, where it took strong root. The effect was an increase in the power of the patriarchs of Alexandria, successors to St Mark as heads of the Egyptian Church, who became the representatives of the Egyptian or **Coptic** people and led the opposition to imperial authority. (Just as the name Egypt is derived from the Greek *Aigyptos*, so the Greek for native Egyptians, which is *Aigyptoi*, gave rise to the term 'Copt'.)

In addition to its problems in Egypt, Rome faced a growing threat from **Persia**, which it met by making **Odainat**, who was ruler of the great Romano-Arab trading city of Palmyra in the Syrian desert, the semi-independent commander of the empire's entire defensive system in the East. When Odainat died in 266, his widow **Zenobia** threw off the mantle of imperial ally, declared herself Roman empress and conquered most of Asia Minor as well as the Near East and Egypt. Her rebellion was short-lived, however; in 272 her armies were defeated by the emperor **Aurelian**, who in the same year suppressed a revolt in Alexandria in which the tomb of Alexander was destroyed and much of the Great Library too.

To remedy the perilous strategic situation, the emperor **Diocletian** (284–305) divided the Roman Empire into eastern and western administrations, each with its own emperor, titled 'Augustus', who was assisted by a 'Caesar' – an arrangement known as the **Tetrarchy** ('rule by four'). Diocletian was Augustus in the East but was also in overall command. In tightening Rome's control over its eastern provinces, he reinforced the claim that as emperor he should be worshipped as a god. Egyptians under their old religion had once readily accorded divinity to their rulers, but now no one offered fiercer resistance to emperor worship than Egypt's Christians, nor did any people suffer greater persecution – which ended only when Diocletian was succeeded by **Constantine the Great** (306–37), who issued an edict tolerating Christianity.

30 BC On 31 August, Egypt becomes a **Roman province** under the direct authority of **Octavian** (r. 30 BC–14 AD), who administers the country through a prefect based in Alexandria.

27 BC Octavian takes the name **Augustus** in January.

> ❝ Egypt, together with the forces designed to keep it in order, has been governed ever since Augustus' day by Romans of equestrian rank acting as successors to the Ptolemies. It seemed politic that a province of this sort – difficult of access, exporting a valuable corn-crop yet divided and unsettled by strange cults and irresponsible excesses, indifferent to law and ignorant of civil government – should be kept under the immediate control of the imperial house. ❞
>
> Tacitus, *The Histories* (early 2nd century AD)

Octavian, the future Augustus, defeated Antony and Cleopatra and made Egypt part of the Roman Empire

25 BC Roman troops are attacked by Nubians, who capture **Aswan** and carry off statues of Augustus. A Roman punitive expedition advances into Nubia as far as **Napata**; the Nubians cede some territory south of the First Cataract, fixing Egypt's southern boundary for the next three centuries.

14 AD **Tiberius** (r. 14–37) becomes Roman emperor on the death of Augustus. Egypt is sufficiently peaceful that he cuts the number of legions stationed there from three to two.

c.30 **Jesus of Nazareth** is crucified at Jerusalem.

38 The **Jews** of Alexandria object to statues of the deified emperor **Caligula** (r. 37–41) being erected in their synagogues and riot in the streets against the demand that they worship him. The city's Greeks take advantage of the situation by persuading the Roman prefect to withdraw the Jews' special privileges; the Greeks also plunder and kill the Jews at will.

Cleopatra's Needles

In the last years of her reign, Cleopatra began a stupendous temple in honour of Mark Antony near the Eastern Harbour in Alexandria, but the pair were defeated by Octavian and committed suicide before it was completed. Rededicated by their conqueror, who was worshipped there as Caesar Augustus, the **Caesareum** remained in imperial hands until Christian times when it became the cathedral of the city. In about 10 BC the Romans adorned the Caesareum with two great **obelisks** brought from Heliopolis which bore inscriptions by Tuthmosis III, Seti I and Rameses II. In time the Caesareum was destroyed, but the obelisks remained and became popularly known as Cleopatra's Needles, though they had nothing to do with her. In 1877 one was removed to **London**'s Embankment and the other was taken to **New York** and erected in Central Park two years later.

40 A Jewish embassy led by the philosopher **Philo** travels from Alexandria to Rome to present its case to Caligula, who instead of insisting on their worship contemptuously offers them his pity that they do not recognize him as god. The Jews at this time amount to perhaps as much as a ninth of the Egyptian population.

41 The emperor **Claudius** (r. 41–54) settles the troubles at **Alexandria**, cautioning the Greeks to accept Jewish customs and telling the Jews to stop agitating for privileged status. The danger of continued disturbances in the city requires that the Romans base the bulk of their legions there, while the rest of the country is controlled by only small detachments of troops.

45 According to legend, **St Mark** comes to Alexandria, where he is said to make the first Christian convert in Egypt – a Jewish shoemaker called **Annianus**.

64 A great **fire** breaks out in Rome; the emperor **Nero** (r. 54–68) makes scapegoats of the Christians and conducts a bloody persecution against them.

66 The Jews of **Judaea** revolt against Roman rule.

69 The prefect of Egypt in Alexandria proclaims **Vespasian** Roman emperor (r. 69–79), who succeeds in his claim partly because he gains control of the **grain supply** to Rome. Vespasian then visits Alexandria, where he is hailed as the son of Amun and Serapis.

70 The Romans suppress the revolt in Judaea; they sack **Jerusalem**, burn the Temple and decimate the Jewish population.

81–96 During his reign as emperor, **Domitian** founds temples to Isis and Serapis in **Rome**.

98 **Trajan** becomes emperor. During his reign (98–117) he builds the Kiosk of Trajan at Philae and a fortress at **Babylon** (within the area of today's Cairo), the Nile crossing

MICHAEL HAAG

Greek settlers in Egypt were mummified at death but buried with expressive portraits of themselves done while alive

point between Heliopolis and Memphis. He also restores the old canal between the Nile and the Red Sea begun by Necho, improving Egypt's trade with India.

c.100 By this date **Christianity** is established in Egypt, as shown by a late-1st-century copy of **St John's Gospel** (found in the early 20th century in the Fayyum).

114 The appearance of a 'messiah' in **Cyrene** sparks off a Jewish revolt there which spreads to Alexandria.

115–17 The **Jewish revolt** in Alexandria turns into a vicious guerrilla war in Egypt which spreads to **Cyprus** and **Mesopotamia**. The massacre of Greeks in the Fayyum, the Nile Valley and the Delta by roving bands of Jewish terrorists leads to the arming of the native population. The insurrection is suppressed, however, and the Jewish community in Egypt is effectively extinguished until the 3rd century.

118 The emperor **Hadrian** (r. 117–38) decrees a reduction in Egyptian **land taxes** to compensate for the loss of agricultural production during the Jewish insurrection.

The Coptic (Egyptian) language

Though the official languages of administration in Egypt were Greek and Latin, Egyptians continued to speak a variation on the language spoken by their ancestors who built the Pyramids. In its written form, it appeared in three scripts: **hieroglyphic**, used mostly for monumental inscriptions; **hieratic**, a cursive form of hieroglyphic used for formal documents on papyrus; and **demotic**, developed around 700 BC, which was a simplified form of hieratic for everyday use. The problem with these scripts, however, was that they indicated only consonants and not vowel sounds, but during the 1st century AD Egyptians adopted the **Greek alphabet**, to which they added a number of demotic signs to express sounds not represented by Greek. By means of this Coptic script, Egyptians developed a flourishing native literature, both secular and religious.

> **"** Those who worship Serapis are Christians, and those who call themselves bishops of Christ are devoted to Serapis. As a race of men they are seditious, vain and spiteful; as a body, wealthy and prosperous, of whom nobody lives in idleness. Some blow glass, some make paper, and other linen. Their one God is nothing peculiar; Christians, Jews and all nations worship him. I wish this body of men was better behaved. **"**

130–31 Hadrian tours Egypt for eight or ten months with his wife and his lover Antinous, who drowns in the Nile – causing the emperor to found **Antinopolis** in his memory. Hadrian's visit to **Thebes** is commemorated by his retinue, who carve graffiti on the leg of one of the Colossi of Memnon, the gigantic statues of Amenophis III which stand before the king's funerary temple. In Alexandria Hadrian disputes with the scholars at the **Museion**, while at the **Serapeum** he confuses Christians with worshippers of the pagan god.

135 The Romans put down a further revolt by the Jews of Judaea (started in 131) and eject them from **Jerusalem**.

138–61 The last significant temple building in Egypt is undertaken during the reign of the emperor **Antoninus Pius**, who makes additions to the temples at **Dendera**, **Medinet Habu** and **Esna**.

c.150 **Claudius Ptolemy**, astronomer, geographer and cartographer, flourishes at Alexandria. He extends and codifies the works of his Ptolemaic predecessors such as **Eratosthenes** (c.276–194 BC), but unlike **Aristarchus of Samos** (fl. 280–264 BC) who realized that the earth went round the sun, Claudius Ptolemy placed the earth at the centre of the universe – an error adopted by all subsequent astronomers until Galileo in the 17th century.

154 The Roman prefect's New-Year edict offers an **amnesty** to those who have fled their villages to escape the growing **poverty** of the countryside owing to years of social disruption, over-taxation and the state's failure to maintain the irrigation system. In the Fayyum, for example, the desert reclaims once productive sites, but Alexandrian prosperity is enhanced by its control of the Indian **mercantile trade** passing through the Red Sea and the Nile Valley to the Mediterranean.

The Catechetical School

Founded as a Christian alternative to the Museion, the Catechetical School sought to disentangle the literature and philosophy of Greek classical education from pagan belief. Next to nothing is known of its founder Pantaneus, but **Clement** (c.160–215), who succeeded him as head of the school in about 190, was a Greek from Athens. Rather than denouncing Greek philosophy and the Jewish law, he presented these as preparations for the Gospel, declaring that Christ was the source of human reason, and that Christianity was the heir to the past and the interpreter of the future. **Origen** (c.185–255), an Egyptian born in Alexandria, continued Clement's teachings when he succeeded him in 202. The two remain among the greatest figures of the Church for their writings and their teachings at the Catechetical School, which gave an intellectual underpinning to Early Christianity and made it attractive to more sophisticated minds – among them foreign scholars such as **Rufinus** and **St Jerome**. But Christian orthodoxy, which built on the foundations laid by Clement and Origen, would not share their enlightenment and respect for the past. A succession of clashes followed with the increasingly powerful patriarchs of Alexandria, who arrogated theological matters to themselves, and towards the end of the 4th century, during the patriarchy of Theophilus (an ignorant thug), the Catechetical School was closed.

c.160 During the reign of the emperor **Marcus Aurelius** (r. 161–80), **plague** sweeps Egypt and much of the Roman Empire.

171–75 Roman forces in Egypt are routed during a fierce revolt led by an Egyptian priest, **Isidorus**, which is subdued only after fresh troops are brought in from Syria.

c.180 The **Catechetical School**, a Christian university and theological school, is founded in Alexandria by **Pantaneus**.

c.193 Ammonius Saccas establishes his **Neo-Platonist school** in Alexandria. His students will include the Christian theologian **Origen** and the Neo-Platonist philosopher **Plotinus**.

199–200 The emperor **Septimius Severus** (r. 193–211) visits Egypt, which for the first time is offered a measure of **self-government** at the local level when he creates town councils in each nome. This is met with resentment, however, as greater responsibility means increased tax obligations.

202 Severus forbids **Christians** to proselytize, affecting the activities of the Catechetical School. Clement flees Egypt to escape persecution, and Origen's father is martyred at this time – though the 17-year-old Origen is prevented from making a martyr of himself when his mother stops him leaving the house by hiding his clothes. Instead, Origen succeeds Clement as head of the Catechetical School.

204 An **imperial edict** prohibits Roman citizens from embracing Christianity. In Egypt, the Delta is studded with Christian communities.

212 The emperor **Caracalla** (r. 198–217) extends **Roman citizenship** to all inhabitants of the Roman Empire, which dilutes its prerogatives but saddles new citizens with tax liabilities. Rivalry between Caracalla and his brother and co-ruler **Geta** culminates with Geta's murder.

> **To any vision must be brought an eye adapted to what is to be seen.**
>
> Plotinus, *The Enneads*

215 Caracalla **visits Egypt**, where the Alexandrian mob mocks him for claiming to have killed Geta in self-defence. In retaliation he allows his troops several days of indiscriminate plunder and murder throughout the city. All native Egyptians are expelled from Alexandria and sent back to the land to increase rural productivity.

c.231 Origen is driven from Alexandria by the patriarch **Demetrius** for his views and settles at **Caesarea** in Palestine.

231–42 **Plotinus** (205–70), the Neo-Platonist philosopher and heir to Plato and Aristotle, studies under Ammonius Saccas at Alexandria.

233 At the death of Demetrius, **Heracles** becomes patriarch; he is the first to bear the title of **'pope'**, which continues to be applied exclusively to patriarchs of Alexandria through the 3rd and 4th centuries.

247–64 **Dionysius** is the first patriarch of Alexandria actively to convert the native Egyptians. With temples closing for lack of funding and priesthoods sinking into poverty, Egypt's traditional religion becomes increasingly less attractive. By now the **Bible** has been translated into Coptic, which, together with Dionysius' preaching of the Gospel in the vernacular, helps create the conditions for the rapid **spread of Christianity**, especially after the **Edict of Milan** in 313 (see p.179). From his time onwards, the Alexandrian patriarchs are accepted as leaders of the Egyptian nation and as great prelates of the international Church.

249 The emperor **Decius** (r. 249–51) mounts a ferocious **persecution of Christians**. He demands proof in the form of certificates called *libelli* that sacrifices have been performed in honour of the communal deities. Some Christians comply, but many others are executed. Also during his reign, a Nubian tribe, the **Blemmyes**, make scattered raids into Upper Egypt, the first disturbances on the southern border since 25 BC.

258 To distract attention from Germanic invasions in the West and a Persian advance in the East, the emperor **Valerian** (r. 253–60) orders persecutions of Christians to begin again.

260 Imperial fortunes reach their nadir when Valerian is captured by the **Persians**. An edict issued by the emperor **Gallienus** (r. 253–68) orders that Christianity should be tolerated and worshippers be permitted to live in peace.

262 The prefect **Aemilianus** leads a rebellion against Rome; before it is put down, there are pitched street battles in **Alexandria**. The city is devastated by the fighting which is followed by the **plague**; the population of Alexandria is reduced by about two-thirds.

268 Taking advantage of Roman troubles with the Germanic tribes, **Queen Zenobia** of Palmyra in Syria lays claim to the eastern half of the Roman Empire and sends an invading army into Egypt.

> ❝ The only way in which Egypt exercised any influence on the course of imperial policy about this time was through its poverty: the inability of the central government to collect the revenue in the Eastern provinces compelled Philip [emperor 244–49] to make peace with the Goths on the Danube. ❞
>
> J. Grafton Milne, *A History of Egypt under Roman Rule* (1924)

270 Zenobia's troops enter **Alexandria**, and for the next two years she is acknowledged as ruler on Egyptian documents.

c.271 After hearing Matthew 19:21 cited during a sermon at church, **St Antony** (251–356), the 20-year-old son of wealthy Egyptian Christian parents, begins his withdrawal from the world. He is the first historically documented **Christian hermit**.

272 Zenobia is defeated by the emperor **Aurelian** (r. 270–75). After destroying **Palmyra**, Aurelian turns to Egypt and crushes a revolt. During the disturbances in **Alexandria**, the tomb of Alexander the Great (the Soma) is destroyed, and the Great Library is damaged and its collection broken up.

284 The accession of the emperor **Diocletian** (r. 284–305) on 29 August marks the beginning of the **Era of Martyrs** from which the Egyptian or Coptic Church dates its calendar, though his persecutions do not begin until the nineteenth year of his reign.

293 Diocletian inaugurates the **Tetrarchy** by dividing the Roman Empire into '**East**' and '**West**', each half ruled by an Augustus with the help of an appointed heir apparent who bears the title of Caesar, but with Diocletian in overall control. The Romans suppress a revolt in Egypt and destroy the town of **Coptos**.

296–97 The Alexandria mint stops issuing its own coins, as Egypt adopts the **Roman Empire's coinage** and ceases to be a closed currency system.

The prefect **Lucius Domitius Domitianus** leads a rebellion, is proclaimed emperor in Egypt and controls the

TRIP/A.GHAZZAL

Pompey's Pillar was actually raised in honour of Diocletian and is all that remains standing on the site of the Serapeum at Alexandria

country independently of Rome for almost a year. Diocletian comes to Egypt and lays siege to **Alexandria**, which falls after eight months. The event is marked by the erection of what later travellers mistakenly call '**Pompey's Pillar**'. Diocletian sails up the Nile and fixes the Egyptian border at **Philae**, after ceding the First Cataract to the Nubades tribe to serve as a buffer against encroachment by the Blemmyes.

303 On 23 February, Diocletian orders the persecution of Christians throughout the Roman Empire: all churches are to be demolished, all Christian officials dismissed and all Christian domestic staff enslaved. In Egypt this is the beginning of the **Great Persecution**, during which 144,000 people are martyred according to the Coptic Church.

> ❝ I was in these places, and saw many of the executions for myself. Some of the victims suffered death by beheading, others punishment by fire. So many were killed on a single day that the axe, blunted and worn out by the slaughter, was broken in pieces, while the exhausted executioners had to be periodically relieved. All the time I observed a most wonderful eagerness and a truly divine power and enthusiasm in those who had put their trust in the Christ of God. No sooner had the first batch been sentenced, than others from every side would jump on to the platform in front of the judge and proclaim themselves Christians. They paid no heed to torture in all its terrifying forms, but undaunted spoke boldly of their devotion to the God of the universe and with joy, laughter, and gaiety received the final sentence of death: they sang and sent up hymns of thanksgiving to the God of the universe till their very last breath. ❞
>
> Eusebius, *The History of the Church*, VIII, 9

305 Diocletian retires. Egypt comes under the jurisdiction of the Caesar-turned-Augustus **Maximinus Daia** (r. 305–13), who continues the persecutions with the aim of completely extirpating Christianity.

311–12 At this time, **Eusebius**, the historian of the Early Church, is in the **Thebiad** (Thebes and the surrounding area), where he is an eyewitness to the persecutions.

312 After having a vision of the Cross in the sky with the words 'In this sign conquer', **Constantine 'the Great'** (r. 306–37) defeats Maxentius in the **battle of the Milvian Bridge** on 28 October outside Rome, and becomes sole emperor in the West.

313 Constantine and **Licinius** (who gains sole control of the Eastern Empire this year) meet in northern Italy, where they issue the **Edict of Milan**. This grants everyone – Christians and pagans alike – the freedom to worship the god of their choice, restores property confiscated from Christians and the Church, and grants Christians the right to hold public office.

Christian Egypt: 313–642

Without Diocletian's dominating personality to steer it, the Tetrarchy quickly broke down, leaving his successors fighting for supreme power until the struggle was won by **Constantine** – who confirmed the Roman Empire's strategic shift eastwards by founding **Constantinople**.

Following the Edict of Milan, **Christianity** spread rapidly in Egypt, aided by the preaching of the Gospel in Egyptian, a process begun by Patriarch Dionysius in the middle of the previous century. The see of Alexandria was the most important in Christendom and its Catechetical School remained the only seat of Christian learning, while Alexandria itself was considered the most important city in the East. It has been argued, too, that Egypt contributed fundamentally to the beliefs and symbolism of Christianity. It may have borrowed from the Osiris cult its doctrine of the Resurrection and personal immortality, while from Isis and Horus came the Virgin and Child, and from the ankh, the ancient Egyptian sign for life, came the paradox of the Cross as representing rebirth.

But now two great issues became fatefully entwined: the founding of Constantinople challenged Alexandria's commercial and spiritual supremacy in the East; while no sooner was Christianity tolerated than the struggle to impose orthodoxy began. The doctrinal arguments turned on the relationship between the human and divine natures of Christ, and at first Alexandria's theologians carried all before them. But when the views of the Egyptian Church were rebuffed at the **Council of Chalcedon** in 451, Egypt's disaffection with the Roman Empire – or **Byzantine Empire**, as the eastern half is usually called after 395 – was complete.

The opening decades of the 7th century saw a titanic struggle between the Byzantine and Persian empires. At first everything went the Persians' way, with **Syria**, **Palestine** and **Egypt** falling into their hands in a series of remarkable victories between 613 and 618. But after reorganizing the Byzantine state and summoning the last forces at his call, the emperor **Heraclius** overcame the Persians in two mighty campaigns between 622 and 627, compelling it to surrender its newly won territories. However, both sides were left exhausted by the confrontation just at the time when the tribes of Arabia were being welded into a formidable united force by **Mohammed**, the founder of Islam.

c.318 No sooner is Christianity tolerated than it is threatened by doctrinal splits. **Arius** (c.250–336), a priest in Alexandria, begins the debate over the nature of Christ that will evolve through various forms and ultimately tear the Church apart.

Athanasius versus Arius

Christ is the Son of God, and so surely he is younger than God – so went the argument of Arius. The notion was appealing, for while the Almighty was distant, **Arianism** brought Christ closer to mankind and emphasized his human nature. The proof of its attraction was the wide popularity of Arianism throughout most of the 4th century and its embrace by the imperial court. But Athanasius saw a danger: if Christ was younger than God, he was not the same as God and therefore his divinity was devalued. Indeed, in time Christ might be seen merely as a good man – as Unitarians or, for that matter, Muslims see him today – while God would be left remote and inaccessible. The counter-argument of Athanasius, for which he fought tenaciously all his life, was that no distinction could be made between Christ and God: they were of the same substance. This became the position adopted at the **Council of Nicaea** in 325 (see p.182) and remains the creed of both the Eastern and Western Churches to this day.

320 St Athanasius (c.296–373), who has been living in the desert with St Antony, returns to his birthplace of Alexandria, and starts his struggle against Arius.

c.320 St Pachom (c.292–346), the son of pagan parents at Esna, founds his first monastery at **Tabennisi** in Upper Egypt and will found ten more. He is the first to organize Christian hermits into a communal life with rules.

321 A synod of Egyptian and Syrian bishops meets in Alexandria and **excommunicates Arius**, but his views continue to gain ground.

324 Constantine defeats Licinius and becomes sole ruler of the Roman Empire and enacts a number of **pro-Christian measures**. By the end of his reign, a quarter to a half of the Egyptian population is Christian.

On 8 November, Constantine marks out the perimeter of

Constantinople. It is to be the new capital of the Roman Empire, undermining Alexandria's position as the chief city in the East.

325 The **First Ecumenical Council** meets at **Nicaea** and is attended by Constantine and by Athanasius in the company of the Patriarch of Alexandria. The Council adopts the **Nicene Creed**, which anathematizes Arianism. It also fixes the **date of Easter** in accordance with the custom of Alexandria – based on calculations that make use of the city's astronomical expertise going back to the time of the Ptolemies.

> ❝ We believe in one God, the Father Almighty, maker of all things, both visible and invisible.
>
> And in one Lord, Jesus Christ, the Son of God, begotten of the Father, God of God and Light of Light, very God of very God, begotten, not made, being of one substance with the Father, by whom all things were made; who for us men and for our salvation came down and was made flesh, made man, suffered and rose again on the third day, went up into the heavens and is to come again to judge the quick and the dead;
>
> And in the Holy Ghost;
>
> But the Holy Catholic and Apostolic Church anathematises those who say that there was a time when the Son of God was not, and that he was not before he was begotten, and that he was made from that which did not exist; or who assert that he is of other substance or essence than the Father, or is susceptible of change. ❞
>
> The Nicene Creed, as passed by the Council in 325

This painted apse, showing Jesus enthroned above the Virgin Mary and saints, dates from the eve of the Arab invasion in the 7th century

328 **Athanasius**, still only in his early thirties, becomes patriarch of Alexandria.

330 At the formal **foundation of Constantinople** on 11 May, Constantine dedicates the city to Jesus Christ and makes it the imperial residence.

Perhaps also in this year, **St Macarius**, a disciple of St Antony, retreats to the **Wadi Natrun** in the Western Desert, midway between Alexandria and Memphis, which soon becomes the greatest centre of monasticism in Egypt.

335 Athanasius is accused of diverting state resources to the Church and is **banished** from Egypt by Constantine. Behind this outward reason lies the emperor's anger at Athanasius' refusal to show tolerance towards Arius and his followers by restoring them to communion. This marks the beginning of a pattern of hostility that will characterize Church-state relations for the next 300 years until the Arab invasion.

Monasticism

With the translation of the Bible into Coptic during the 3rd century, **Christianity** spread beyond Alexandria and other Greek-speaking communities to the native population of Egypt. During that century and more of persecution, nowhere in the Roman Empire suffered more than Egypt, where hundreds of thousands were martyred in the final holocaust under Diocletian. A few sought refuge in the desert, but only after the Edict of Milan in 313, when the need to flee had passed, did the great exodus begin. A direct route to God had been found in martyrdom, but now the way would be found in the desert.

This was a peculiarly Egyptian response, for the first hermits and monks were natives nearly to a man. Egyptians headed in their thousands for the barren wilderness with the aim of shedding all worldly possessions and distinctions, wishing even to shed their sense of self, the better to unite with God. St Antony said: 'Let no one who hath renounced the world think that he hath given up some great thing. The whole earth set over against heaven's infinite is scant and poor.' That quiet voice from the Egyptian desert, which found eternity in each living moment, was to have as profound an impact on the imagination of the wider Christian world as all the Greek sophistication of Alexandrian thought.

336 Arius dies in Alexandria.

337 Constantine **converts to Christianity** on his deathbed, though he chooses baptism in the Arian mode. He leaves the empire to his three sons, **Constantine II**, **Constans** and **Constantius** (r. 337–61), the last receiving Constantinople and the East, including Egypt. Under Constantius, **Arianism** becomes the religion of the royal court. Nevertheless, Athanasius is permitted to return to Egypt – where he is received in triumph, but where the Arians resume their attacks against him, aiming their propaganda at the monasteries to turn the monks against him.

338 St Antony leaves his hermit's cell and appears in **Alexandria** to support Athanasius. In spite of this, Constantius has Athanasius and his followers expelled from the churches. Athanasius leaves Egypt and takes refuge in **Rome** with Constans.

341 The formal persecution of traditional **pagan beliefs** begins in Egypt, Constantius decreeing: 'Let superstition come to an end, and the insanity of sacrifices be abolished.'

346 Athanasius again returns to Alexandria, where he remains for the next ten years. During this time, Alexandria extends its influence into Christian **Ethiopia**, gaining the right to appoint the head of its Church (the **abuna**) and its bishops – a practice continued into the twentieth century.

350 Constantius donates the **Caesareum**, the temple built in Alexandria by Cleopatra for Mark Antony, to the Church.

353 Imperial edicts begin to prohibit cultic ceremonies and to force temple closures.

356 After further disturbances between Athanasius and the Arians, Constantius attempts to have Athanasius arrested, but he is smuggled to safety in the desert, where he spends time at various monasteries. During this **third exile**, which lasts for six years, the authorities allow the Arians to take over the churches. Together with the pagans, the Arians attack the Caesareum, which Athanasius had earlier claimed for his own followers.

St Antony dies, aged 105.

c.361–63 St Antony's monastery is built near the site of his hermit's cave.

361 The emperor **Julian** (r. 361–63), a convert to paganism from Christianity, restores official patronage to the **pagan cults** and also allows the orthodox bishops, followers of Athanasius, to return to their churches.

> It is more than probable that we are indebted to the remote hermits for the first preaching of the gospel in England where, till the coming of St Augustine, the Egyptian monastic rule prevailed. But more important is the belief that Irish Christianity, the great civilising agent of the early Middle Ages among the northern nations, was the child of the Egyptian church.
>
> Stanley Lane-Poole, *A History of Egypt in the Middle Ages* (1901)

362 Athanasius returns to **Alexandria**, but Julian, who regards him as the epitome of intolerance, has him thrown out again. During this fourth banishment, Athanasius takes refuge in the **Thebiad**, the area around Thebes.

364 The emperor **Valens** (r. 364–78), though an Arian, allows Athanasius to return to Alexandria.

373 Briefly banished by Valens, Athanasius spends the time in his father's sepulchre, then returns to Alexandria, where he dies.

380 The emperor **Theodosius I** (r. 379–95) announces that the **Nicene faith** is the one true religion, thus ending imperial support for Arianism.

381 Theodosius summons the **Second Ecumenical Council** at Constantinople, which amends the Nicene Creed and declares that the patriarch of **Constantinople** is second only to that of Rome, relegating Alexandria to a secondary position in the East.

391 On 24 February, Theodosius issues an edict banning all expressions of **paganism** throughout the empire.

On 16 June, a second edict banning paganism is specifically addressed to **Alexandria** and **Egypt**. The edict, which makes paganism treasonable, encourages the patriarch

Theophilus to lead a mob against the **Serapeum**, which is vandalized and gutted, and its library of 40,000 books destroyed. By this time about half to three-quarters of the Egyptian population are **Christian**.

In their eagerness to renounce worldly desires and bring themselves closer to God, some Egyptians became hermits, while others founded the first monasteries

394 The latest known **hieroglyphic inscription**, found at Philae, records the birth festival of Osiris on 24 August.

395 Theodosius is succeeded by his sons, who formalize the division of the Roman Empire, with **Honorius** ruling in the West and **Arcadius** (r. 395–408) in the East. This is taken as the notional date for the beginning of the **Byzantine Empire** (though some would put it as early as 324, others as late as 527).

407 A demotic graffito at Philae shows that the **worship of Isis** continues unabated.

410 The Bedouins sack the monasteries of the **Wadi Natrun**, and the Visigoths capture **Rome**.

412 The patriarch Theophilus is succeeded by his nephew **Cyril** (r. 412–44) who has previously spent five years at monasteries and can count on Egyptian monks as his supporters. He directs the monks and the Alexandrian mob against the **Jews**, destroying their property and driving them out of the city. During his lifetime, Cyril's influence and opinions prevail in both the Eastern and Western Churches.

415 Cyril determines to suppress the philosophical schools in Alexandria and sets his mob of monks on **Hypatia**, a pagan Neo-Platonist philosopher. They drag her to the Caesareum church, where they tear her apart with broken-up tiles.

c.421 The Blemmyes renew their incursions from **Nubia** into Upper Egypt, causing 20,000 refugees to seek protection at the **White Monastery** near Sohag.

444 **Dioscorus** (r. 444–54) succeeds Cyril as patriarch of Alexandria. He inherits a very strong position, both spiritually and temporally, and is regarded as a **'Pharaoh of the Church'**. During his term, **Eutyches**, a monk from Constantinople, argues that Christ has only one nature as the human and divine are fused, the doctrine that becomes known as **'monophysitism'**.

448 Flavian, the patriarch of Constantinople, excommunicates Eutyches, affirming the **'diophysite'** or dual nature of Christ, in which the human and the divine are clearly differentiated. He is supported by **Pope Leo** of Rome. But Dioscorus supports Eutyches.

449 Large numbers of Egyptian monophysites attend a Church Council at Ephesus which is later known as the **Robber Council** because of the disorderly behaviour of the monks. Dioscorus dominates the proceedings and has the pope of Rome excommunicated and the bishops of Antioch and Constantinople deposed. The Council marks the pinnacle of Alexandrian influence in the Church.

Nationalism and the nature of Christ

In the argument between Arius and Athanasius, it was decided that Christ and God were one, though as the Nicene Creed acknowledged in 325, Christ was also a man. This was ratified at the **Council of Chalcedon** in 451, when a majority decided that Christ had two natures, the human and the divine, adding that these were unmixed and unchangeable but at the same time indistinguishable and inseparable.

This is the view of almost all Christian Churches to this day, but the Egyptian Church, while not denying the two natures, put emphasis on their unity at the Incarnation. For this, the Copts were called **monophysites** (*monophysis*, 'single nature'), and were charged with the heretical belief that Christ's human nature had been entirely absorbed in the divine. What exactly the parties to the dispute meant when they talked of the nature of Christ was affected by shades of language and culture, and these were taken to the limits of contrast by opposing political ambitions. Apart from its theological import, the argument over the single or dual nature of Christ provided slogans by which the opposing political groupings denounced one another. Nationalism, as much as theology, placed Alexandria on the opposite side to its rivals Constantinople and Rome.

450 At the death of the Eastern emperor **Theodosius II** (r. 408–50), who has been a weak and vacillating figure, particularly on theological matters, he is succeeded by his stepfather **Marcian** (r. 450–57), a man of strong character and a soldier of note. He uses his authority to set in train the reversal of what was done at the Robber Council.

451 Marcian concludes a **peace treaty** with the Blemmyes, allowing them yearly access to the temple of Isis at Philae and the right to borrow the cult statue for processional oracles, thus sparing Philae from conversion to a church for a century. Marcian also convenes the **Council of Chalcedon**, a turning point against the power of Alexandria. The Council reasserts the diophysite position and declares monophysitism a heresy, effectively expelling the Egyptian Church from the main body of Christianity. Dioscorus is brought to trial for behaviour unbecoming a man of the Church and misappropriation of Church property, and also for considering himself to be the real ruler of Egypt, not the imperial prefect. He is excommunicated, deposed and exiled, and dies three years later. Chalcedon is a political defeat for Egypt, which retreats into xenophobia. Monophysitism is now the Egyptian nationalist religion, and stands opposed to diophysitism, the religion of the empire whose adherents in Egypt are known as **Melkites**, from *melk*, the Semitic word for 'king'. From now on, no Greek is safe in Alexandria.

452 The final **demotic inscription** is carved on 11 December – at the temple of Isis at **Philae**.

476 The Roman Empire in the West falls to the barbarians.

480 Despite the suppression of paganism by the Christians, villagers at **Menouthis**, near Canopus, east of Alexandria, are found worshipping the ancient Egyptian deities in a private house.

c.530 St Catherine's Greek Orthodox Monastery is

founded in Sinai by the emperor **Justinian** (r. 527–65).

c.540 The Nubades and the Blemmyes tribes of Nubia begin converting to **Christianity**.

543 The emperor Justinian closes the temple of Isis at **Philae**, imprisons the priests and has the cult statues carried off to Constantinople.

c.553 Part of the temple of Isis at Philae is turned into a **church**, commemorated by a contemporary inscription in Greek: 'This good work was done by the well-beloved of God, the Abbot-Bishop Theodore. The Cross has conquered and will ever conquer.'

570 From now on, there are two coexisting if antagonistic patriarchs of **Alexandria**, **Melkite** (diophysite) and **Coptic** (monophysite). To some extent this reflects the ethnic division within the city between Greeks and Egyptians, the Greeks tending to hold the churches near the harbour, the Egyptians holding those near the ruined Serapeum in the vicinity of what used to be Rhakotis.

613–15 The Persians under Chosroes attack the Byzantine Empire and take **Jerusalem**, from where many refugees flee to Alexandria.

616 The **Persians** advance into Egypt.

617 In spring, the Persians take Trajan's fortress of **Babylon** between Heliopolis and Memphis, and towards the end of the year they take **Alexandria**.

618 The Persians, who are Zoroastrians, subjugate the whole of **Egypt**. They show violent hostility towards Egypt's Christians, forbidding the ordination of bishops and massacring 700 monks in their caves.

622 The Byzantine emperor **Heraclius** (r. 610–41) opens his campaign against Persia in the spring.

On 16 July, **Mohammed** flees from Mecca to Medina.

This flight is known as the *hegira*, from which the Muslim calendar is reckoned.

627 Heraclius invades **Persia**, which sues for peace. Egypt is restored to Byzantine rule.

631 Heraclius appoints **Cyrus** as prefect of Egypt and patriarch of Alexandria. Zealously anti-monophysite, over the next ten years Cyrus tries to kill the Coptic patriarch, expels monophysite bishops from their sees and monks from their monasteries. But his measures succeed only in further alienating Egyptians against Byzantine rule on the eve of the Arab invasion.

632 Mohammed declares a **holy Islamic war** against the Byzantine Empire, which is exhausted – as are the Persians – from years of fighting. The Byzantines regard Islam as a Christian heresy, another version of Arianism, and do not feel greatly threatened. Mohammed dies before the *jihad* begins, however.

636 The Arabs defeat a Byzantine army and take **Damascus**.

637 The Persian empire is destroyed by the invading Arabs.

638 **Jerusalem** falls to the Arabs.

> ❝ People of the Book, do not transgress the bounds of your religion. Speak nothing but the truth about God. The Messiah, Jesus the son of Mary, was no more than God's apostle and His Word which He cast to Mary: a spirit from Him. So believe in God and His apostles and do not say: 'Three'. Forbear, and it shall be better for you. God is but one God. God forbid that He should have a son! ❞
>
> The Koran, 4:171

639 Amr ibn al-As, operating under the Muslim caliph **Umar** in Medina, the capital of the growing Arab empire, crosses the border from Gaza into **Egypt** with a small force of 3500 to 4000 cavalry on 12 December.

7: The Arab period

640–1250

Mohammed, the founder of Islam, died in Mecca in 632, having united the Arabian tribes by a combination of warfare and faith. Over the next ten years, under Mohammed's successors, known as 'caliphs' (from *Khalifat rasul-Allah*, 'Successor to the Apostle of God'), the Arabs destroyed Persia's Sassanian empire, overran the Byzantine Near East and invaded Egypt.

The **Arab conquest** marked the beginning of the complete cultural and political transformation of Egypt. Significant elements of pharaonic civilization had survived intact into the Ptolemaic and Roman periods, and aspects of Egypt's ancient religion had found their way into Christianity too, but Islam uprooted Egypt from its past – for example by its ban on images, which closed the door on thousands of years of Egyptian sculptured art and its interplay with Graeco-Roman civilization.

Some cultural continuity was provided by the **Copts**, as it was three or four centuries before the majority of native Egyptians ceased to be Christians: they kept alive their language and their artistic traditions, which went back to pharaonic times. But deprived of patronage, the Coptic Church was a feeble institution for propagating a culture, though something of its techniques and motifs survived where Coptic builders and artists were pressed into the service of Islam.

The Arabs rejected Alexandria as their capital in Egypt, the caliph complaining that it was on the wrong side of the Nile and the Delta and so meant crossing water to reach it from Arabia. The same applied, though with less emphasis, to ancient Memphis on the west bank of the Nile, which by this time was in any case becoming ruinous. But in founding **Fustat** near the Roman fortress of Babylon, it was clear that the Arabs appreciated Menes's genius in siting a capital where the valley of the Nile meets the apex of the Delta. By avoiding Alexandria, the Arabs turned their backs on the Mediterranean world, but by building Fustat they meant to grip Egypt by the neck.

If the Romans had mismanaged Egypt, the Arabs mismanaged it still worse. From three million inhabitants at the time of the Arab conquest, Egypt's **population** fell dramatically over the next three and a half centuries. By 1000 AD, there were not many more than 1.5 million Egyptians, though a fall in land level in the Delta and an unusual number of low Niles probably contributed to the problem.

Dates from the Arab invasion to the end of the Ottoman period – that is, for what can be called Egypt's 'Islamic period' – are liable to be slightly imprecise, owing to the absence or inexactitude of Arab and Turkish chronologies. In fact, for the first 200 years after the conquest there was no Arab history of Egypt at all.

The conquest of Egypt and its rule by the Umayyads, Abbasids, Tulunids and Ikhshidids: 640–969

Amr ibn al-As, the leader of the Muslim invasion of Egypt, began his expedition in the winter of 640–41 with no more than 4000 horsemen, though he was soon joined by 12,000 more. Against them stood 25,000 to 30,000 Byzantine troops – about the same number as the Romans had once stationed in Egypt. Unlike the battle-seasoned Arabs, fresh from their victories in Palestine and Syria, the defenders were a motley force, many of them Egyptian irregulars. Even so, they had the powerful advantage of a well-built fortress at Babylon (at present-day Cairo) and the great walled city of Alexandria. Why Egypt fell as easily as it did is, therefore, something of a mystery.

The Byzantines' loss of Syria and Palestine blocked the land route between Constantinople and Egypt, but nothing hindered the sea route to Alexandria. There were few in Egypt who at first believed that the Muslim invasion was irrevocable, but with the fall of Alexandria in 642 its reversal became almost impossible. Behind Alexandria's all but impregnable walls, the city could have been kept supplied with troops and provisions indefinitely, ready to serve as a base for a counterattack, yet the city was surrendered to the Arabs without offering any serious resistance.

Even before the demoralizing death of the emperor **Heraclius** in 641, Byzantine political, Church and military authorities in both Egypt and Constantinople were embroiled in rivalries that prevented a coherent response to the Arab threat. There was also the old religious antagonism between the Byzantines and the Copts, which was exacerbated by the imperial patriarch and prefect **Cyrus**, who for the last ten years had been fiercely persecuting the monophysites. Certainly the Byzantines took no steps to arm the Egyptian population, which in turn showed no eagerness to fight to the death against the invaders. But it is wrong to assume that the Copts gave willing support to the Muslims. In fact, the evidence points to betrayal among several of the highest ranking Byzantines in Egypt, above all Cyrus himself, though he died in 642 before he could reap the benefits; but it is perhaps telling that three Byzantine regional governors succeeded in retaining office under their new Arab masters, in return for transferring their political and their religious allegiance to Islam.

Though the rapidly expanding Muslim empire was at first ruled from Medina in Arabia, from 661 it was governed from **Damascus** in Syria by caliphs of the Umayyad dynasty. But after a violent transfer of power to the Abbasid dynasty in 750, the caliphate was moved to **Baghdad** in Iraq. Throughout these changes, however, Arab policy towards Egypt remained the same – namely, to extract the maximum revenue from the country. This was the chief task of the Arab governors based at Fustat, the new Egyptian capital founded near the fortress of Babylon. During the first decades following the conquest, a stern law prevented Arabs from settling on the land – they were needed for military service – and as nomads they were in any case disinclined to become farmers. Instead, the Muslim Arab warrior caste lived off the **poll tax** (*jizyah*) and the **land tax** (*kharaj*), which was paid by the Egyptians in return for the protection of their lives and property and for the right to worship their own religion. The surplus revenue was then sent to the caliphs in Medina, Damascus or Baghdad, who during the first two centuries of Arab rule sent a succession of eighty governors to milk the country, the level of taxation soon proving more burdensome than it had ever been under the Byzantines.

Because the *jizyah* could be imposed only on non-Muslims, there was little interest in making converts to Islam, but the conquerors imposed restrictions on their subjects to keep them firmly in place. The building of new churches and synagogues was prohibited, the ringing of church bells was forbidden, and festivals and public expressions of faith were curtailed. Jews and Christians also had to distinguish themselves by their clothing from Muslims, they could not ride horses, only asses, and any who attempted to convert Muslims to their own religion paid with the death penalty – as did any Muslim who apostasized.

Muslim discrimination and oppressive taxation stoked up resentment among the Copts, whose national pride was already wounded by the coming of the Arabs and the continuing infiltration of Egypt by nomadic tribes, and led to repeated **Coptic revolts** which were only suppressed with much bloodshed. After one such revolt in 726, the authorities arranged for the first large-scale settlement of Arabs in Egypt. Many Copts converted to Islam after the ferocious repression of 832; being unable to meet taxation demands, partly because the irrigation system was falling into further disrepair, they migrated into the towns, leaving large areas of land uncultivated.

In 870 the Abbasids sent a Turkish general, **Ibn Tulun**, to Egypt as governor. Instead he asserted his autonomy from Baghdad, and for the first time since the Ptolemies Egypt was ruled by someone who set out to develop the country's economic potential for its own benefit. Ibn Tulun restored the irrigation system, thereby increasing agricultural productivity, and reformed taxation, so releasing Egyptians from an oppressive burden. The magnificent mosque that bears his name is still the largest in Cairo and, apart from Amr's much rebuilt mosque at Fustat, is the oldest in Egypt.

The Abbasids regained Egypt from Ibn Tulun's less able descendants in 905, but Baghdad's authority lasted only thirty years before another Turkish governor, **Ikhshid**, established his own dynasty. In 969 that too was swept away, this time by the Arab **Fatimids**, who built on the strong autonomous regimes of Ibn Tulun and Ikhshid, and established Egypt as an independent state.

640 In January, the Arab general **Amr ibn al-As** takes the Mediterranean port of **Pelusium** at the northeast corner of the Delta after a one-month siege. In the spring, he comes up before the walls of the Byzantine fortress of **Babylon**. The Muslims are worn down by several weeks of fighting, and Amr, realizing that he lacks the forces to take the fortress, sends to Arabia for **reinforcements**. In the meantime he crosses the Nile and marches south past **Memphis**, which has fallen into decay since the founding of Alexandria, and launches a raid against the **Fayyum** – where he meets spirited resistance and is forced to retreat.

In June, Arab reinforcements – about 12,000 in all – arrive in the vicinity of **Heliopolis**, where they join forces with Amr's men. A great battle is fought at Heliopolis the following month: 15,000 Arabs defeat 20,000 Byzantine defenders who retreat to the fortress of **Babylon**, to which the Muslims now lay siege.

> Many of the soldiers in that army must have seen beautiful cities in Palestine, like Edessa, Damascus, and Jerusalem; some may even have gazed on the far-famed splendours of Antioch or the wonders of Palmyra; but nothing can have prepared them for the extraordinary magnificence of the city which now rose before them, as they passed among the gardens and vineyards and convents abounding in its environs. Alexandria was, even in the seventh century, the finest city in the world: with the possible exception of ancient Carthage and Rome, the art of the builder has never produced anything like it before or since. Far as the eye could reach ran that matchless line of walls and towers which for centuries later excited the enthusiasm of travellers. Beyond and above them gleamed domes and pediments, columns and obelisks, statues, temples, and palaces ... and in the background, towering from the sea, stood that stupendous monument known as the Pharos, which rightly ranked as one of the wonders of the world. Even these half-barbarian warriors from the desert must have been strangely moved by the stateliness and grandeur, as well as by the size and strength, of the city they had come to conquer.

Alfred J. Butler, *The Arab Conquest of Egypt* (1902)

641 After a long illness, the Byzantine emperor **Heraclius** dies in Constantinople on 11 February. With his death the fight goes out of his commanders in Egypt. On 9 April, the Byzantine prefect and patriarch **Cyrus** surrenders the fortress of **Babylon** to Amr's forces, making it all but impossible for Byzantine forces in Upper Egypt to coordinate its defence with Lower Egypt, or to receive instructions from Constantinople.

At the end of June, Amr lays siege to **Alexandria**, the Egyptian capital, and meanwhile attempts to beat the Delta into submission, though without much success.

On 8 November, Cyrus signs a **treaty** with Amr by which Egypt will pay a tribute and Alexandria will be surrendered to the Muslims in eleven months – this despite the fact that the city was impregnable and could have held out for years. Amr meanwhile extends his control over Upper Egypt as far as Thebes.

In December, ships laden with tribute and gold for the caliph **Umar** sail from Alexandria.

642 At the site where Amr's forces originally pitched camp during the siege of Babylon, the invaders build a permanent military camp during the winter which acquires the name **Fustat** – probably from the Greek *phossaton* or the

> The yoke they laid on the Egyptians was heavier than the yoke which had been laid on Israel by Pharaoh. Him God judged by a righteous judgement by drowning him in the Red Sea after He had sent many plagues both on men and cattle. When God's judgement lights upon these Muslims, may He do unto them as He did aforetime unto Pharaoh!

John of Nikiou, 7th century Coptic bishop and historian, on the forced labours imposed by the Arabs on the Egyptians

> **" "** I have taken a city of which I can only say that it contains 4000 palaces, 4000 baths, 400 theatres, 1200 greengrocers and 40,000 Jews. **" "**
>
> Amr to the caliph in Arabia, describing his entry into Alexandria

Latin *fossatum* ('camp'). Here they build the **mosque of Amr**, the first in Egypt. Amr also clears Necho's **canal** and restores it to use.

Byzantine forces evacuate **Alexandria** on 17 September, and Amr makes a peaceful entry into the city on the 29th.

643 Amr conquers **Cyrenaica**. On his return to Egypt, he wishes to retain his seat of government at Alexandria but is ordered by the caliph to make **Fustat** the Arabs' capital.

644 Uthman succeeds to the caliphate at the murder of Umar by a Christian slave.

645 A Byzantine fleet and troops under the command of general Manuel retake **Alexandria**. The Byzantines march south towards the apex of the Delta, where, after a fierce battle at **Nikiou**, they are defeated by Amr's army and retreat to Alexandria.

646 Alexandria is betrayed by a gatekeeper and the Arabs rush in, plundering, burning and slaying all before them, and taking women and children as prizes of war.

652 The Arabs send an expedition south to **Nubia**, but are unable to conquer the country. Instead a **treaty** is agreed between Muslim Egypt and Christian Nubia, fixing the border at **Aswan**.

655 The caliph Uthman makes his cousin governor of Egypt after removing Amr from office.

656 Angered by the removal of Amr and stirred up by

eminent companions of Mohammed and by his widow **Aisha**, insurgent Arab troops in Egypt march on **Medina** and murder the caliph Uthman. **Ali**, who is married to Mohammed's daughter Fatima, becomes caliph, but his accession is not universally accepted and civil war breaks out.

658 Amr is reinstated as governor of Egypt.

The wound to Islam: Shia versus Sunni

At the death of the caliph Uthman, who was a member of the powerful Umayyad family of Mecca, **Ali** put himself forward as the natural inheritor of the caliphate, basing his claim on his marriage to Mohammed's daughter Fatima as well as on his considerable religious learning. But Ali was opposed by **Aisha**, who had been Mohammed's favourite wife, along with her Umayyad family and many of Mohammed's surviving companions. He took to arms and won his first battle, but later saw his authority dissolve when rebels advanced on his army with copies of the Koran fixed to the points of their spears and his troops refused to fight. Ali was assassinated and the Umayyads were installed once again in the caliphate.

But the real wound to Islam occurred when Ali's son by **Fatima**, and therefore of Mohammed's blood, led a revolt against the Umayyads and was killed with all his men after a fanatical struggle. In a sense the Prophet's own blood had been shed, so that for the partisans, or **Shia**, of Ali, Hussein's death was a martyrdom and also a stain on the **Sunni** (orthodox) Muslims, who have always constituted the greater part of Islam. From then on, the Shia refused to accept as caliph any but Ali's descendants, while the Sunni barred the caliphate to the Prophet's descendants for all time. Almost three centuries after the death of Ali, his followers, in the form of the **Fatimids**, would invade Egypt with the intention of using it as a base for the Shia domination of the entire Islamic world.

661–750: The Umayyad dynasty

661 Ali is murdered and is succeeded as caliph by the Arab governor of Syria, Muawiya, a member of the Umayyad clan of Mecca. Muawiya is the founder of the **Umayyad dynasty**, which rules from Damascus over a united Arab empire stretching from the borders of China to the shores of the Atlantic and up into France. Fustat in Egypt remains unimportant during this period, and little of note is built there.

664 Amr dies at Fustat on 6 January.

674–78 The Arabs lay siege to **Constantinople** by land and sea. With little knowledge of seafaring, the Arabs rely on the resources of ports in Egypt and Syria for the construction and crewing of their fleet. The siege fails when the Byzantines defeat the Arab army on land.

680 **Hussein**, the son of Ali and grandson of Mohammed, is massacred along with his followers by Umayyad forces in the **battle of Karbala**.

681 Amr's nephew **Uqba** begins the Arab conquest of **North Africa**.

683–90 Arab tribal rivalry over control of the caliphate erupts in a second **civil war**.

697–98 **Carthage** falls to the Arabs, who advance to **Morocco** and the Atlantic.

c.700 The lantern at the top of the Pharos falls.

705 A decree makes **Arabic** the sole official language of Egypt, at the expense of Greek.

710–11 Muslim Berbers cross the Strait of Gibraltar into **Spain**, where they capture **Córdoba** and **Toledo**.

712 An Arab army follows the Berbers into Spain and takes **Seville**.

> ❝ Usama ibn Zaid al-Tanukhi, commissioner of revenues, oppressed the Christians still more, for he fell upon them, robbed them of their possessions, and branded with an iron ring the name of every monk on the monk's own hand, and the name of his convent, as well as his number; and whosoever of them was found without this brand, had his hand cut off ... He then attacked the convents, where he found a number of monks without the brand on their hands, of whom he beheaded some, and others he beat so long that they died under the lash. He then pulled down the churches, broke the crosses, rubbed off the pictures, broke up all the images. ❞
>
> Al-Maqrizi, 15th-century Egyptian historian

715–17 The complete destruction of the Arab fleet and army before the walls of **Constantinople** contributes to the weakening of Umayyad power.

725–26 The **Copts** – the native Christian Egyptians who still compose the overwhelming majority of the population – revolt against discrimination and the burden of taxation under Muslim rule.

727 In the first large-scale settlement of Arabs in Egypt, the Umayyad caliph **Hisham** orders the migration of several thousand **Yemenis**.

732 The Arabs are defeated by **Charles Martel** at the **battle of Poitiers** in France, checking their northern advance, though for several decades yet the Arabs occupy coastal **Provence** and **Languedoc**.

The Abbasid dynasty (750–868)

750 In a violent transfer of power, the Umayyads are overthrown by the Iraqi-based **Abbasids**, whose line of descent issues from Abbas, an uncle of Mohammed. **Marwan II**, the last Umayyad caliph, flees to Egypt where he is murdered by Abbasid sympathizers.

755 Abd al-Rahman, an Umayyad prince who has escaped from Syria, lands in **Spain** where he establishes an independent Umayyad dynasty with its capital at **Córdoba**.

762 The Abbasids turn their backs on the Mediterranean world by founding **Baghdad** in Iraq as their new capital, where they begin to build up a standing army of Turkish slaves (Mamelukes).

786 Harun al-Rashid (r. 786–809) becomes Abbasid caliph at Baghdad. *The Thousand and One Nights*, a treasurehouse of Arab, Persian and Indian fable, begins to take shape around him, though it will not reach its final form until the fifteenth century in Egypt.

815–16 Arab exiles from Córdoba, unhappy under the rule of the Spanish Umayyads, land at **Alexandria** and seize control of the city.

827 The Córdoban exiles leave Alexandria and conquer **Crete**, from where the Arab navy disrupts shipping in the Eastern Mediterranean and protects Arab maritime trade between Egypt, Syria, North Africa and Spain.

828 The Venetians, according to their own account, steal the body of **St Mark** from Alexandria, concealing it in a barrel of pickled pork to repel the attentions of Muslim harbour officials.

832 A widespread **Coptic revolt** in the Delta is fiercely suppressed by Harun al-Rashid's son, the caliph **al-Mamun** (r. 809–833), and is followed by large-scale conversions to Islam to escape discrimination and high taxation. While in Egypt, al-Mamun breaks into the **Pyramid of Cheops** to search for treasure.

833 With the accession of **al–Mutasim** (r. 833–42), the domination of the caliphate by **Mamelukes**, Turkish military slaves, begins. From Baghdad, they extend their influence throughout the Arab empire.

856–68 Egypt is ruled for the Abbasids by a succession of Turkish generals.

The Tulunid dynasty (868–905)

868 Ahmad Ibn Tulun (r. 868–84), a Turkish general, is appointed governor of Fustat, from where over the following years he creates a powerful army of black slaves and Turks, extends his authority over the whole of Egypt, and rules autonomously of Baghdad – though he maintains a nominal allegiance to the caliph. Under his rule, taxes are reduced, the economy prospers, and harmonious relations are established with Egypt's Jews and Christians.

c.870 After Bedouin attacks in 817 and 866, Christian monks take the first steps to fortify the **monasteries** of the Wadi Natrun.

878 Ibn Tulun gains control of Palestine and Syria.

879–80 Immediately northeast of Fustat, Ibn Tulun founds a new city, **al–Qatai** ('The Concessions'), where he builds the **mosque of Ibn Tulun**. In Alexandria he restores the top storey of the Pharos.

884 Ibn Tulun is succeeded by his son **Khumarawayh** (r. 884–96), who inherits an empire extending from Cyrenaica to the Euphrates. He counts himself the equal of the caliph – to whom he marries off his daughter – but dissipates his wealth.

896 Khumarawayh is assassinated by his eunuchs in Damascus. The Egyptian **economy** suffers further over the next nine years as Khumarawayh's sons contest the succession.

Ibn Tulun, the Abbasid governor of Egypt, broke away from Baghdad and built a new capital north of Fustat – only his mosque remains

905 Taking advantage of Egyptian weakness, an **Abbasid army** enters the country, destroys al-Qatai (except for Ibn Tulun's mosque) and brings Egypt under Abbasid control for the next thirty years.

> ❝ Ibn Tulun was a man of distinguished intelligence, learning, and character. His son Khumarawayh inherited his love of building but few of his other qualities, yet we owe to this fainéant an image that evokes the wealth and luxurious splendour of the Tulunid capital. Suffering from insomnia he laid out, in association with a palace that was greater than his father's, a pool of quicksilver surrounded by a loggia supported on silver columns; here, rocked on the softest of couches, he courted sleep guarded by a blue-eyed lion. ❞
>
> Robin Fedden, *Egypt: Land of the Valley* (1978)

From papyrus to paper

Papyrus, the flexible writing material of ancient Egypt, was finally superseded in its homeland by paper in the 10th century. Paper was first made in China in the late 2nd century BC, but only began its travels westwards in 751 AD when the Arabs defeated a Chinese force north of Samarkand in Central Asia and captured some Chinese papermakers. The use of paper spread rapidly across the Islamic world, reaching Egypt by 800, though at first its manufacture was confined to the eastern provinces of the Arab empire. Sometime after 900, however, paper mills were founded in Egypt. The decline of the papyrus industry might have hit the fellahin of the Delta, but for two new crops which were also introduced by the Arabs during the 8th and 9th centuries, sugar and rice.

910 The **Fatimids**, originally from Syria, establish a Shia caliphate in North Africa.

912 The **Caesareum**, the temple built by Cleopatra for Mark Antony and since refurbished as the cathedral of Alexandria, is finally destroyed in a fire.

914 The Fatimids briefly seize **Alexandria** but fail to take Fustat and retreat to North Africa.

919–21 The Fatimids launch a second campaign against Egypt, occupying **Alexandria** and the **Fayyum**, but their fleet is destroyed at the western Delta port of **Rosetta** and their army is beaten at Fustat.

The Ikhshidid dynasty (935–69)

935 The Fatimids take Alexandria for the third time before being driven out by the new governor, a Turk called **Mohammed ibn Tughj al-Ikhshid** (r. 935–46), whose victory bolsters his authority over Egypt.

944 The caliph confirms Ikhshid's authority over **Egypt**,

A survival from Egypt's Byzantine past, St Catherine's monastery in Sinai is Greek Orthodox, not Coptic, and is home to Egyptian-born Greek monks

Syria, **Palestine** and the **Hejaz**.

946 Ikhshid is succeeded by his son **Unujur** (r. 946–61), but real power is held by **Kafur**, an extremely able Nubian who is tutor to Ikhshid's two sons.

961 Unujur dies and is succeeded by his brother **Ali** (r. 961–66), but power remains with Kafur. The Byzantines retake Crete from the Arabs.

966 Ali dies and is openly succeeded by **Kafur** (r. 966–68).

967 Egypt suffers a calamitous **drought** and **famine**. Ensuing disorder assists Fatimid takeover of Egypt, as does the death of Kafur the following year.

968 Amid the disorder following the drought of the previous year, Kafur dies and is succeeded by **Ahmed** (r. 968–69), the son of Ali, who flees to Syria on the approach of a new Fatimid army.

Egypt under the Fatimids and Ayyubids: 969–1250

In 909, an Arab dynasty originally from Syria and claiming descent from Mohammed's daughter Fatima established its own Shia caliphate centred on **Tunisia**. With the ultimate intention of overthrowing the Abbasids' Sunni caliphate in Baghdad and making themselves masters of the entire Islamic world, in 969 the Fatimids invaded Egypt, where they founded **Cairo** and built the great **mosque of al-Azhar** to propagate their version of the faith. Egypt ceased to be a colony and became an independent state – though also the seat of a religious schism. Yet the Fatimids failed to impose their Shia beliefs at all widely on the country, which remained largely Sunni.

The conquest of Egypt and the founding of Cairo were in fact the work of the Fatimid general **Jawhar**, a Greek convert to Islam, while an Islamicized Jew, **Yaqub ibn Killis**, bore the responsibility for organizing the civil service and the taxation system. Anxious to preserve the expertise that came with continuity, the Fatimids showed a preference for Copts in their administration – especially in the **irrigation** department, where traditional techniques and exact knowledge were essential; and in the closely linked **revenue** department, where the Copts' carefully devised system of record-keeping was indispensable. During the first century of Fatimid rule, however, the Copts ceased to form a majority of the Egyptian population.

Egyptian **foreign trade** during the preceding Arab regimes had been negligible, but under the Fatimids Egypt was at the centre of a flourishing network of commercial relations extending from India to Spain, and the harbour at Alexandria bristled with ships sailing to Amalfi, Pisa and Venice. At the height of their prosperity and power in the mid-11th century, the Fatimids controlled North Africa, Sicily, Egypt, Palestine, Syria and western Arabia, but natural calamities, internal disorders and the rise of the **Seljuk Turks** sent their fortunes into a steep decline, and their fate was sealed in 1099 when the First Crusade took Fatimid-held **Jerusalem** amid scenes of bloody slaughter.

Christian counterattacks against the Muslim conquests came almost simultaneously in Spain and the Near East. The ultimate success of the **'Reconquista'** in Spain had much to do with the support received from neighbouring Christian powers, but in the Near East the antagonism between the Latin Church and the Orthodox Church caused the West to sideline the Byzantines, who were then betrayed by the Fourth Crusade. The Crusades in the Near East also failed because of the religious significance they attached to Jerusalem at the expense of the strategic significance of Egypt, which they fully appreciated only in 1218 when the Fifth Crusade captured the Delta port of **Damietta**, for which the terrified Egyptian sultan al-Kamil offered Jerusalem in exchange. Al-Kamil was the nephew of **Saladin**, the founder of the Ayyubid dynasty, who in 1171 overthrew the Fatimid caliphate in Cairo, returned Egypt to the Sunni fold, and in 1187 had taken not only Jerusalem but much else of the Holy Land from the Latins. With the passing of the Fatimids and the advent of Saladin, who was a Kurd, Egypt would never again be ruled by Arabs.

Further attacks on Egypt followed after Saladin's death, most notably the Seventh Crusade led by the French king **St Louis**, which occupied Damietta in 1249. As the Crusaders were advancing through the Delta, Sultan al-Salih Ayyub died in Cairo, but his death was kept secret by his widow Shagarat al-Durr, who conducted the campaign in his name, relying on an army of Turkish slaves, who would soon see their opportunity to seize power for themselves – inaugurating over 250 years of **Mameluke rule** in Egypt.

969 The Fatimid army under **Jawhar**, a freed Greek slave and now a general, enters Egypt without encountering any serious resistance. Jawhar founds a new capital three kilometres north of Fustat, which is at first called **al-Mansuriyya**, after al-Mansur, the father of the **Fatimid caliph al-Muizz** (r. 953–75).

970 The **Seljuk Turks** enter the territories of the Abbasid caliphate from the east.

971 In the heart of their new capital, the Fatimids inaugurate their **mosque of al-Azhar**, which serves also as a theological college to propagate the Shia faith in Egypt.

973 In June, **Caliph al-Muizz** comes to Egypt and takes up residence at the new city of al-Mansuriyya, which is now proclaimed the ' City of al-Muizz's Victory', al-Qahira al-Muizziyya, or **al-Qahira (Cairo).**

975 At the death of al-Muizz, **Abu Mansur al-Aziz** (r. 975–996) becomes the second Cairo caliph. The Fatimid empire reaches its apogee during his reign, extending across **North Africa**, **Egypt**, **western Arabia**, **Palestine**, **southern Syria** and **Sicily**. Egypt's foreign trade is

The mosque of al-Azhar, depicted on an Egyptian banknote, was founded by the Shia Fatimids but later became the world's leading centre of Sunni teaching

Coptic-Arab art and architecture

The nomads who emerged from the deserts of Arabia were not craftsmen or builders, so that after their invasion of Egypt they necessarily relied on the Copts. Coptic craftsmen made no distinction between their own churches and the mosques they built to order for the Arabs, employing the same ideas for both. In consequence, there is no clear distinction between Coptic and Arabic art and architecture from the conquest of Egypt to the end of the Fatimid period.

Being Shia, the Fatimids did not observe the Sunni prohibition on the representation of living creatures and had their palaces and mosques decorated with animal and human figures; the woodwork at the **al-Azhar mosque**, for example, is carved with typically Coptic lions. At both Christian and Muslim places of worship, it is possible to see a cross figuring in the middle of a geometrical design, or a polygonal medallion surrounded by a border containing the mystic hare, or the symbol of Osiris as the protector of the dead, and so on. Likewise, the pointed arch is characteristically Coptic; the Copts used it in their churches at least as far back as the 4th century and repeated it in the **mosque of Ibn Tulun**. Even as late as the 14th century, the Mameluke sultan Hassan employed a Coptic architect to build his mosque. As A.J. Butler wrote in *The Arab Conquest of Egypt*, 'The more the history of Egypt, both Byzantine and Saracen, is studied, the clearer becomes the truth that in all the handicrafts –

---

expanded, and its taxation is reduced. Abu Mansur also introduces **Turkish slave troops** into the army, who become a source of tension as they rise to prominence at the expense of the Berbers who brought the Fatimids to power.

996 Al-Hakim (r. 996–1021), the third Cairo caliph, takes power – he is an all-powerful psychotic who eventually proclaims himself God.

1021 After the disappearance of al-Hakim, he is succeeded

in goldsmith's work, in enamelling, in metal-work, in glass-work –
and in every province of design and construction, it was the Copts
who kept alive the artistic traditions of the country.'

The mosque of al-Aqsar in Cairo displays a typical feature of Fatimid
architecture, an arch in the form of an upturned keel, derived from the
Coptic pointed arch

by his son **al-Zahir** (r. 1021–35). Famine and unrest mark
his period of rule.

1035 Al-Mustansir (r. 1035–94) succeeds to the Cairo
caliphate. During the early years of his long reign, Egypt
enjoys considerable prosperity.

1055 The Seljuk Turks take **Baghdad** and establish their
hegemony over the Sunni caliphate. The Seljuks' martial
prowess leads to a resurgence in the fortunes of Sunni Islam
in **Iraq**, **Syria** and **Iran**.

Caliph al-Hakim (d.1021)

Fatimid rule had been marked by its tolerance towards Christians, Jews and Sunni Muslims – a tradition that al-Hakim, whose mother was a Greek Orthodox Christian, gave early signs of continuing. He also showed a keen interest in mathematics and the sciences, endowing Cairo with an astronomical observatory and a scientific institute to which he attracted such figures as the mathematician **Ibn al-Haytham**, famous for his treatise on optics, which first described the camera obscura.

But al-Hakim had always been highly capricious, and he suddenly turned violently against everything he had once favoured, throwing scientists into prison and from 1004 persecuting Christians and Jews. Christians were forced to walk around carrying heavy crosses, and Jews had to wear clogs around their necks, while many outwardly converted to Islam to save their lives. Over the next ten years al-Hakim destroyed 30,000 churches in Egypt and the Near East, including the **Church of the Holy Sepulchre** in Jerusalem. The persecutions only stopped when al-Hakim became convinced that he was God, which was publicly proclaimed in 1016 at Friday prayers in Cairo. When Muslims protested, he burnt down half of Cairo and went about decapitating the well-to-do, claiming the assistance of Solomon and Adam in angelic guise. At this point, he restored his favours to Christians and Jews, thousands of whom returned to their faith from Islam, while he struck at Muslims by forbidding them to fast at Ramadan and to go on the pilgrimage to Mecca. Al-Hakim disappeared, it is said, while in the Moqattam Hills overlooking Cairo where he liked to look for portents in the stars; probably he was killed by his ambitious sister, **Setalmulq**, who put his young son on the throne and ruled as regent.

1061 The Normans begin the conquest of **Sicily**.

1065–73 A series of **low Niles** brings drought and famine to Egypt. So desperate are conditions in Cairo, say chroniclers at the time, that meathooks are fixed to ropes and lowered to catch pedestrians, who are lifted from the streets and eaten.

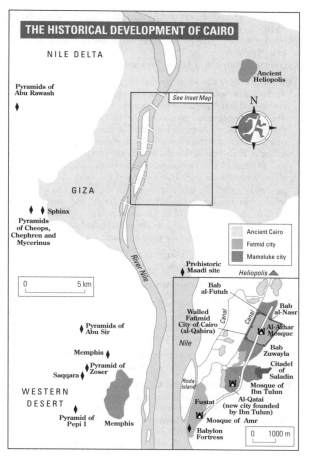

THE HISTORICAL DEVELOPMENT OF CAIRO

NILE DELTA

Pyramids of
Abu Rawash

Ancient
Heliopolis

See Inset Map

N

GIZA

Sphinx

Pyramids
of Cheops,
Chephren and
Mycerinus

Ancient Cairo
Fatmid city
Mameluke city

0   5 km

River Nile

Prehistoric
Maadi site

Heliopolis

Bab
al-Futuh

Bab
al-Nasr

Walled
Fatimid
City of Cairo
(al-Qahira)

Al-Azhar
Mosque

Nile

Bab
Zuwayla

Citadel
of
Saladin

Pyramids of
Abu Sir

Memphis

Roda
Island

Mosque of
Ibn Tulun

Pyramid of
Zoser

Saqqara

Al-Qatai
(new city founded
by Ibn Tulun)

WESTERN
DESERT

Fustat

Mosque of Amr

Pyramid of
Pepi I

Memphis

Babylon
Fortress

0   1000 m

1071 The Seljuks defeat the Byzantine army at the **battle of Manzikert**, opening the whole of Asia Minor to conquest by the Turks. The Seljuks also turn south, taking **northern Syria** from the Byzantines, who had recaptured it a century before, and taking **Jerusalem** from the Fatimids.

1073 Famine is followed by fighting between the black and Turkish slave soldiers in **Cairo**, forcing the caliph **al-Mustansir** to sell off his treasures to appease the army. But the situation degenerates into open revolt, and **Badr al-Jamali**, the governor of Acre in Palestine, arrives in Egypt with his private army of Armenian soldiers in answer to the caliph's call for help. Badr puts down the rebellious Turkish troops in Cairo and suppresses the factional fighting in the provinces, which along with the drought has devastated the land. Assuming the powers of vizier, he suspends taxes for three years to allow the fellahin time to begin cultivating their fields, and with the support of the merchant class he restores law and order. After Badr, the Fatimid state and its enfeebled caliphs will effectively be ruled by viziers who are military men.

1076 The Seljuks take **Damascus** from the Fatimids, whose control over Syria is now limited to a thin coastal strip.

1085 In Spain, the Christians capture **Toledo**.

1095 The **First Crusade** is proclaimed at Clermont-Ferrand in France on 27 November, in response to the Byzantine emperor's appeal after the battle of Manzikert and the Seljuks' mistreatment of pilgrims to Jerusalem.

1098 The Fatimids regain control of **Jerusalem** and welcome the approach of the Crusaders.

1099 Jerusalem falls to the Crusaders on 15 July, who massacre its Muslim inhabitants and also its Jewish population for helping the Muslims. The Crusaders establish the **Kingdom of Jerusalem**, on which are dependent the Western feudal states of the County of Edessa, the Principality of Antioch and, from 1109, the County of Tripoli.

> Viewed as an episode in the sequence of contacts between the East and the West, the Crusades appear as the first counter-stroke of the Occident to the forward march of Islam. Orientals, however, unlike Europeans, have always included in this sequence the Spanish reconquista, that is the gradual conquest of the Iberian peninsula by Christian states, and they date the beginning of the Crusades from the loss by Islam of Toledo in 1085. It must not be forgotten that the community of Mohammed was attacked simultaneously there and in the east and that on one occasion a crusading army was purposely directed to Spain … The results of the two offensives were very different; the one led to the definite expulsion of Islam from Spain, while the other was only transitory in its effects, both political and cultural, on the East. It cannot be too strongly emphasized that the Crusades had no such fundamental significance for the East as they did for Europe. For the East they were a side-show, running solely in Syria, Palestine and on the coast of Egypt, which even at its height meant little or nothing to Mesopotamia and the Caliphate, let alone to Persia or Central Asia or even to Middle and Upper Egypt. The political evolution of these lands was in no way affected and their inhabitants had no contact whatever with the Crusaders.

Bertold Spuler, *The Muslim World* (1960)

c.1100 An **earthquake** at Alexandria destroys Ibn Tulun's restored upper storey of the Pharos.

1127 Zangi, a Seljuk officer appointed governor of Mosul in Iraq, begins the Muslim reaction against the Crusaders; over the next ten years he extends his control over northern Syria, capturing **Aleppo** and threatening **Damascus**.

1144 The Crusaders' County of Edessa falls to Zangi.

1146 Zangi dies; his son **Nur al-Din** continues the Muslim offensive against the Crusaders from Aleppo.

1147–48 The **Second Crusade** is launched in a vain attempt to recover Edessa.

1154 **Nur al-Din** captures Damascus from its local Muslim ruler and establishes his authority over the whole of **Syria**, in preparation for an assault on the Kingdom of Jerusalem.

1167 Taking advantage of divisions within Fatimid Egypt, Nur al-Din's forces invade the country. The Fatimids invite an alliance with **Amalric**, the king of Jerusalem, and Frankish-Egyptian forces drive out Nur al-Din's army.

1168 In turn, Amalric **attacks Egypt** and the Fatimid caliph calls on Nur al-Din, while as a defensive measure the caliph orders the burning of **Fustat**. Nur al-Din's forces drive Amalric out of Egypt.

1169 The Fatimid caliph appoints as his new vizier **Saladin (Salah al-Din)**, a Kurd, whose father Ayyub is close to Nur al-Din.

The Ayyubid dynasty (1171–1250)

1171 **Saladin** (r. 1171–93) overthrows the Fatimid caliphate, becomes sultan of Egypt and founds the **Ayyubid dynasty**.

1173 Saladin's brother **Turanshah** attacks Nubia in retaliation for its support of the Fatimids. Peace is made soon afterwards, but Nubia suffers continued attacks from the desert by Muslim Bedouins.

1174 Nur al-Din dies, and Saladin seizes the opportunity to take **Damascus**.

1176 Saladin consolidates his position in Egypt by constructing the **Citadel** of Cairo, home of all Egypt's rulers for nearly 700 years to come, and building the **city walls** joining Cairo and Fustat.

Saladin (1138–93)

Saladin's achievement was to unite the Muslim world against the Crusader states, which he did with a sure sense of strategy, understanding that he needed to bring into play the great resources of wealth and manpower of Egypt. With Egypt in his grasp and using Damascus and Aleppo in Syria as forward bases, he enjoyed the advantages of ample resources, strategic depth and interior lines of communication when he unleashed his campaign. **Jerusalem** fell to him in 1187 after he destroyed a Crusader army at the battle of Hattin in Galilee.

Saladin could be ruthless, and in the interests of policy he did not shrink from bloodshed. He was a devout Muslim who abhorred free-thinkers, and though he made many friends among the Christians, he never doubted that their souls were doomed to damnation. Yet as men the Crusaders had his respect, and he treated them fairly and as equals; he never broke his word to anyone. His genius in war, his sense of honour and his many gestures of gallantry and kindness won him the admiration of his adversaries.

Saladin died at the age of 54, exhausted by his many years of battle and after having to concede some ground to the Third Crusade and Richard I 'the Lionheart' of England in particular. Another century would pass before the Crusaders were driven entirely from the East, but meanwhile Saladin had shifted the centre of the Islamic world from Baghdad to Egypt.

1183 Saladin captures **Aleppo** and gains full control of Syria. He is now ready to unleash his *jihad* against the Christians.

1187 Saladin defeats the Crusaders at the **battle of Hattin** near the Sea of Galilee and a few months later takes **Jerusalem**.

1190–92 The **Third Crusade**, which brings King Richard I 'the Lionheart' of England to the Holy Land, wins back some coastal territory. Saladin accepts a truce and makes agreements with the Crusaders to bolster trade.

1193 At his death, Saladin's empire, which has extended over **Egypt**, **North Africa**, **Palestine**, **Syria**, **Yemen**, the **Hejaz** and **northern Iraq**, disintegrates, with only Egypt remaining in Ayyubid hands.

1199 After a period of struggle between Saladin's sons for control of Egypt, Saladin's brother **al-Adil I** (r. 1199–1218) is made regent.

1200 Al-Adil is proclaimed sultan in Cairo. Low Nile floods between 1199 and 1202 depopulate the countryside and cause **famine** throughout Egypt. Al-Adil responds by directing his soldiers to work the land directly, ensuring an early economic recovery.

1202 Ayyubid authority is reasserted over **Syria** by Sultan al-Adil.

1204 Byzantine **Constantinople** falls to the Venetian-led **Fourth Crusade**.

1215 Sultan al-Adil decides to sell off the stones from the Pyramids of Giza to building contractors. His workmen begin with the **Pyramid of Mycerinus**, the smallest of the three, but they find it more difficult to dismantle than it was for the ancient Egyptians to construct it, and after eight months they give up.

> ❝ The poor, pressed by famine … ate carrion, corpses, dogs and the excrement and filth of animals. This went on for a long time, until they began to eat little children … When the poor people began to eat human flesh, such was the horror and shock that these crimes became the chief topic of conversation … But soon they grew used to such things, and developed quite a taste for these detestable foods. ❞
>
> Abd al Latif, 13th-century historian

> Considering the vast masses that have been taken away, it might be supposed that the building would have been completely destroyed, but so immense is the structure that the stones are scarcely missed.
>
> Abd el Latif, 13th-century historian

1218 Al-Adil is succeeded as sultan by his son **al-Kamil** (r. 1218–38). The **Fifth Crusade** attacks the eastern Delta port of Damietta, where **St Francis of Assisi** crosses the lines in an attempt to convert Sultan al-Kamil.

1219 Al-Kamil is so unnerved by the Crusaders' capture of Damietta that he offers them **Jerusalem** in exchange and a thirty-year truce, which they refuse.

St Francis and the sultan

Among the besiegers at Damietta in 1218 was **St Francis of Assisi**. He had come to the East to preach peace, and courageously crossed the lines to confront Sultan al-Kamil in person. St Francis told the sultan that he had come to convert him and his people to Christ, unaware that al-Kamil was surrounded with Coptic advisers and was fully familiar with the Christian faith. The sultan was charmed by someone so simple, so gentle, so dirty and so evidently touched by God, but when St Francis offered to enter a fiery furnace on the condition that, should he come out alive, al-Kamil and all Egypt would embrace Christianity, the sultan replied that gambling with one's life was not a valid proof of one's God. Instead he said, 'Pray for me, that God may deign to show me the law and the faith that are most pleasing to Him', and offering gifts, which St Francis refused, the sultan put him in the care of a safe escort and returned him to the Crusader lines.

1220 The Mongols under **Gengis Khan** conquer the eastern territories of the Abbasid caliphate, but instead of heading towards Baghdad and the Near East they first advance into **southern Russia**.

1221 After making a blundering march on **Cairo**, the Crusaders are driven out of Egypt by al-Kamil.

1227 The death of Gengis Khan postpones further conquests as the Mongol empire is reorganized.

1229 In return for help against a hostile brother, al-Kamil cedes **Jerusalem** to the Crusader **Frederick II**, emperor of Germany and king of Sicily.

1236 In Spain, the Christians capture **Córdoba** from the Muslims.

1238 The death of al-Kamil leads to complete disintegration of the Ayyubid empire, which becomes divided among various rivals within the dynasty. In Egypt, al-Kamil's son **al-Adil II** becomes sultan (r. 1238–40).

1240 Adil II is deposed and his brother **al-Salih Ayyub** (r. 1240–49) is made sultan. Owing to factionalism in Egypt, al-Salih is unable to rely on its army; instead he builds up his own by purchasing **Mamelukes** in large numbers. These military slaves are mostly Kipchak Turks from the steppes of southern Russia, whom he installs on the island of Roda in the Nile at Cairo, and who become known as **Bahri (river) Mamelukes**.

1244 Jerusalem falls to allies of al-Salih, the **Khwarazmians**, a Turkic people displaced from Transoxiana and parts of Iran and Afghanistan, by the advancing Mongols. Later in the year near **Gaza** in Palestine al-Salih defeats a combined Christian-Muslim army composed of Crusader remnants from the Kingdom of Jerusalem and troops of his Ayyubid rival in Damascus.

1249 The **Seventh Crusade** under **King Louis IX of France** captures **Damietta** in June.

In November, the death of al-Salih is kept secret by his wife, **Shagarat al-Durr**, who directs the campaign against the Crusaders in his name.

1250 The French advance south to **Mansura** in the Delta, where they are checked by the Mamelukes in February. A stalemate follows and the Crusaders are weakened by illness. In April, the Crusaders retreat and are captured by the Mamelukes along with King Louis himself, who is released only after a huge **ransom** is paid.

8: Mamelukes and Ottomans

1250–1798

The rise of the Turks went back to the beginning of the Abbasid period, and already during the reign of caliph Mutasim (r. 833–42) they were in charge of affairs in Baghdad. Within a few more years, Ibn Tulun and Ikhshid, Turkish governors nominally loyal to the caliph, had established autonomous dynasties in Egypt. The Fatimids represented a return to Arab rule, but after 80 years under Saladin's Kurdish Ayyubid dynasty, Egypt again fell under the thumb of the Turks – first in the form of the **Mamelukes**, later as part of the **Ottoman Empire**. In fact, in the 1156 years between the Arab and French conquests, Egypt was only under any kind of Arab rule for 458 years – well under half – while for 698 years it was under some kind of rule by Kurds or Turks. As for the Egyptians themselves, apart from those few Copts and Jews and converts to Islam who administered the finance and irrigation systems, their role was as it had always been – to till the land for their masters.

Nevertheless, the Mamelukes, an oligarchy of Turkish military slaves, were considered entirely legitimate rulers of Egypt as they were orthodox **Sunni Muslims** and proved their ability to protect the lands of Islam by repelling the Mongols and driving the Crusaders from the Near East. But as for the most part they rejected the dynastic principle, Mameluke sultans came to power more through the blood on their hands than by the blood in their veins, and the factionalism, violence and chaos that characterized so much of the period did little for the sound maintenance of the Egyptian infrastructure, particularly the irrigation system. The fate of **Memphis** offers an illustration. As late as the 13th century, the historian Abd al Latif could write: 'The ruins still offer, to those who contemplate them, a collection of such marvellous beauty that the intelligence is confounded, and the most eloquent man would be unable to describe them adequately.' But towards the end of the Mameluke period the dykes around Memphis fell into disrepair and at every inundation the mud swept in, until it swallowed the city completely.

At first the **Ottoman conquest** was an advantage, bringing relative security and prosperity, but by the 18th century the Ottoman Empire's own decline was translated into corruption, anarchy and stagnation in Egypt. The Mamelukes were at least Egyptian by adoption; it stood at the centre of their world and was no mere province. They adorned medieval **Cairo** with many of its most magnificent mosques, mausoleums, maristans (hospitals) and madrasas (theological schools), while in the three centuries of Ottoman rule that followed, not a single monument was built that could compete with the grace and splendour of Mameluke architecture. The neglect suffered by Egypt under later Ottoman rule – or rather an almost complete absence of rule – went a long way towards ruining the country and leaving it defenceless. When **Napoleon** landed at Alexandria in 1798, Egypt once again was drawn into the Mediterranean and European worlds as it had been 2200 years before with the arrival of Alexander the Great.

The Mamelukes: 1250–1517

Mamelukes were youths born outside the lands of Islam to non-Muslim parents, usually inhabitants of the Eurasian steppe and preferably of Turkish stock, who were captured or sold into slavery, then bought, raised, converted to Islam and trained as highly disciplined horse archers. Already at the beginning of the Abbasid dynasty in Baghdad, such boys or adolescents were being imported into Muslim territory. Far from being regarded as degrading, slavery guaranteed a career structure which offered the satisfaction of belonging to the military elite and might carry a Mameluke to high administrative office, such as provincial governor or treasurer of the sultan's household. Indeed, in the 9th century, the Abbasid caliphs were more the slaves of the Mamelukes than the other way around. But not until the 13th century did **al-Salih**, the last of the Ayyubid sultans, introduce Mamelukes to Egypt, where they proved themselves to be the most formidable fighting force of their time.

Among his Mamelukes, al-Salih created an elite corps composed predominantly of Kipchak Turks from the southern Russian steppes whom he garrisoned on an island in the Nile at Cairo, and who for that reason became known as **Bahri Mamelukes** (*bahr* means 'river'). It was this corps, about 1000 in all under their leader **Baybars**, who successfully defended Egypt against the Seventh Crusade in 1249–50, and when al-Salih died during the course of the campaign it was only the manoeuvrings of his widow **Shagarat al-Durr** that prevented them from capturing outright power. Instead, it would take the further shock of the Mongol invasion a decade later to establish the Bahri Mamelukes as the legitimate defenders of Islam against the infidels of East and West.

A long period of security and prosperity followed, during which, in 1291, the Bahri Mamelukes drove the last Crusaders from the Near East, but by the middle of the 14th century their rule had descended into incompetence and vicious rivalries. From 1382 their place was taken by the **Burgi Mamelukes**, a corps composed of Circassian Turks from the Caucasus whose barracks occupied a tower at the Cairo Citadel (*burg* means 'tower'), and who governed Egypt until the Ottoman invasion in 1517. Wherever the Mamelukes came from, the Egyptians called them 'Turks', because they spoke Turkish and had Turkish names, which set them apart as a ruling military caste from their subjects who spoke Arabic and had Arabic names.

In the late 14th century, Sultan Barquq deflected **Timur** (Tamerlane) from Egypt by keeping him at bay in Syria, though the campaign imposed a considerable financial strain. Famine, plague and Portugal's discovery of a sea route round Africa into the Indian Ocean combined to weaken Egypt's economic position during the 15th century. And Egypt's **Christians** paid the price. The Copts had remained in the majority until Fatimid times and were still a substantial minority nationwide. But the internecine struggles of Egypt's Mameluke rulers from the mid-13th century to the 16th century produced an atmosphere of insecurity and distrust which, combined with the growing impoverishment of the country, had sultans and mobs alike turning against the Christians. In 1321, fanatical Muslims looted and destroyed all the principal churches of Egypt, and Christians suffered wholesale massacre, while surviving Copts were expelled from official positions and subjected to a range of indignities. Even so, Copts continued to outnumber Muslims in Upper Egypt until the great wave of persecutions in 1354. Each of these events was followed by mass conversions to Islam, which reduced Egypt's Christian population to about ten percent – the proportion persisting to this day. Meanwhile the **fellahin**, whether Christian or Muslim, were so ruthlessly taxed and oppressed that even by contemporary standards elsewhere in the Islamic world, their exploitation and harsh living conditions were appalling. Not surprisingly, **Sufism**, an otherworldly form of Islam, took strong hold in the countryside.

Though prosperity returned to Egypt and Cairo regained its splendour under the rule of sultan **Qaytbey** in the late 15th century, the country's economy was gradually being sapped by European commercial successes in the Indian

Ocean and the Mediterranean. For that reason alone the Mameluke regime was doomed, but it now also faced the **Ottomans** – a rising and modernizing Islamic military power possessing cannon and muskets, which the bow-and-arrow Mamelukes rejected as unmanly.

Shagarat al-Durr (d.1257)

Of Armenian or Anatolian Turkish stock, Shagarat al-Durr, whose name means 'Tree of Pearls', shares with Hatshepsut and Cleopatra that rare distinction of having been a female ruler of Egypt. Al-Salih purchased her as a slave and made her one of his concubines; though he would obligingly lend her out to friends, when he became sultan he married her. They had a son, prince **Mansur Khalil**, who died in infancy, and Shagarat al-Durr was also stepmother to al-Salih's son **Turanshah**.

In 1249, as the **Seventh Crusade** seized the Delta port of Damietta, al-Salih was dying of cancer and the French king imagined that it was just a matter of time before the government collapsed and Egypt fell into his hands. But Shagarat al-Durr hid her husband's corpse and kept morale alive by pretending to transmit the sultan's orders to his army, while awaiting the return of Turanshah to Egypt. By then the Crusaders had been defeated by the elite Bahri Mameluke corps, who now expected to taste the rewards of power; instead, when Turanshah arrogantly swept them aside, appointing his own Mamelukes to high posts, the Bahris murdered him. Now Shagarat al-Durr made her own bid for power, basing her claim to the succession on having borne al-Salih a son, though the child had predeceased his father. In May 1250 she became sultan, coins issued in her name proclaiming her as 'Queen of the Muslims, Queen Mother of Prince Mansur Khalil'. Though forced to surrender her title after only 80 days, Shagarat al-Durr remained at the centre of power for seven more years, when she was caught out in a murderous intrigue and her naked body was thrown over the Citadel walls to be eaten by dogs – but not before she spent her last days grinding up all her jewels so that no other woman should wear them.

1250 After al-Salih's son **Turanshah** belatedly arrives in Egypt from across the Euphrates in May, he is murdered by a group of Bahri Mamelukes. Though lacking the support of the Bahris, **Shagarat al-Durr** (r. 1250) lays claim to Ayyubid legitimacy and is proclaimed sultan, becoming the first and last female ruler of Muslim Egypt. The Abbasid caliph in Baghdad will not accept a woman, however, and as she also lacks sufficient support in Cairo, Shagarat al-Durr abdicates in July, after 80 days in charge. But she marries **Aybak** (r. 1250–57), a non-Bahri Mameluke, who is made sultan by anti-Mameluke elements eager to keep the Bahris from power.

During this year, the formerly Shia mosque and theological college of **al-Azhar** in Cairo is reopened as a centre of the Sunni faith.

1254 Aybak invites the Bahri leader for a meeting at the Cairo Citadel, where he has his head struck off and tossed out to the other Bahris waiting at the gates. Most of the Bahri Mamelukes flee Egypt.

1257 Hearing rumours that Aybak intends another marriage, Shagarat al-Durr has him murdered in his bath. She then appeals to those Bahri Mamelukes who have remained in Egypt, but none offer her their support, and Shagarat al-Durr is killed by Aybak's supporters. Aybak's young son **Mansur** (r. 1257–59) becomes sultan, but only as a front-man for contesting groups of Mamelukes.

1258 On 10 February, the **Mongols**, led by Hulagu, a grandson of Gengis Khan, capture **Baghdad**, which is plundered and destroyed. Ten days later the Abbasid caliph is put to death, and with him passes any lingering pretence of the unity of Sunni Islam.

1259 In November, **Qutuz** (r. 1259–60), a non-Bahri Mameluke, deposes Mansur and becomes sultan.

> It was God's benevolence that He rescued the faith by reviving its dying breath and restoring the unity of the Muslims in the Egyptian realms, preserving the order and defending the walls of Islam. He did this by sending to the Muslims, from this Turkish nation and from among its great and numerous tribes, rulers to defend them and utterly loyal helpers, who were brought from the House of War to the House of Islam under the rule of slavery, which hides in itself a divine blessing. By means of slavery they learn glory and blessing and are exposed to divine providence; cured by slavery, they enter the Muslim religion with the firm resolve of true believers and yet with nomadic virtues unsullied by debased nature, unadulterated with the filth of pleasure, undefiled by the ways of civilized living, and with their ardour unbroken by the profusion of luxury. The slave merchants bring them to Egypt in batches, like sandgrouse to the watering places, and government buyers have them displayed for inspection and bid for them ... Thus, one intake comes after another and generation follows generation, and Islam rejoices in the benefit which it gains through them, and the branches of the kingdom flourish with the freshness of youth.

Ibn Khaldun, 14th-century North African historian

1260 The Mongols take **Aleppo** in January, and **Damascus** falls in March. When Mongol ambassadors arrive in **Cairo** demanding Egypt's submission in the summer, Qutuz has them killed. On 3 September, a Mameluke army under Qutuz inflicts a stunning defeat upon the Mongols in the **battle of Ain Jalut** in northern Palestine.

On 23 October, Qutuz is murdered by a mixed group of Bahri and other Mamelukes, among them the Bahri

Mameluke Baybars, who becomes sultan. **Baybars I** (r. 1260–77) becomes the founder of the **Bahri Mameluke sultanate**, which will last until 1382.

1261 Baybars invites a surviving member of the Baghdad Abbasids to Cairo to take the title of caliph, though he and his successors are mere court functionaries of the Mameluke sultans.

1261 The Byzantines retake **Constantinople** from the Latins.

1279 **Qalaun** (r. 1279–90) becomes sultan. During his reign he fends off another Mongol attack and campaigns against the Crusaders in the Near East, where he reduces their holdings in **Acre** in northern Palestine and **Tortosa** (modern Tartus) in Syria. He also buys in Circassian Mamelukes whom he stations at the Citadel – hence their name, **Burgi** or 'tower' Mamelukes.

1291 The Mamelukes under Sultan **Khalil** (r. 1290–93) take **Acre** and **Tortosa**, expelling the last Crusaders from the mainland of the Near East.

1293 For most of the next fifty years, Egypt's sultan is **Mohammed al-Nasr** (r. 1293–94, 1299–1309 and 1310–41).

1302 Egypt signs a **commercial treaty** with Venice, granting protection to Venetian lives, property and trading privileges.

> ❝ The Turkish Mamelukes installed as Caliph a man to whom they gave the name and titles of Caliph. He had no authority and no right to express his opinion. He passed his time with the commanders, the great officers, the officials and the judges, visiting them to thank them for the dinners and parties to which they had invited him. ❞
>
> al-Maqrizi, 15th-century Egyptian historian

Bab Zuwayla, one of the sixty gates that encircled medieval Cairo, was the place of public execution and the starting point of the Mecca pilgrimage

1312 After being invited to intervene in the succession to the **Nubian throne**, Sultan al-Nasr succeeds in replacing Nubia's Christian king with a Muslim, who establishes Islam as the state religion, though Christianity lingers in some regions for another 200 years.

1321 Resentment among Muslims against Copts in high administrative positions boils over into widespread **anti-Christian riots**, quite possibly stirred up by Sultan al-Nasr to divert anger away from his tampering with payments to officers in his forces. Muslims loot and destroy all the principal churches of Egypt, and Christians suffer wholesale massacre. Copts are expelled from official positions and are subjected to a range of indignities, such as being forbidden to ride horses or asses unless they sit backwards, being forced to wear distinctive clothing, and even being required to have a bell around their necks when entering a public bath. Mass conversions to Islam follow.

1322 A **peace treaty** brings the Mameluke-Mongol conflict to an end. Mamelukes begin attacks against the coast of **Cilicia** in a struggle with Cyprus for control over the ports and commerce of the Eastern Mediterranean.

1341 Al-Nasr dies. Twelve sultans, all al-Nasr's sons, come and go over the next forty years, usually as puppets of rival Mameluke factions.

1345 Since the fall of Acre in 1291 there has been little **trade** between Western Europe and the Mameluke sultanate, partly due to papal embargos, and partly because of the rival commercial attractions of Byzantium, Turkish Anatolia, the Black Sea and Armenian Cilicia. But following a new treaty this year granting further commercial privileges, the **Venetians** send annual convoys of galleys to Alexandria which return to Europe laden with spices. Soon other European commercial powers obtain privileges and follow suit.

> One particular feature of medieval Egypt's population history has drawn comment from modern historians – namely the alleged failure of the mamluk elite to reproduce themselves genetically. It has been noted that it is difficult to trace a mamluk family for more than three generations. ... The difficulty seems to reflect the fragility of tenure on status and wealth, rather than some specific mamluk genetic failing. Incidentally, such modern speculations are interestingly anticipated by medieval Western observers who attempted to explain from a distance the mamluk phenomenon. According to William of Adam, writing in the early fourteenth century, Egypt ate up its inhabitants, and abortion ravaged its population. Therefore merchants imported specially fattened-up boys for the homosexual pleasure of the mamluk elite.
>
> Robert Irwin, *The Middle East in the Middle Ages* (1986)

1347 Of al-Nasr's many sons, the only one to rule as sultan for any length of time is **al-Hassan** (r. 1347–51 and 1354–61). In the autumn, **Bubonic plague** (the 'Black Death') strikes Egypt, and over the next two years kills about a third of the population.

1354 Another wave of **anti-Christian rioting** leads to further conversions to Islam, particularly in Upper Egypt where until now Copts had remained in the majority. **Coptic**, the ancient tongue of pharaonic Egypt, ceases to be a spoken language and is henceforth confined to liturgical use.

1355 The Mamelukes occupy the Cilician ports of **Tarsus** and **Adana** (on the Mediterranean coast of today's Turkey). These are staging posts for strategically important supplies of timber, iron and white slaves, and are also the western termini for much of the overland trade in silk and spices.

Plague

Bubonic plague originated in Central Asia and reached Alexandria aboard merchant ships from the Black Sea in the autumn of 1347. A low Nile flood that year brought widespread famine conditions, so resistance was already low and soon the plague was taking a terrible toll throughout the whole of the country. By the following spring the Delta was in the grip of the Black Death, and the first fatalities were reported in Upper Egypt in the autumn of 1348. In Cairo, more than a thousand people were dying every day. By the time the plague began to subside in 1349, a third of the Egyptian population had died.

Europe also suffered from the Black Death, but population levels soon recovered. That did not happen in Egypt, however, partly owing to bouts of drought and famine, and also to the periodic occurrence of the yet more deadly **pneumonic plague**. Until the 19th century Egypt was struck by a major epidemic on average every ten years and by minor outbreaks every two to three years, which, along with the neglect of the irrigation system, had a devastating effect on agricultural productivity and caused the population level to fall even below what it had been at the time of the Arab conquest.

1356–63 Sultan Hassan builds the great Cairo **mosque** that bears his name, reputedly using stone from the Pyramid of Cheops.

1365 Peter I of Lusignan, the ruler of Cyprus, attacks **Alexandria** in response to Mameluke attempts to control Cilicia, which has been in Cyprus' sphere of influence and since the fall of Acre has been the Western commercial bridgehead to the Orient.

1382 Barquq (r. 1382–89 and 1390–98) seizes the throne, marking the beginning of the **Burgi Mameluke** period (to 1517). Though of different ethnic origin to the Bahris, the Burgis too speak Turkish, which remains the unifying language.

Mamelukes were trained to be the elite warriors of Islam, but began their lives as non-Muslims on the Eurasian steppes

Construction of **Khan el Khalili**, the great Cairo market, begins.

The North African historian **Ibn Khaldun** (1332–1406) arrives in Egypt, where he is appointed to important diplomatic and judicial positions.

1394 Barquq confronts the Turco-Mongol forces of **Timur (Tamerlane)** in Syria, who for the time being withdraws beyond the Euphrates.

1399 The Ottomans, now the dominant Turkish group in **Anatolia**, penetrate Mameluke territory. Timur takes **Aleppo** in northern Syria.

1400 Timur sacks **Damascus** and ravages Syria during the following year.

1401–13 Taking advantage of the army's distraction in Syria, the Bedouin rise in revolt and sweep **Upper Egypt** clear of Mameluke officials, thus preventing the collection of taxes.

1402 Pressure on the Mameluke sultanate is temporarily relieved when Timur turns north against the Ottomans, whom he defeats at **Ankara** in northern Anatolia.

1403 A low Nile brings **famine** to Egypt.

1405 **Plague** strikes Egypt which, along with the famine, adds to the country's financial and administrative woes, and the economy again goes into decline.

1415–17 A new **plague** epidemic hits Egypt.

> ❝ What one can imagine always surpasses what one sees, because of the scope of the imagination, except Cairo, because it surpasses anything one can imagine. ❞
>
> Ibn Khaldun, 14th-century North African historian

1420 Egypt suffers yet another attack of **plague**, which will be followed by minor outbreaks every two to three years and major epidemics every ten years or so, regularly cutting back the population and drastically reducing productivity.

1425 **Sultan Baybars II** (r. 1422–38) establishes **state monopolies** over the transit trade in sugar, pepper and other spices from India and China, which since the depredations of Timur in Iraq now follows the Red Sea route and passes through Egypt. In the face of recent plagues, famines and political disruptions at home and abroad, Baybars' move is intended to squeeze the maximum revenues out of the transit trade, and at first the sultanate is enriched.

1453 The Ottomans under their sultan **Mehmet II** (r. 1451–81) capture **Constantinople** on 29 May and extinguish the Roman Empire in the East (the Byzantine Empire).

1468 With the accession of **Qaytbey** (r. 1468–95) the Burgi Mameluke sultanate embarks on its most stable, prosperous and magnificent period, but after thirteen years Egypt goes into sharp decline.

1480 Qaytbey builds a fort in **Alexandria** on the site of the Pharos, which had finally been totally destroyed by an earthquake in the 14th century.

1481 At the death of Mehmet II, Qaytbey gives shelter in Cairo to a fleeing Ottoman crown prince who has claims to the throne at Constantinople. This gives rise to a decade of aggression by the Ottomans against the Mameluke sultanate.

1484 Bedouins attack **St Antony's monastery**, a noted centre of scholarship, burning the books in its library and killing all the monks.

1491 The Mamelukes press as far as **Kayseri** in Anatolia and extract a peace treaty from the Ottomans.

1492 Christians capture **Granada**, driving the last Muslims out of Spain.

Mameluke magnificence

Though *The Thousand and One Nights* was ostensibly set in Baghdad, when the tales were set down in their final written form, the city of mystery and beauty that was being described was really the Cairo of the Mamelukes. Ruthless and often brutal and barbarous, the Mamelukes at their best were resourceful and vital. They patronized learning, encouraged the writing of history, and showed an incomparable flair for architecture, where their grandiose designs – bold, vigorous and voluminous – were gracefully decorated with the play of arabesques and the embroidery of light through stained-glass windows. Bahri and Burgi sultans alike built magnificent buildings in Cairo and elsewhere in Egypt, and also in Syria, which they financed with the revenue from agriculture and international commerce, particularly the Eastern spice trade which passed through Cairo en route to Europe.

But where previously the state had merely taxed the trade in spices, the monopolies created by **Baybars II** (r. 1422–38) and continued by his successors had the long-term effect of putting Egyptian merchants out of business, causing higher prices and acting as a spur to European countermeasures – notably Portugal's success in bypassing Egypt by finding a sea route to India. In addition, the dispute touched off with the Ottomans in 1481, when Sultan Qaytbey gave refuge to a pretender to the Ottoman throne, proved immensely costly in terms of Mameluke armies that had to be equipped and sent to the Anatolian front; internal security was left to falter, so that by the mid-1480s the Bedouins in Egypt had become uncontrollable. Perhaps the most magnificent thing about the Mamelukes was their proud refusal to adapt to **gunpowder** in warfare; and that too contributed to the ease with which the Ottomans, only 20 years after Qaytbey's death, swept the Mameluke sultanate aside.

1498 The Portuguese explorer **Vasco da Gama** reaches **India** by sailing round the Cape of Good Hope, becoming the first person to find a way round Africa since the expedition sent out by the Egyptian king Necho (r. 610–595 BC) over two thousand years before.

1500 Lacking a navy and modern firearms to resist the Portuguese presence in the Red Sea, Sultan **al-Ghuri** (r. 1500–16) sends to the Ottomans for help.

1508 Trials to create an Egyptian **artillery unit** begin in response to the European threat, though the concept seems unmanly to the Mameluke way of fighting on horseback with bows and arrows.

1511 Ottoman consignments of guns and powder reach Alexandria, accompanied by shipwrights and sailors. Al-Ghuri creates a corps of **fusiliers** (light musketeers) recruited from outside the Mameluke tradition.

MICHAEL HAAG

An earthquake destroyed the Pharos in the 14th century, but Sultan Qaytbey used some of its stones to build a harbour fortress at Alexandria in 1480

1514 The new Ottoman sultan **Selim** (r. 1512–20) employs cannon and firearms to defeat the Safavids (Persians) in the **battle of Chaldiran**, but resenting the lack of help from Egypt he now directs his aggressive policy against the Mamelukes.

1516 With the Mameluke fusiliers based at the Red Sea looking out for the Portuguese, the Ottoman fusiliers decimate the Mamelukes in battle north of **Aleppo**, where al-Ghuri is killed on 24 August. The Ottomans go on to conquer the whole of **Syria**.

The Ottomans: 1517–1798

Under the Ottomans, Egypt once again became a province, though it was never fully integrated into the empire and was governed with the minimum of interference from Constantinople. The Ottomans were content to leave the traditional system of administration in place, which was supervised by the **pasha**, the Ottoman governor. The value of Egypt for the empire was both strategic and economic. The land tax (*kharaj*) and port duties supported the garrison and administration, and also paid for the upkeep of the Ottoman army and navy based in Yemen, coastal Ethiopia and the Red Sea, where they countered the Portuguese and gave protection to the holy cities of Medina and Mecca in the Hejaz. Any surplus was sent to Constantinople, along with large quantities of agricultural products on demand. The caliphate was also stripped from the Mamelukes' Abbasid stooge; instead the office was assumed by the Ottoman sultan, who now claimed both temporal and spiritual authority.

In return for drawing off revenues and introducing a debased coinage which robbed Egyptians of a third of the value of their money, the Ottomans left their province to rot. After the military disturbances of 1586 and 1607–11, even the Ottoman pashas began to lose power, and throughout the 17th and 18th centuries were no more than straw men, as Egypt muddled along on shifting alliances between merchants, army regiments, religious functionaries and a revived Mameluke caste. Indeed, by the second half of the 18th century, certain **beys** – the institutional successors of the old Mameluke high command – had gathered up so much power that they became almost absolute masters of Egypt, and under **Ali Bey** all payments of revenue to Constantinople were stopped. But despite the fact that native chroniclers now took to describing the Mameluke beys as 'Egyptians' rather than 'Turks' – as though their self-seeking opposition to Constantinople corresponded to a benevolent interest in Egypt – it was under the rapacious misrule of Ali Bey in the 1760s and particularly his successors **Murad Bey** and **Ibrahim Bey** that the richest province of the Ottoman empire was brought to ruin.

The **French**, who only recently had been enjoying a booming trade with Egypt, were particularly hard hit by the failure of Murad and Ibrahim to honour their obligations under the Capitulations. Along with other Europeans, their merchants were twice driven out of Cairo, and several of their commercial houses had gone into bankruptcy. Furthermore, Russian military successes against the Turks threatened to undermine the Ottoman empire and to give Russia control of Constantinople and a large share of the Levant trade. So, largely to protect France's trading position in the Eastern Mediterranean, in 1798 the Directory gave **Napoleon** authority to invade Egypt. Ibrahim Bey and Murad Bey were as unprepared for the French invasion as they were unaware of the significance of the event.

1517 In January, the Mameluke sultan **Tumanbey** (r. 1516–17) hastily puts together fusilier and artillery corps to confront Selim and his Ottoman army outside **Cairo**, but the Mamelukes are outflanked and defeated. Ottoman troops pillage the city for three days, the Mamelukes are hunted down and slaughtered, and anyone suspected of helping or hiding them is put to death – as many as 10,000, it is alleged, though the figure is probably inflated. Nevertheless, the shock of events causes the inhabitants of Cairo to compare their city's fate to the destruction of Baghdad by the Mongols in 1258 – a symbol for Muslims of a disaster of immense magnitude. Egypt is reduced to being a province of a foreign empire.

In April, Tumanbey (who had escaped from Cairo in January) is captured by the Ottomans and hanged at **Bab Zuwayla**, one of the main gates of the city, as a demonstration to the populace that the Mameluke sultanate is finished. Notables, officials and craftsmen are **deported** to Constantinople, along with Cairo's Abbasid caliph, underlining that Egypt is now a province of a foreign empire. In the 18th century, the Ottomans will claim that it was at this time that the caliph transferred his rights to Selim and his descendants. The surviving Mamelukes are pardoned and the killings are stopped just before Selim leaves Egypt in September.

1520 Mameluke morale in Egypt rises on the accession to the Ottoman throne of **Suleyman the Magnificent** (r. 1520–66). Under his milder rule, most of the exiles in Constantinople are allowed to return to Cairo.

1522 Suleyman uses Mameluke troops for the conquest of **Rhodes** and expresses his astonishment that such magnificent fighters had been put to death by his father.

1523 Some Mamelukes in Egypt rise up against the Ottomans, and those who remain loyal to the Ottomans and march against their companions do so with little enthusiasm. The revolt is crushed nevertheless, but the episode adds further strain to Ottoman-Mameluke relations.

1524 A more serious rebellion against Constantinople in February is led by the Ottoman governor **Ahmet Pasha**, who assumes the title of sultan. Ahmet is captured and beheaded in March, but the country remains unsettled for another year. This is the last serious effort to separate Egypt from the Ottoman empire until 1760.

1525 Ibrahim Pasha, Suleyman's grand vizier, comes to Egypt in April and restores Ottoman authority.

1528 The Ottomans seal their occupation of Lower Nubia by garrisoning **Qasr Ibrim**, north of Abu Simbel, with Bosnian troops, who intermarry with the local population.

1535 Suleyman grants special rights to **France** to promote trade with the Ottoman Empire. Known as the **Capitulations** (from the Latin *capitula*, meaning the 'heads' or 'chapters' of an agreement), they guarantee to French traders the safety of their persons and property, their freedom of worship, and their right to be tried by the French consul, not by an Islamic court.

1538 The Ottomans send their navy to **India** via the Red Sea under the command of their Egyptian governor **Suleyman Pasha**, but the fleet is defeated by the Portuguese.

> ❝ At Ibrim, as at Derr, there are 'fair' families [whose] light hair and blue eyes ... date back to Bosnian forefathers of 360 years ago. These people give themselves airs, and are the haute noblesse of the place. ❞
>
> Amelia Edwards, describing the inhabitants of Qasr Ibrim in Nubia in *A Thousand Miles up the Nile* (1877)

1568 The Ottomans fail in their attempt to build a **canal** through the isthmus of Suez.

1580 The Ottoman Empire grants Capitulations to **England**.

Of eunuchs, coffee and culture

Egypt's loss of its central position in the international trade in Indian spices was compensated to some extent by the burgeoning 17th-century trade in **coffee**, with dealers in Cairo importing coffee beans from Yemen and exporting them to Europe. Payment for the beans was made in wheat, which offered opportunities to defraud both the imperial government in Constantinople and the holy cities of Medina and Mecca. Certain wheat-growing estates in Egypt were endowed to huge Ottoman pious foundations whose purpose was to provide for the poor in the holy cities, but those in charge of the estates and the foundations enriched themselves by diverting a portion of the wheat to pay for the coffee. At Constantinople, the person in ultimate charge of these pious foundations was always the chief black African eunuch in charge of the Ottoman sultan's harem. Having become a coffee mogul, he would also take care to amass property in Egypt – with almost predictable regularity chief black harem eunuchs were deposed from office, and it was to Egypt that they were exiled. Having received the best education at the imperial palace, exiled eunuchs were frequently known to bring their private libraries with them to Cairo, where they lived grandly, wielded great influence, and played a critical role in transmitting the intellectual and spiritual culture of the Ottoman court to the province. But they will also have played an important if indirect role at the level of popular culture, for soon there were so many **coffee houses** in Cairo that they competed for customers by entertaining them with the best storytellers and poets, giving a stage to Egypt's lively oral culture, whose use of colloquial Arabic injected life into a wide range of written literature – so creating a culture from below.

1586 Economic misrule brings inflation, which hurts the soldiery who impose an illegal tax, the *tulba*, on the fellahin. The soldiers, some but not all of them Mamelukes, rise up against the Ottoman pasha (governor), and attack officials and officers.

1604 Egyptian military mutineers kill the Ottoman pasha in Cairo.

1607–11 A new governor, **Mehmet Pasha**, suppresses the unruly soldiery and abolishes the *tulba*.

1630 Violent **feuding** breaks out between high-ranking figures within the Egyptian military caste, known as **beys**, who seek to gain dominance over Egyptian affairs. Meanwhile, Ottoman governors become mere creatures of the beys.

1639 The Ottomans conquer **Iraq**, the last stage in bringing almost the entire Arabic-speaking world under their rule.

1660 The fierce and often bloody rivalry between the **Faqariyya** and **Qasimiyya** groups of beys (named after their supposed founders) reaches a climax with the **massacre** of a group of Faqari beys by a coalition of the governor, the Qasimi beys and an Ottoman regiment, the **Azab**.

1662 The Ottoman governor has the leader of the Qasimi beys **assassinated**. The power of the beys declines, while the seven regiments of the Ottoman garrison become powerful at the expense of both the governor and the beys. The largest and richest of these regiments is the **Janissaries**, to whom the centre of political power now shifts.

1711 Armed **battles** break out between the Janissaries and the second-largest regiment, the Azab, over lucrative tax revenues. Cairo's Citadel is bombarded, and the fighting ends with the defeat of the Janissaries and their allies, the Faqari beys. The Qasimi beys are now dominant, though the old vicious rivalry between them and the Faqariyya soon resumes.

Popular religion

Built by the Fatimids in the 11th century, **Bab Zuwayla** was one of 60 gates that once encircled medieval Cairo. Perhaps because it once led out to the city's cemeteries, it long had the reputation of being an unlucky place, and also because it was the site of public executions. Tumanbey, the last Mameluke sultan, was hanged here by the Ottomans; twice the rope broke, the third time his neck. But the populace also endowed Bab Zuwayla with a special spiritual aura, saying it was inhabited by the **Qutb**, the master of the saints, who could flit to Mecca and back again in the twinkling of an eye. He reproved the impious and exposed the sanctimonious, and distributed evils and blessings; the sick would attach locks of their hair and bits of their clothing to the gate in the hope of receiving a miracle. Here during the month of Ramadan the Sufis gathered to perform their prayers, and on this occasion were attacked with swords and cudgels by a mob of Turks issuing out of the nearby mosque of Muayyad. The incident was part of the long antagonism between the Egyptians and their alien rulers, with 'Egyptian' now meaning the Arabic-speaking population, the overwhelming number of whom were Muslims. Opposition took religious rather than political form, however, and was often expressed through **Sufism**, which at first was a purely individual mystical experience but became popular among the common people, so that the authorities saw it as a social movement with an antipathy towards the existing order, which ought to be suppressed. More generally, popular religion was an expression of cultural continuity – the origins of many a Muslim saint can be found in a Christian saint who preceded him, and in an ancient Egyptian deity before that; and the ancient past arose too in such popular practices as bringing flowers and fragrant herbs to the tombs of the dead and having a meal there, which the more purist Ottomans also wanted to suppress – as though they could suppress 5000 years of history.

Meanwhile, there are disturbances between Ottoman soldiers and Egyptians at **Bab Zuwayla**, one of the gates of Cairo, when a Turkish preacher incites a crowd of Turks to attack Egyptian Sufi dervishes who are performing their whirling prayer.

1736 By now the hostile Faqariyya and Qasimiyya factions have exhausted themselves and power passes to another group of beys, the **Qazdagli**, from within whose ranks comes the leadership of Egypt until the arrival of Napoleon and indeed beyond. For the next two and a half decades, until 1760, Egypt enjoys an unusual period of stability, prosperity and freedom from plague. Foreign trade flourishes, particularly with France; the population increases; and wealthy Cairenes endow the capital with a plethora of mosques, schools, fountains and palaces.

1760 Ali Bey al-Kabir (r. 1760–72) becomes sheikh al-balad (commander of the city [Cairo]) and consolidates his position by wiping out the Janissaries and stripping the other regiments of almost everything but their names. He further aggrandizes himself through the extortion of foreigners, Copts and Jews.

1768–69 Ali challenges Ottoman authority by dismissing the governors and not permitting the appointment of new ones, and he declares his effective **independence** from Constantinople by having his name proclaimed at Friday prayers and inscribed on coins rather than the Ottoman sultan's.

1770 Ali intervenes in the Hejaz, replacing the Ottoman governor at **Jedda** with an Egyptian one.

1771 Ali campaigns in **Syria**, where he relies on the Russians who are at war with the Ottoman sultan. But Ali's power begins to crumble as his lieutenants, after defeating an Ottoman army, back off from the decisive step of openly declaring themselves in alliance with the Russians and in revolt against Constantinople. Instead of taking **Damascus**, they return to Cairo and turn on Ali, who flees.

1773 Ali returns to Cairo and is poisoned by his enemies.

1775 A **power struggle** begins between Ismail Bey, the Ottoman governor, Ibrahim Bey, the sheikh el balad and Murad Bey, who is in charge of the lucrative Mecca pilgrimage.

1778 Ismail Bey is driven from Egypt to **Constantinople**, while Ibrahim and Murad, distrusting one another, struggle for advantage.

1783 **Ibrahim Bey**, the sheikh el balad who also controls the customs houses of Suez and Alexandria, and **Murad Bey** who claims control over the provinces of Lower Egypt, begin a period of fractious joint rule. They are unusually exploitative and oppressive, and things are made worse by plagues, cattle murrain and low Niles, which cause great economic hardship.

> **❝** The land turned to waste, highway robbery flourished, marauders indulged in looting, security was nonexistent, and the roads were impassable except with a protective escort, then at a dangerous risk. The peasants abandoned their villages because of a lack of irrigation and because of the oppression. **❞**
>
> Al-Jabarti (1753–1825), Egyptian historian

> **❝** I have come to restore to you your rights and to punish the usurpers. I worship God more than the Mamelukes do, and I respect his Prophet Mohammed and the admirable Koran. We are the true Muslims. **❞**
>
> Napoleon's proclamation to the people of Alexandria, 2 July, 1798

1784 During one of several fallings-out, Ibrahim drives Murad from **Cairo**, and they fire cannon at one another across the Nile, but soon make peace – only for Murad to drive Ibrahim out of Cairo in turn.

1786 Constantinople attempts to impose **direct rule** on Egypt by sending an invading force under Admiral **Hasan Pasha**. Ibrahim and Murad retreat to Upper Egypt, from where Hasan cannot dislodge them.

1787 Hasan is recalled to Constantinople to take command of the Ottoman forces in the looming war against **Russia**. He leaves Ismail Bey in Cairo as sheikh el balad.

1791 **Plague** kills virtually the whole regime in Cairo, including Ismail Bey and most of the Mameluke beys. The ports of Rosetta and Damietta lose about half their populations, Cairo loses about a sixth, and the population of Alexandria falls to a few thousand. In the midst of this, Ibrahim and Murad return to **Cairo**, where their regime goes unchallenged.

1795 The government of revolutionary **France** sends a mission to Ibrahim and Murad warning them of the consequences of their extortions against French merchants and their failure to honour the Capitulations, but the beys dismiss the threat.

1798 On 12 April, the government in Paris gives its authority to **Napoleon** for an invasion of Egypt. On 1 July, he lands near **Alexandria**.

9: Egypt's encounter with the West

1798–1914

When the 29-year-old **Napoleon** landed in Egypt in 1798 with 40,000 men, his instructions from the Directory, the government of revolutionary France, were to advance French mercantile interests in the Eastern Mediterranean, to obtain the wealth of Egypt, and to cut a canal through the isthmus of Suez to ensure 'the free and exclusive possession of the Red Sea for the French Republic'. Behind these commercial aims was a political objective that centred not on Egypt but on affairs in Europe, where since 1792 France had been waging wars of conquest. Its one undefeated enemy was **Britain**, which, though it lay in sight across the English Channel, was protected by a formidable fleet. Rather than attempt a direct assault, the Directory saw greater promise in strangling British trade with the Near East and India, major sources of its wealth, by launching an attack on Egypt.

The Egypt encountered by Napoleon was economically impoverished, politically in a state of anarchy and culturally decadent. It was a backwater of the Ottoman Empire that had stagnated outside the mainstream of ideas and events for the last 300 years. But as bad as things had been under the Turks and Mamelukes, they were co-religionists who allowed Egypt to inhabit the delusion that the heartlands of Islam were safely isolated from European influence and that Muslims were superior to the infidel. Napoleon might claim that the French had come to liberate the country from rapacious and alien masters, but his arrival challenged Egypt's complacency and faith, and he was not welcomed for it.

In fact, the French occupation, which lasted only three years, made very little difference to the Egyptians themselves. There was no significant cultural interaction between the French and the Egyptians, no change in agricultural methods, land tenure or taxation. These would come over the following decades under the rule of **Mohammed Ali**.

The real effect of Napoleon's adventure was to make Egypt interesting to Europe. Politically, Egypt became a preoccupation of European strategists and diplomats, who were concerned not just with the control of Egypt but also with the flow of Eastern trade and the survival of the Ottoman Empire, had it disintegrated could have had unpredictable consequences for the balance of power in Europe if Russia, the Austro-Hungarian Empire, France and Britain had to fight over the pieces. Instead their policy was to prop up the 'Sick Man of Europe', notably against the energy of Egypt's Mohammed Ali. No longer drowsing in its historical backwater, Egypt was now caught up in wider and uncertain currents.

The age of Mohammed Ali: 1798–1849

British seapower in the Mediterranean proved as effective as in the English Channel and made the French position in Egypt untenable. The British had no interest in occupying Egypt for themselves and after the French evacuation the country was restored to Ottoman rule. Among Ottoman troops that were landed in Egypt was **Mohammed Ali**. He came from Kavalla in Macedonia, which was then part of the Ottoman Empire but today is part of Greece, and he sailed from there to Egypt with a Macedonian company that had joined up with a contingent of Albanian soldiers of which he was made second in command. Whether he himself was Albanian is not clear; he was blond, grey-eyed and spoke Greek as well as Albanian and Turkish. Mohammad Ali was always mysterious about his origins, and he may well have modified his year of birth to 1769 so that it would be the same as Napoleon's, his hero. That he was born in Macedonia added to his legend; later, people spoke of him as another Ptolemy Soter to Napoleon's Alexander the Great.

The incompetent Ottoman army was unable to impose itself upon the chaos that followed the French and British withdrawals from Egypt, and instead a struggle for power began between the surviving Mamelukes, the Ottoman Janissary corps and the Albanians, who, after the assassination of their leader in 1803, fell under the command of Mohammed Ali. With the Albanians behind him, he took his chance to fill the power vacuum, and in 1805 at about the age of 35 he made himself the master of Cairo, forcing the sultan in Constantinople to recognize him as the Ottoman governor (pasha) of Egypt. Though he was to govern for another 43 years, he remained haunted by doubts about his political legitimacy and gratefully accepted the sultan's offer of hereditary rule when in fact he twice had the chance – in 1833 and 1839 – to overturn the Ottoman Empire and become sultan himself.

Mohammed Ali was an admirer of the West and devoted his energies to **modernization**, encouraging European immigration, especially from Greece, and forging close relations with France, using foreign expertise and capital to develop the country while avoiding falling into foreign debt. After his massacre of the Mamelukes in 1811, which consolidated his power, he instituted wide reforms in the military, agriculture, education and health, and he also made an attempt to bring the industrial revolution to Egypt. By the end of his reign towards the middle of the nineteenth century, he had laid the foundations for the infrastructure of a modern Egyptian state.

1798 On 3 July, the French army begins its march from Alexandria to **Cairo**. Frequent massacres of stragglers and small parties of Frenchmen in the countryside are demonstrations of the **hostility** with which the French are met by the local population.

In the **battle of the Pyramids** on 21 July – in fact eight miles away at Embaba, in present-day western Cairo – Napoleon Bonaparte's army defeats the Mameluke forces. Ibrahim Bey flees to Syria and Murad Bey withdraws into Upper Egypt. The French are now in full possession of **Cairo**, **Alexandria** and **Rosetta**.

In the **battle of the Nile** on 1 August, near the mouth of the river east of Alexandria at Aboukir Bay, the British admiral **Horatio Nelson** destroys the French fleet, cutting off Napoleon's army from home. In consequence, Murad refuses Napoleon's offer of the government of Upper Egypt under French authority.

Napoleon establishes the **Institute of Egypt** on 22 August, drawing its members from the **Commission on the Sciences and Arts**, a body of 167 scientists, mathematicians, naturalists, engineers, irrigation experts, Arabists and artists who accompanied the voyage to Egypt. The aims of the Institute are to advance the spread of science in Egypt, to study the natural, historical and industrial aspects of the country, and to publish the results, and to provide advice to the French administration in Egypt. The most lasting achievement of Napoleon's scholars will be the famous 24-volume *Description de l'Egypte,* published over a decade later.

The Ottoman Empire **declares war** on France in early September. A *firman* (decree) from the sultan is read out in

Napoleon considers his place in history as he confronts the Sphinx at Giza at the outset of the French occupation of Egypt

all the mosques of Cairo calling on Muslims to resist the French and promising the imminent arrival of Ottoman forces. In Cairo on 21 October, there is a call for a *jihad* against the French, whose military governor is killed. The insurgents are surrounded in the vicinity of the **Azhar mosque** and are subjected to artillery fire from the Citadel. The uprising is suppressed within 36 hours at a cost of 300 French dead and perhaps 3000 Cairenes. Six sheikhs (clerics) of the Azhar are executed.

> " The work of the savants filled a gap in human knowledge that had persisted since Roman times. There is hardly an aspect of Egyptian life that is not carefully examined in the twenty-four volumes of their monumental Description de l'Egypt, and the illustrations ... give us a picture of the country that has never been surpassed. It was one of the most ambitious publications ever attempted ... This was a true census of Egypt. "
>
> Alan Moorehead, *The Blue Nile* (1962)

The first Arabic printing press

When the French enquired into the library of a scholar at the university attached to the mosque of **al-Azhar** in Cairo, they found that its only nonreligious works were a treatise on love, an anthology of songs and poems, a book of historical curiosities, instructions for drawing up marriage and divorce contracts, and a manual on sexual techniques. There were no printed works, not because Egyptians were ignorant of the technology – Jews had been operating their own Hebrew printing press in Cairo since the sixteenth century. But when the French introduced the first Arabic printing press, it was seen as the devil's work: according to the sheikhs of the Azhar, the Koran was the fount of all truth and they were its learned interpreters, so that a printing press could only further the proliferation of falsehood.

1799 Napoleon's civil engineer **Lepère** mistakenly concludes that the surface of the Red Sea is 33 feet higher than that of the Mediterranean, causing plans for the construction of a **canal** through the isthmus of Suez to be shelved.

In spring, Napoleon leads 13,000 men into **Palestine** to deny its ports to the British, but he is checked at **Acre** by the British navy and by local resistance loyal to the Ottomans. In the **Delta**, two uprisings against the French are suppressed. **General Desaix** manages to pacify Upper Egypt, though Murad Bey and his Mamelukes escape into **Lower Nubia**, from where they make occasional forays.

Napoleon retreats from Palestine in June, and arrives back in Egypt, where it is clear that his position is hopeless owing to Britain's mastery of the seas. His army has suffered damaging losses from battle and disease, and Napoleon reports to France that it will be reduced to an effective force of only 12,000 by spring 1800.

In July, French sappers at Rosetta under the command of

P.F.X. Bouchard find a basalt stone bearing ancient hieroglyphic and demotic inscriptions. Through the activities of the Egyptian Institute, Bouchard appreciates that the **Rosetta Stone**, as it comes to be known, may be of considerable importance, as its uncomprehended Egyptian inscriptions are accompanied by a parallel inscription in readable Greek.

Napoleon defeats an Ottoman force which the British have landed at **Aboukir** on 25 July.

Leaving word that his army should be commanded by **General Kléber**, Napoleon secretly sails from Alexandria to France on 23 August. Once back in Paris in November, Napoleon overthrows the Directory and establishes the Consulate with himself as **First Consul** – that is, dictator of France.

1800 On 6 June, Kléber is **murdered** in Cairo by a Syrian Muslim whom the French impale, and they also behead three sheikhs of the Azhar mosque.

> " At nine o'clock, in making a sharp turn round a projecting point, we discovered all at once the site of the ancient Thebes in its whole extent. This celebrated city … enveloped in the veil of mystery and the obscurity of ages, whereby even its own colossal monuments are magnified to the imagination, still impressed the mind with such gigantic phantoms that the whole army, suddenly and with one accord, stood in amazement at the sight of its shattered ruins, and clapped their hands with delight, as if the end and object of their various toils, and the complete conquest of Egypt, were accomplished and secured by taking possession of the splendid remains of this ancient metropolis. "
>
> Vivant Denon, describing the arrival of the French army at Luxor, 1799

1801 A British force lands at **Aboukir** in early March and meets only feeble resistance from the French, whose army in Egypt is now under the command of General Menou. On 25 March the British are joined at Aboukir by an Ottoman force. Among the Ottoman troops is **Mohammed Ali**, a member of a Macedonian company. **Rosetta** is quickly taken and the advance through the Delta begins. Another Ottoman army enters Egypt from Syria, meanwhile.

Surrounded by enemies and with plague afflicting **Cairo**, the French forces in the city capitulate on 27 June and agree to evacuate Egypt. General Menou holds out for a while longer in **Alexandria**.

The last French soldiers embark in September, having surrendered all their antiquities to the British, who deposit them at the British Museum. Among these is the Rosetta Stone, though copies of it are made and widely circulated. The **Ottomans** have their fleet at Alexandria and their army occupies Cairo, but they are unable to establish full control over Egypt owing to the poor quality of their forces and organization and to the still significant power of the Mamelukes.

1803 Having seen off the French, the British complete their **evacuation** of Egypt on 11 March, as strife between the Ottomans and the Mamelukes reduces the country to chaos and misery.

During the summer, Mohammed Ali becomes commander of the Ottoman army's Albanian contingent in Egypt.

1805 In May Mohammed Ali gains the support of the *ulama* (Muslim legal scholars) in **Cairo**, who are desperate for order in Egypt to be restored. In August, they declare the Ottoman pasha (governor) deposed and offer the post to Mohammed Ali. With their backing, and with the armed assistance of the populace of Cairo, Mohammed Ali lays siege to the Citadel and forces out the Ottoman governor. As the new governor, **Mohammed Ali** (r. 1805–48) is ruler of an effectively autonomous Egypt, though he recognizes Ottoman sovereignty and continues to pay an **annual tribute** to Constantinople.

1808 With the aim of developing Egypt through the acquisition of Western skills, Mohammed Ali begins a programme of **educational missions**, sending students from Egypt to Europe, at first mainly to Italy.

1809 The first volume of the *Description de l'Egypte*, the massive study undertaken by the scientists and artists who accompanied Napoleon to Egypt, is published in Paris, with 23 more volumes to follow until 1828.

> **❝** That Mohammed Ali is an extraordinary man, cannot be disputed. His address, his restless activity and spirit of enterprise, and his superiority to national and religious prejudices, justly entitle him to be considered as one of the most accomplished Turks, and one of the greatest of Mohammedan princes, that have ever vaulted into a throne. When he first assumed the government of Cairo, complete anarchy prevailed in every department … During the sixteen years of his energetic administration, a mutinous soldiery has been transformed into a regular army; the revenue has been prodigiously increased; new articles of produce have been raised; trade has been carried on to an extent previously unknown; several important public works have been undertaken and executed; and the whole country from Alexandria to Syene [Aswan], has been rendered perfectly safe for the European traveller. **❞**
>
> Josiah Condor, *The Modern Traveller* (1827)

This engraving from the *Description de l'Egypte* reconstructs the Hypostyle Hall in the temple of Amun at Karnak

> **66** No considerable power was ever amassed by any nation, whether in the West or in Asia, that did not also turn that nation towards Egypt, which was regarded in some measure as its natural lot. **99**
>
> Preface to the *Description de l'Egypte*

The rise and fall of Mohammed Ali's Egyptian empire

Mohammed Ali's foreign military campaigns began when the Ottoman sultan called on him to intervene in **Arabia**, where Abdullah ibn Saud, the champion of the Wahhabi sect, a puritanical and fundamentalist version of Islam, had overrun the Hejaz and taken the holy cities of Mecca and Medina, and was now threatening Syria and Mesopotamia. Mohammed Ali responded to the invitation, and in 1818 an Egyptian army broke the power of the Wahhabis.

With the Hejaz under Mohammed Ali's control, and the **Sudan** by 1825, the Red Sea had become an Egyptian lake. In that same year, again at the request of the sultan, Egyptian troops were sent to **Greece**, where Ibrahim Pasha, Mohammed Ali's son, very nearly succeeded in extinguishing the Greek revolt against the Ottoman Empire but for the intervention of the British fleet at Navarino in 1827. Nevertheless, Ibrahim was discovering his genius as a general, the capabilities of his well-trained troops and the weakness of the Ottomans, and in late 1831 he invaded the Ottoman province of **Syria**. Mohammed Ali now possessed something like the classic Egyptian empire of a Ptolemy or a Tuthmosis, when Ibrahim made a spectacular advance against the Ottoman armies and early in 1833 stood within a few days' march of **Constantinople**. At this moment – and it happened again in 1839 – Mohammed Ali had the chance to overthrow the sultan and make himself master of the Muslim world.

But perhaps because he was too much an Ottoman himself, Mohammed Ali recoiled. He turned to the European powers instead, suggesting that they recognize his domain as an independent state, but even his friends, the French, rejected the proposal. They feared that without Egypt, Syria and Arabia, what remained of the Ottoman Empire would disintegrate, setting European states against one another in the race to gather up its pieces for themselves and igniting a continental war. While Mohammed Ali hesitated, the European powers forced him to become again a vassal of the Ottoman Empire.

1810 After two years of campaigning in **Upper Egypt**, Mohammed Ali loosens Mameluke control there.

1811 Mohammed Ali invites 480 **Mamelukes** to a gala dinner at the Citadel and massacres them as they leave. Over the next few days, he kills about 1000 more throughout Cairo. Except in Upper Egypt, his authority is now absolute. With the freedom to act abroad, he launches his campaign against the Wahhabis in **Arabia**. The Egyptian army under the command of Mohammed Ali's second son Tusun captures **Mecca** and **Medina** in the Hejaz, but fails to advance further against the forces of Abdullah ibn Saud.

1812 Mohammed Ali establishes a **monopoly** over rice cultivation in the Delta and cereal production in Upper Egypt, part of his long-term scheme to organize the commercial exploitation of agricultural produce and to concentrate it in the hands of his government.

1813 The Swiss traveller **John Lewis Burckhardt** is the first European since Graeco-Roman times to see Rameses II's great temple at **Abu Simbel** in Lower Nubia on 22 March.

1814 The **Mecca pilgrimage**, suspended for a decade owing to the aggressive activities of the Saudi-led Wahhabis, is resumed under Egyptian protection, and Mohammed Ali's stock rises throughout the Islamic world.

> **❝** At one hour and a half, ascended a steep sandy mountain … I fell in with what is yet visible of four immense colossal statues cut out of the rock … they stand in a deep recess, excavated in the mountain, but it is deeply to be regretted, that they are now almost entirely buried beneath the sands, which are blown down here in torrents. **❞**
>
> John Lewis Burckhardt, *Travels in Nubia* (1819)

> We order you and your subordinates to make sure of the proper functioning of the irrigation system and to work diligently to protect and maintain the dykes and to see to it that the waters are not unnecessarily wasted. Should any dyke show a crack or a break, or be emptied of its waters, the official in charge of the district will merit execution.

An order from Mohammed Ali to his chief engineer

1815 Napoleon is defeated by the Duke of Wellington at the **battle of Waterloo**.

Mohammed Ali takes over sugar production in Upper Egypt after his eldest son, **Ibrahim Pasha**, who has been governor there, breaks the last resistance of the Mamelukes and pacifies the Bedouin. Another attempt by Tusun to reach the Saudi capital of **Derayah** fails, and Mohammed Ali entrusts the task to Ibrahim.

1818 Ibrahim Pasha lays siege to **Derayah** in April and takes it in September, capturing Abdullah ibn Saud and sending him to Constantinople for execution. The campaign, conducted with great difficulty through the desert against an elusive enemy, convinces Ibrahim and Mohammed Ali that the Egyptian army needs to be organized on more European lines. Following Waterloo, there are plenty of French officers and soldiers available as advisers and troops.

1818–19 Excessive **floods** cause terror among Egypt's rural population. The high water razes settlements, destroys food stores, endangers seed stock for the next season and decimates livestock. It also destroys the transverse dykes subdividing basins, which need to be rebuilt and maintained to ensure proper irrigation in future years.

1820 The Frenchman Joseph Sève (later known as **Suleyman Pasha** after his conversion to Islam) establishes

Egypt's first school of infantry.

Mohammed Ali completes construction of the **Mahmoudiya Canal**, which links Alexandria to the Nile, spurring the city's revival – thanks particularly to its trade in long staple (long fibre) **Jumel cotton**, whose commercial promise is first demonstrated this year.

1820 To gain control of the resources of Nubia and the Sudan, principally gold and slaves, Mohammed Ali places his third son, **Ismail**, in charge of an expedition of conquest which sets out from Aswan in June.

1821 An uprising at **Patras** in the Peloponnese on 25 March marks the beginning of the **Greek war of independence** against the Ottoman Empire.

The rebirth of Alexandria

When Napoleon landed near Alexandria in 1798, it was hardly more than a large village of perhaps 6000 people. But with the completion of the **Mahmoudiya Canal** in 1820 it became the major point of population and economic growth in Egypt. Greeks, Italians, Jews, Lebanese Christians and others from around the Mediterranean settled in the city, which developed into a cosmopolitan port – the rival of Genoa or Marseilles. It also became the favourite summer residence of Mohammed Ali himself and the focus of his wider ambitions. He built dockyards here and a fleet, and government warehouses which he filled with agricultural products such as sugar, grain and cotton, over which he had established monopolies, shipping them downriver to Alexandria – just as the Ptolemies had done – for export abroad. In particular the new **long staple** variety of cotton, developed with Mohammed Ali's encouragement by a Frenchman called Louis Jumel, became recognized as the finest cotton in the world and attracted a premium price; in Alexandria, which was largely built on its trade, they called it 'white gold'. By the end of Mohammed Ali's reign in 1848, the population of Alexandria had reached 150,000.

Ibrahim assumes overall command in the **Sudan** in autumn. Ismail pushes southwards up the **Blue Nile** in a vain search for gold, while of the 30,000 slaves he captures, most are women and children and only half survive the journey to Cairo.

1822 Frustrated after two years of campaigning in the Sudan, Ismail turns back towards Egypt but is murdered by a Sudanese chief. His death provokes the Egyptian forces to horrific **reprisals** which remain a byword for brutality in the Sudan for generations to come.

In Cairo, Mohammed Ali establishes the first Muslim-run Arabic-language **publishing house** in the world, which mainly prints textbooks for Egypt's new schools and training colleges.

In Paris, **Jean-François Champollion** (1790–1832), who has been studying the Rosetta Stone, deciphers **hieroglyphs**, opening up three millennia of ancient Egyptian history.

1823 During the spring, Egyptian troops in the service of the Ottoman sultan put down Greek revolts in **Crete** and **Cyprus**. By the autumn, the Greeks have gained control of almost the entire **Peloponnese**.

1824 **General Boyer**, head of a French military mission, replaces Sève and over the next two years makes further improvements to the Egyptian army.

1825 Ibrahim, who has sailed from Alexandria with an Egyptian expeditionary force, lands in the Peloponnese in February. By the end of the year, his forces restore almost the whole of the Peloponnese to Ottoman control.

1826 Mohammed Ali develops closer ties with **France**, one aspect being his decision to send Egyptians on educational missions there instead of Italy.

1827 British, French and Russian fleets, which are operating together in an attempt to enforce an armistice on the

Ottomans and Greeks, arrive on 20 October outside the port of **Navarino** in the western Peloponnese, where the Egyptian-Ottoman fleet is at harbour. But when Admiral Codrington sails into the harbour a shot is fired and general action begins; the Egyptian-Ottoman fleet is destroyed with considerable loss of life. Ibrahim's army is now cut off from Egypt.

1828 After agreeing with the British and French to a peaceful withdrawal of Egyptian forces from Greece, Ibrahim arrives at Alexandria with his army in October.

1830 Mohammed Ali begins construction of the huge Ottoman imperial-style **mosque** that bears his name, atop the Citadel in Cairo.

A British engineer's report states that a canal through the isthmus of **Suez** is technically possible, but the European powers are divided on its desirability, with France and the Austro-Hungarian empire in favour but Britain and Russia opposed to the idea – as is Mohammed Ali, who fears that it will lead to European interference in Egypt.

The French invade and occupy **Algeria**.

1831 In October, Mohammed Ali sends his army into **Syria** under the command of Ibrahim, one motive being to obtain timber from the mountains of Lebanon for Egypt's navy. But from the outset Ibrahim conceives the bolder idea of eventually advancing into Asia Minor and overthrowing the Ottoman dynasty.

A heavy **cholera outbreak** in Egypt in the same month leads Mohammed Ali to establish a board of health and a quarantine service.

1832 Greek independence is recognized and guaranteed by Britain, France and Russia in May.

Damascus falls to Ibrahim in June, and in August he crosses into Asia Minor and captures **Adana** in Cilicia.

A bronze equestrian statue of Mohammed Ali dominates the central square of Alexandria, the city he refounded

1833 After defeating the Ottomans in the **battle of Konya**, Ibrahim reaches Kutahia, less than 150 miles from Constantinople, where Mohammed Ali orders him to stop.

At the **treaty of Kutahia** in May, the Ottomans cede **Syria**, **Lebanon** and **Palestine** to Egypt. Ibrahim establishes centralized control over the whole of Greater Syria, giving its people unity, security, justice, an equitable system of taxation and a considerable increase in prosperity.

1834 Work begins on the **Delta Barrage** in an attempt to ensure perennial irrigation for the cultivation of cotton.

1835 Mohammed Ali founds the **School of Languages** in Cairo, which facilitates the translation of European works into Arabic and helps stimulate the intellectual atmosphere in Egypt. It leads to a revival of **Arabic**, which begins to replace Turkish as the language of administration and leads to the development of an Egyptian cultural and political consciousness.

Plague kills about a quarter of Cairo's 250,000 population. Free clinics are opened to identify suspicious cases and to carry out post-mortem examinations and research.

1836 A regular **steamship service** between Britain and Egypt is inaugurated.

> ❝ For my part I hate Mohammed Ali, whom I consider as nothing but an ignorant barbarian, who by cunning and boldness and mother wit has been successful in rebellion ... I look upon his boasted civilisation of Egypt as the arrantest humbug; and I believe that he is as great a tyrant and oppressor as ever made a people wretched. ❞
>
> Lord Palmerston, British foreign minister, 1839

Advances in education and health

Rather than limiting himself to the traditional activities of raising taxes, internal security and the defence of Egypt's borders against foreign armies, Mohammed Ali assumed governmental responsibilities that were modern even in European states. **Education** was an important part of his plan for the development of Egypt, and he established a system of government secondary schools and also sent students to Europe. These in turn became teachers, or doctors or engineers, and became a professional elite which eventually formed the core of Egypt's new middle class.

One of Mohammed Ali's most impressive achievements was in **health reform** and medical training, which was carried out under the supervision of the Frenchman **Dr Clot Bey**. Doctors and midwives were educated in Egypt and many were sent to France to finish their training, returning to assume important posts in the expanding medical service. By the middle of the 19th century, plague and smallpox were all but eliminated owing to mass vaccinations of children and the quarantine measures taken against Mecca pilgrims.

As a gift from Mohammed Ali, an **obelisk** of Rameses II at the temple of Luxor is erected by the French in the Place de la Concorde in Paris.

Mohammed Ali creates a **ministry of education**; by now Egypt has 67 European-style primary schools and 23 specialist schools where music, medicine, art and technical subjects are taught, though mostly they are devoted to military studies.

1838 In May, Mohammed Ali proposes to the European powers that he should declare Egypt **independent** of the Ottoman Empire, but they – including his main supporter, France – reject the suggestion, preferring to keep the Empire intact.

1839 The Ottomans send their army into Syria, where it is heavily defeated on 24 June in the **battle of Nezib**, north of Aleppo, by the Egyptians under the command of Ibrahim Pasha.

The Ottoman high admiral declares for Mohammed Ali and sails the entire **Ottoman fleet** into Alexandria harbour on 1 July, where he hands it over to the Egyptians. The Ottomans have now lost their army and their navy, and Mohammed Ali is the most powerful man in the Empire.

1840 Alarmed by the success of Mohammed Ali's ambitions, the 'great powers' meet at the **London Conference** on 15 July, where Britain, Russia, France, Austria and Prussia pledge to protect the Ottoman Empire.

On 11 September, a British and Ottoman force lands at **Beirut** and calls on the Syrians to rise up against the Egyptians – a call widely heeded by a local population wanting an end to Ibrahim's 'un-Islamic' reforms. In November, a British fleet arrives outside Alexandria harbour and threatens Mohammed Ali, who signs an **armistice** and agrees to the withdrawal of Egyptian forces from **Syria** and the return of the Ottoman fleet.

1841 In **Constantinople**, the sultan issues a *firman* (decree) in May, accepting Mohammed Ali's submission to Ottoman sovereignty – though in reality this is owed to European power while Ottoman authority is as feeble as ever. Mohammed Ali restores **Syria** and **Crete** to the Empire and accepts a limitation of 18,000 men to his **army**, which had numbered 90,000 at its peak. In return he gains Ottoman and European recognition of his hereditary rule over Egypt.

During the summer, an exceptionally high **Nile flood** drowns crops and villages throughout Egypt.

1842 European merchants win their fight to have an **Ottoman law** extended to Egypt, which places a limit on the duties that can be imposed on their imports and exports.

Egyptian agriculture suffers from more **Nile floods**.

> **❝** The attachment and veneration of all classes in Egypt for the name of Muhammad Ali are prouder obsequies than any which it was in the power of his successor to confer. The old inhabitants remember and talk of the chaos and anarchy from which he rescued this country; the younger compare his energetic rule with the capricious, vacillating government of his successor; all classes whether Turks, or Arabs, not only feel, but do not hesitate to say openly that the prosperity of Egypt has died with Muhammad Ali ... In truth my Lord, it cannot be denied, that Muhammad Ali, notwithstanding all his faults was a great man. **❞**
>
> British Consul Murray, describing Mohammed Ali's funeral to Lord Palmerston, the foreign minister, 1849

1844 A murrain ravages Egypt's cattle herds.

1847 Mohammed Ali suffers a nervous breakdown and goes to **Naples** for treatment and rest. From now on, effective rule passes to his son **Ibrahim**.

1848 In July, **Ibrahim** (r. 1848) is invested as ruler of Egypt by the sultan in Constantinople but dies on 10 November. He is succeeded by Tusun's son and Mohammed Ali's grandson **Abbas Hilmi I** (r. 1848–54).

1849 Mohammed Ali dies at **Alexandria** on 2 August.

The European takeover: 1850–1914

The sultan's *firman* of 1841 acknowledged Egypt's return to the Ottoman imperial fold and confirmed Mohammed Ali as its hereditary ruler, but behind the arrangement stood the

European powers, who regarded themselves as its guarantors. In effect, Europe had gained direct influence in Egyptian affairs – an influence that would enlarge, as Mohammed Ali's successors fell into Europe's financial debt until they lost all control over Egypt's political destiny.

Railway building in Egypt began during the reign of **Abbas Hilmi I** (r. 1848–54), but it was under his successor **Said** (r. 1854–63) that the new rush for **development** truly got underway. He encouraged a free-market economy through the organization of banking and credit on European lines, by giving cultivators the right to inherit the land on which they worked, and by abandoning the state's monopoly over agricultural produce. The fellahin could now sell their cotton directly to exporters, for example, rather than it passing through the government as an intermediary. Said also abolished the *jizya*, the tax that non-Muslims had been obliged to pay since the Arab conquest, and in place of Necho's long-abandoned canal he granted a concession for constructing a waterway directly linking the Mediterranean and the Red Sea through the isthmus of Suez.

During the reign of Said's successor, **Ismail** (r. 1863–79) the Suez Canal was completed, over 8000 miles of new irrigation canals were dug and vast tracts of desert land were reclaimed. Egypt also saw a four-fold increase in railway mileage, a ten-fold extension of its telegraph lines, the construction of 430 bridges and major improvements to the ports of Suez and Alexandria. The number of primary schools rose from 185 to 4685, customs and postal services were improved, and vigorous attempts were made to stamp out the slave trade in the Sudan. In 1867 the sultan gave Ismail the honorary title of **khedive** (meaning 'lord' or 'master'), partly in recognition of his unique autonomous position within the Ottoman Empire – though also in exchange for a large bribe.

The benefit of Ismail's achievements to Egypt's long-term wealth and welfare was immense, but the immediate cost was greater than Egypt could afford and drove it to the brink of **bankruptcy**. When Ismail found himself unable to meet payments on his debts to his European creditors in 1876, the French and British took direct charge of Egypt's revenue and expenditure, effectively placing the country into receivership by instituting the **Anglo-French Dual Control**. But in 1879, after refusing to accept further limitations to his authority, Ismail was declared deposed by the Ottoman sultan under pressure from France and Britain.

The next three years saw the earliest manifestation of **Egyptian nationalism**, which culminated in 1882 with a military rebellion led by **Colonel Ahmed Arabi** (Orabi or Urabi). At first Arabi represented the constitutionalist opposition to misgovernment under the khedive **Tewfik**, and there were many in Britain who thought him a moderate figure worthy of support. But the British and the French chose to back the khedive instead and sent their fleets to Alexandria. At the last moment the French had a change of mind, leaving the British to act alone, which they did by bombarding the harbour defences at Alexandria and **occupying Egypt**, one motive being to safeguard the Suez Canal and the route to India, another to maintain naval supremacy in the Eastern Mediterranean – the same reasons that would keep a British military presence in Egypt for over 70 years to come.

The outward forms of Egypt's government were left intact, while the British consul-general **Evelyn Baring** (who later became the Earl of Cromer) ran the country behind the scenes. One of the greatest achievements during these last decades of the 19th century was the introduction of **perennial irrigation**, owing to the network of dams, barrages and canals built by British engineers. Egyptian agriculture, no longer reliant solely on the Nile's annual inundation, enjoyed several harvests a year, its increased productivity both reducing the debt and raising living standards.

Nationalism was revived again in the 1890s by **Mustafa Kamel**, a young lawyer with great oratorical powers, whose immediate aim – to get the British out – became an end in itself. His traditional Islamic values remained intact, so that he supported, for example, conservative Muslim opposition to the emancipation of Egyptian women. And because the Ottoman sultan also bore the title of 'caliph', and thereby asserted his leadership of the entire Muslim world, Kamel's Islamic sympathies likewise led him to support an Ottoman claim in 1906 to a portion of Egyptian Sinai, and in this he won the backing of the mass of the fellahin, while other nationalists such as **Lufti al-Sayyed** and **Saad Zaghloul**, who had a territorial and secular view of what it meant to be an Egyptian, gave their support to the British, who opposed the Ottoman claim. Egypt would face similar divided loyalties during World War I, when Britain defended it against attack by the Ottoman Empire, allied with Germany. Political confusion between pan-Islamic and pan-Arab affinities on the one hand and national interest on the other persists up to the present day.

1851 In response to Britain's desire to improve communications with India, construction of Egypt's first **railway** begins when Abbas Hilmi I gives the contract for an Alexandria-Cairo-Suez line to **Robert Stephenson** (son of George Stephenson, inventor of the world's first locomotive, *The Rocket*). The railway is financed, owned and operated by the Egyptian government, and when completed in 1857 it makes Egypt more attractive to British investment.

Modern Egyptology begins when **Auguste Mariette** discovers the Serapeum at **Saqqara**, including the tomb of Khaemwaset, high priest of Ptah at Memphis during the reign of his father Rameses II, and also the undisturbed tomb chamber of an Apis bull, its sandy floor still bearing the footprints of the last priest to leave before the chamber was sealed over 3000 years before. Mariette is later appointed director of antiquities in Egypt and is authorized to establish a **museum of antiquities** in Cairo.

1854 After Britain and France join the Ottoman Empire against Russia in the **Crimean War** (which lasts until 1856), the demand of the allied armies for provisions triples the price of many agricultural products in Egypt and sends cereal prices sky-high. With greatly increased **tax revenues**, the Egyptian government gains the means to spend on large-scale projects.

Abbas Hilmi dies in mysterious circumstances in July, probably murdered by his eunuchs in a personal dispute, and is succeeded by **Said** (r. 1854–63), a son of Mohammed Ali.

In November, **Ferdinand de Lesseps**, formerly French consul in Cairo, obtains a concession from Said to build a canal through the isthmus of **Suez**, but it is blocked by Constantinople the following year under British pressure. **Lord Palmerston**, now prime minister, is concerned that the French might use the canal concession as an excuse to occupy Egypt again.

> " We do not want Egypt or wish it for ourselves, any more than any rational man with an estate in the north of England and a residence in the south would have wished to possess the inns on the north road. All he could want would have been that the inns should be well-kept, always accessible, and furnishing him, when he came, with mutton-chops and post-horses. "
>
> Lord Palmerston, British prime minister

1855 The *jizya*, the tax on non-Muslims, is abolished.

1859 In April, Lesseps begins work on the **Suez Canal** without authority from Said or the Ottoman sultan.

The Suez Canal

In 1858, Ferdinand de Lesseps, known as the master of the *fait accompli*, issued shares for his **Suez Canal Company** on the European money markets. In France the flotation was successful, but elsewhere it was a failure, leaving Lesseps with thousands of unsold shares. Having already falsely stated in his prospectus that flotation had been authorized by Said, he now put the unsold shares, a quarter of the total, down to Said's account.

That Lesseps, who was a cousin of Napoleon III's wife Eugénie, should get away with such sharp practice demonstrated the way in which Mohammed Ali's successors felt overawed by prominent Europeans and their governments. The Ottoman sultan was in a similar position: he did not want to offend the British by allowing the project to go ahead, but neither did he wish to offend the French by stopping it. In the event, he did nothing at all, and eventually the British too accepted the *fait accompli*. In addition to Said's financial contribution, Lesseps was granted the right to use forced labour, with 60,000 fellahin involved at a time: 20,000 of them digging, 20,000 en route to the canal, 20,000 returning to their villages; the practice was both inhumane and damaging to Egypt's agricultural economy.

The Company's 99-year concession ran from the canal's completion in 1869, by which time Said had died and his successor Ismail was struggling under accumulating debt, leading him to sell his shares to Britain in 1875. The canal itself – at 100 miles, still the longest without locks in the world – further increased Egypt's strategic significance and became, as Mohammed Ali had predicted, an additional reason for European interference. When King Farouk was asked after World War II what should be done with it, his answer was 'Fill it in'.

The Suez Canal, which allowed ships to pass between the Red Sea and the Mediterranean without sailing round Africa, became of enormous strategic importance

1861 The **American Civil War**, which lasts four years, interrupts the export of **cotton** from the Southern states to British textile mills and creates a worldwide boom in the price of cotton, which increases four-fold between 1860 and 1864. Great wealth pours into Egypt, and cotton acreage increases five-fold between 1861 and 1866.

1863 Said dies in January and is succeeded by Ibraham Pasha's son **Ismail** (r. 1863–79).

In April, **Abdul Aziz** makes the first visit to Egypt of an Ottoman sultan since Selim in 1517.

1866 Ismail creates an unelected **advisory assembly**. The cotton boom comes to an end, and over the next ten years the Egyptian treasury falls deeper and deeper into debt.

1867 The Ottoman sultan gives Ismail the honorary title of **khedive** in recognition of his unique status as a semi-independent vassal of the Ottoman Empire.

Nubar Pasha, an Armenian Christian who is Ismail's foreign minister, puts forward proposals for reforming the **Capitulations**, so that the law in Egypt should be territorial and its administration should be independent of foreign consuls and the Egyptian government alike.

1869 Ismail appoints the explorer **Samuel Baker** to lead an expedition into Africa in an attempt to suppress the **slave trade**.

1869 The **Suez Canal** opens on 17 November, making Egypt again a crossroads of international trade – a position

---

The Mixed Courts

In the 16th century, Ottoman sultans exempted non-Muslims who established themselves within the empire for purposes of trade from taxation and gave them the right to be tried in their own consular courts. With the decline of Ottoman power, foreigners living in Egypt who were citizens of the Capitulary powers (Britain, France, Holland, Austria, Germany, Italy, Russia, Belgium, Spain, Portugal, Greece, Denmark, Sweden and the United States) took full advantage of these Capitulations until they were virtually above the law.

But in 1875 foreigners became subject to the Mixed Courts in all but criminal cases, which continued to be heard in the consular courts until 1937. They were called 'mixed' because in these courts Egyptians, including the Egyptian government, could bring suits against foreigners and vice versa. The Courts represented the assertion of a degree of Egyptian sovereignty as they fell under Egyptian jurisdiction, but they were also reassuring to foreigners whose cases were heard by panels of both Egyptian and foreign judges who dispensed justice in accordance with the *Code Napoléon* instead of Islamic and customary law. These courts became a training-ground for Egyptian lawyers of high calibre, who eventually became the country's political elite and helped shape the national movement.

> Egypt was made to pay heavily both for the concession of the [Suez Canal] site and for the construction of the greater part of the Canal, and was left with no share in the concern. The sufferings of the Egyptian fellaheen, both in the years of forced labour and the subsequent fiscal exactions to meet interest on the Canal debt, put Europe heavily in their debt, a debt of honour of Europe to Egypt as to which we have not heard so much as we have of the less worthy liabilities of Egypt to Europe … Egypt deserved well of Europe in this matter and was in return most ruthlessly defrauded.

George Young, *Egypt* (1927)

it had lost in the fifteenth century when the Portuguese opened up the route round Africa to the Indian Ocean.

1871 **Jamal el Din Afghani** (born c.1839) arrives in Egypt. He claims to be an Afghan but is probably a Shia Persian; his idea is to regenerate Islam by sloughing off the accretion of tradition and adopting Western values that are not in conflict with Islam's essential dogma. He wants to revive the cultural and military ascendancy of Islam, using political revolution and religious reform to unify the *umma Islamiya* ('Islamic nation'). His influence will be felt on generations of Egyptians.

1874 Ismail follows up Samuel Baker's expedition into the interior of Africa by appointing **General Charles Gordon** to suppress the slave trade in the Sudan.

1875 *Al Ahram* ('The Pyramids'), a newspaper, is founded in Alexandria by Lebanese Christians and furthers the widespread use of Arabic over Turkish; later it moves to Cairo and becomes the leading newspaper in the Arab world.

Ismail sells his **shares** in the Suez Canal to the British.

> **❝** I am appealing to his Majesty the Sultan to defend me against foreign pressure. I have now completed sixteen fruitful years. Under my administration Egypt has been covered with a railway network; she has greatly extended the canal system which brings forth the riches of her soil; she has built two great ports, Suez and Alexandria; she has destroyed the sources of slavery in Central Africa and hoisted the flag of the Empire over those formerly unknown lands; and finally after long resistance, she has established efficient courts which in future will provide the means of bringing the harmony of justice into relations between the foreigner and those of Eastern cultures. **❞**
>
> Khedive Ismail, writing to the Ottoman sultan, June 1876

The Capitulary powers agree to the creation of the **Mixed Courts**, which set to work the following year.

1876 Ismail's attempts to agree terms for the payment of Egypt's debt to its European creditors leads to the establishment of the Anglo-French **Dual Control** in November. British and French Controllers of Revenue and Expenditure for the whole of the Egyptian government are appointed, with the effect that Egypt is no longer in the position of a debtor nation in charge of its own affairs, rather a bankrupt in receivership with half its annual revenues going to service and pay off the debt.

1877 **Yaqub Sanu**, an Egyptian-Italian Jew and a follower of the Islamic reformer **Jamal el Din Afghani**, founds a satirical newspaper with a nationalist bent and coins the slogan 'Egypt for the Egyptians'.

In the summer, a low Nile leaves over a third of the Nile Valley unirrigated and initiates **crop failure** in the spring of 1878, bringing Egypt's financial problems to a head.

An **obelisk** from the vanished Caesareum in Alexandria (one of 'Cleopatra's Needles') is transported to London and erected on the Thames Embankment.

1878 Following Egypt's inability to meet its **debt payments** without causing arrears of pay to its troops and government employees and imposing an oppressive tax burden on the fellahin, an international **commission of inquiry** is established. In an interim report, the commission condemns the corruption and abuses of Ismail's government, laying the chief blame on the khedive's unlimited authority. Ismail accepts the Dual Control's recommendations for limitations on his powers, including the requirement that he delegates to his ministers and accepts the so-called European Ministry with **Nubar Pasha** as prime minister, an Englishman as minister of finance and a Frenchman as minister of public works.

1879 The second of **'Cleopatra's Needles'** is removed from Alexandria and is erected in New York's Central Park.

In March, the international commission announces that Egypt has been **bankrupt** since 1876. Ismail rejects the claim, and makes it clear that he will not cooperate with the Europeans in reducing his authority to that of a figurehead. In April, he creates an elected assembly.

Under British and French pressure, but also to increase his own authority over Egypt, the Ottoman sultan issues a

> ❝ My country is no longer in Africa; we are now part of Europe. It is therefore natural for us to abandon our former ways and to adopt a new system adapted to our social conditions. ❞
>
> Khedive Ismail, responding to the 1878 recommendation that limitations be placed on his powers

firman deposing Ismail on 26 June. Ismail sails to Italy on the royal yacht *Mahroussa* at the end of the month, being succeeded by his son **Tewfik** (r. 1879–92).

In November, **nationalist protest** stirs among large landowners, both Turkish and Mameluke, and also among the religious establishment and a number of army officers, among them **Colonel Ahmed Arabi**, of native Egyptian descent. Tewfik responds by suppressing nationalist newspapers, exiling prominent nationalists – among them Afghani – and dismissing the assembly. He governs through his autocratic prime minister, **Mustafa Riaz Pasha**.

1881 Villagers near **Luxor** reveal a large cache of royal mummies, among them those of Sekenenra of the Seventeenth Dynasty, Amosis I and Tuthmosis III of the Eighteenth Dynasty, Seti I and Rameses II of the Nineteenth Dynasty, and Rameses III of the Twentieth Dynasty, high among the cliffs at **Deir el Bahri**, where they were hidden by priests of the Twenty-First Dynasty. As the boats carrying the mummies sail downriver to Cairo, local village women run along the riverbanks throwing dust on their heads and ululating as a sign of mourning for their departing kings.

The French occupy **Tunisia**, while on the White Nile south of Khartoum, **Mohammed Ahmed** (born c.1844) proclaims himself the **Mahdi**, the 'Rightly Guided One', and leads a *jihad* against the Egyptians and their attempts to abolish the slave trade.

In September, a military **demonstration** led by Colonel Ahmed Arabi against the khedive at Abdin Palace in Cairo demands the recall of Ismail's assembly, the dismissal of Riaz, the granting of a constitution and the enlargement of the army, which is now the one remaining voice of Egyptian nationalism. Arabi develops his political ideas through talks with **Mohammed Abdu**, a disciple of Al Afghani, who runs a nationalist newspaper and wants a constitution that is established on Islamic principles.

As Arabi's popularity grows through October, his call becomes more strident and arouses Muslim feelings against the infidel. To maintain calm in **Cairo**, the government sends Arabi and his regiment into the provinces, but as he departs he again stirs up the crowd.

1882 The assembly votes a **nationalist government** into power in January. Arabi is appointed undersecretary for war.

After relations between the khedive and his government deteriorate into open conflict, on 11 April Tewfik calls on foreign help. The British and French send warships to **Alexandria**, where a fifth of its 230,000 population is European, but at the same time public excitement obliges the khedive to appoint Arabi **minister for war**.

> ❝ Henceforth the Parliament, made up of our own flesh and blood, will stand between us and Tyranny. Justice and the People will provide its strength. The Europeans, unjust as they always are, made blind and cruel by their greed for money, pretend that the army has risen to steal the nation's wealth and cheat the creditors of Ismail. ... Were they in our place, Jews and Christians as they are, they would have unanimously repudiated the debt imposed on them by an abominable tyrant! Brothers, you have understood me. Be patient and prudent, I am not going far away and I will soon return. ❞
>
> Ahmed Arabi, addressing the crowd as his regiment leaves Cairo
>
> on 3 October, 1881

Agricultural revolution in the Delta

The **Delta Barrage** begun by Mohammed Ali in 1834, planned as the largest structure of its kind in the world, ran into difficulties when the Delta's shifting alluvial soil made its foundations insecure. From 1867, it lay useless – until 1884, when preliminary repairs were undertaken by Sir Colin Scott-Moncrieff. When he completed rebuilding the barrage in 1890, the effect on the Delta's agricultural productivity was spectacular. For the first time in its history, a large portion of Egypt enjoyed the benefits of **perennial irrigation**, which the barrage achieved by permanently raising the level of water running through the Delta's irrigation canals. It was no longer necessary to rely on the shaduf, saqiya or other devices with their great expenditure of labour in order to irrigate the fields year-round.

With the British and French fleets already outside Alexandria harbour, on 11 June there is a **riot** in the city in which up to 150 Europeans are killed and a similar number of Egyptians, but the fleets do not intervene. Neither do the Egyptian troops in Alexandria, without orders from Arabi. When he finally acts towards evening, the disorders cease. The deaths move British opinion towards intervention, and finally the Liberal prime minister **William Ewart Gladstone** acts. On 11 July, the British bombard the harbour defences at **Alexandria**, which are being prepared against them, including Fort Qaytbey (built on the site of the Pharos and using some of its remains), but the French government has not authorized its admiral to take part, and in the morning the French fleet sails away. The bombardment does little damage to the city itself, and that evening the Egyptian army withdraws to new positions outside Alexandria. With no one in control of the city, **Bedouin** swarm in from the desert the following day and join with the local Egyptian population in **rioting**, looting and spreading fires; by evening the entire centre of the city is in flames and a great number of lives are lost. On 13 and 14 July, the

British land a force of **marines**, who take control of Alexandria and restore order. Though as yet there is no intention to remain, in effect the British **occupation** of Egypt has begun.

The British defeat Arabi's forces at the **battle of Tell el Kebir** on 14 September, and a day later British troops occupy **Cairo**. In London, however, the government promises an early evacuation of Egypt.

Arabi is tried for treason and condemned to death in December, but British pressure ensures that his sentence is immediately commuted, and he is **exiled** to Ceylon.

According to Egypt's first modern **census**, its population reaches 6,800,000 – matching or exceeding that of Ptolemaic times.

1883 **Evelyn Baring** (who in 1892 becomes Earl of Cromer) is appointed British **consul general** in September, a position he holds until 1907. He is the effective ruler of Egypt, though he operates behind the screen of Egyptian institutions.

Among those induced to come to Egypt is **Sir Colin Scott-Moncrieff**, an irrigation engineer who has worked on the vast canal system in northern India; between 1883 and 1890 he comprehensively reorganizes the country's **irrigation system**.

In November, **Colonel William Hicks**, a British soldier in the Egyptian service, is appointed to lead an Egyptian army against the Mahdi in the Sudan, but Hicks is killed and his force of 10,000 men is annihilated.

1884 Following preliminary repairs to the **Delta Barrage** by Scott-Moncrieff, the Delta cotton crop increases by twenty percent.

Nubar Pasha again becomes prime minister (until 1888); he accepts Baring's recommendation that Egypt withdraw all its forces from south of **Wadi Halfa** at the Second Cataract. **General Charles Gordon** is employed by the Egyptian government to organize the withdrawal, but he is cut off by the Mahdi's forces at **Khartoum**, and a British rescue mission under General Wolseley is despatched in August.

1885 Gordon is killed as **Khartoum** falls to the Mahdi on 26 January. General Wolseley's relief force arrives two days later.

On 22 June, the Mahdi dies at Omdurman and is succeeded by the **Khalifa Abdullah**, whose Dervish followers have free run of the Sudan and pose a threat to Egypt. Baring proposes that the withdrawal of British forces from Egypt should be indefinitely postponed, a view accepted by the Egyptian and British governments.

> ❝ You have erred in many ways and are suffering great loss, from which there is no refuge for you save by turning to God and entering among the people of Islam and the followers of the Mahdi, grace be upon him ... But if you will not turn from blindness and self-will you will be crushed by the power of God. ❞
>
> Letter from the Khalifa Abdullah to Queen Victoria

Evelyn Baring, later Lord Cromer, held the modest title of British consul, but was in reality the most powerful man in Egypt

1887 The Khalifa, who announces that his aim is to conquer Egypt and the world, summons **Queen Victoria** to Omdurman, where she is to offer her submission and become a Muslim. The Queen does not reply.

1890 Scott-Moncrieff completes the rebuilding of Mohammed Ali's **Delta Barrage** in June, with the result that crop production, particularly cotton, increases phenomenally during the 1890s. The consequent growth in Egypt's **revenue** accelerates the reduction of its debt, permitting Baring to reduce taxation. At the instigation of its foreign population, **Alexandria** becomes the first city in Egypt to acquire a municipal government, nearly six decades before Cairo in 1946.

1892 The first indication that Egypt once possessed a Predynastic civilization is unearthed when the British Egyptologist **Flinders Petrie** discovers a vast cemetery of 3000 graves at the village of **Naqada** in Upper Egypt.

At Tewfiq's death, his 17-year-old son, **Abbas Hilmi II** (r. 1892–1914), comes to the throne.

The all-powerful Baring is created **Earl of Cromer**, whereafter he is widely known as 'The Lord'.

The British government, with the French and Italians particularly in mind, is concerned to keep rival powers out of the lands of the upper Nile. Meanwhile, feeling is growing among the British public that Gordon's death at Khartoum is a stain on British honour and must be avenged – a view shared by **Sir Herbert Kitchener**, who is appointed Sirdar (commander-in-chief) of the Egyptian army.

1895 **Kaiser Wilhelm II** of Germany makes a state visit to **Constantinople**. Germany is cultivating an alliance with the Ottoman Empire and is financing the construction of a railway across **Anatolia** that will link Berlin with Baghdad.

1896 Kitchener advances into the **Sudan**, building a railway at the rate of nearly a mile a day between Wadi Halfa and Abu Hamed, 200 miles north of Khartoum.

A young Egyptian lawyer, **Mustafa Kamel**, makes common cause with the 21-year-old Abbas Hilmi II, and with secret funding from the khedive sets himself to revive and organize Egyptian nationalism.

1898 British engineer **Sir William Willcocks** begins construction of the **Aswan Dam**, in February, its purpose to control the level of the Nile all year round.

On 2 September, Kitchener's army defeats the Khalifa's just north of **Omdurman**. One of the British cavalry officers is the 22-year-old **Winston Churchill**.

1899 The **Anglo-Egyptian Condominium** is established over the Sudan, effectively securing British rule through its governor general in Khartoum.

1900 Mustafa Kamel emerges as a political figure in his own right and asserts his independence from the Palace, when he publishes his own nationalist newspaper and calls for a parliamentary government for Egypt.

> **"** The whole of the Khalifa's army, nearly 60,000 strong, advanced in battle order from their encampment of the night before, topped the swell of ground which hid the two armies from one another, and then rolled down the gently-sloping amphitheatre in the arena of which, backed upon the Nile, Kitchener's 20,000 troops were drawn up shoulder to shoulder to receive them. Ancient and modern confronted one another. The weapons, the methods and the fanaticism of the Middle Ages were brought by an extraordinary anachronism into dire collision with the organisation and inventions of the nineteenth century. The result was not surprising. **"**

Winston Churchill, *My Early Life* (1930)

Construction begins on the British dam at Aswan as workmen lay stones across the Nile at the First Cataract

1902 Willcocks completes construction of the **Aswan Dam** in December, which at this time is the largest dam in the world and the longest until the building of the High Dam at Aswan in the 1960s. Following Willcocks' plans, British engineers also complete the **Assiut Barrage**.

1906 In June, a party of British officers on a bird shoot near the Delta village of Denshaway are set upon by angry pigeon farmers; later one officer later dies of concussion. To Cromer the **'Denshaway Incident'** is one more example of the dangerous xenophobic fanaticism, fanned by the nationalists, that is sweeping the countryside. A special tribunal sentences four of the villagers to death, and they are hanged outside Denshaway, where their fellow villagers are made to watch. Overnight, Egyptian sentiment turns against the British, and Mustafa Kamel's nationalists gain a million new followers. Kamel goes to Britain to win over liberal opinion; he meets the Liberal prime minister **Campbell Bannerman**, and pleads for an advance towards self-government – to some effect. Following Kamel's visit to London, and under instructions from the British government, in October Cromer grudgingly tells the khedive that the powers of Egyptian ministers are to be enlarged.

1907 Cromer resigns as British consul general in March. He is succeeded by **Sir Eldon Gorst**, who restricts British intervention in Egyptian affairs to issues in which Britain is directly interested and gives the assembly some say in policy-making.

The end of the Nile flood

Since at least 3000 BC, Egyptians had been practising **basin irrigation** to even out the effects of the Nile's annual flood: farmers dug basins to capture water during the inundation and to hold it for some time after the river receded. Following the construction of the Delta Barrage, the completion of the **Aswan Dam** and the **Assiut Barrage**, both designed by Sir William Willcocks, now finally eliminated the inundation throughout the whole of Egypt, permitting a controlled flow all year long. The barrage at Assiut regulated (and still does) the amount of water entering the Ibrahimiyya Canal, which distributes irrigation waters to farmers' fields between Assiut and Beni Suef; while the dam at Aswan, which also included a hydroelectric power station, did the same for agriculture between the First Cataract and Assiut, though since 1971 its functions have largely been taken over by the **Aswan High Dam**. Willcocks' achievement was to place the entire length of the Nile in Egypt under human control for the first time in history, thereby furthering agricultural production. There was now no season when Egypt's agriculture lay idle owing to the summer inundation – a necessary factor particularly when growing cotton, which requires year-round irrigation.

In the autumn, Mustafa Kamel forms the anti-British **Watan ('Homeland') Party**, which adopts Yaqub Sanu's slogan, 'Egypt for the Egyptians' and calls for complete **independence** under a constitution in which the executive would be responsible to an assembly elected by universal suffrage; he also wants the early evacuation of British forces. Yet Kamel is also pan-Islamic and traditionalist in his outlook and clings to the notion of Egypt's dependent relationship with the Ottoman Empire. Believing that pan-Islamism is more damaging to the growth of Egyptian nationhood than the British occupation, **Lufti al-Sayyed** breaks with Kamel and founds the **Umma**

> The Englishman, I have said, came to Egypt with the fixed idea that he had a mission to perform, and, with his views about individual justice, equal rights before the law, the greatest happiness of the greatest number, and similar notions, he will not unnaturally interpret his mission in this sense, that he is to benefit the mass of the population. There lie those nine or ten million native Egyptians at the bottom of the social ladder, a poor, ignorant, credulous, but withal not unkindly race, being such as sixty centuries of misgovernment and oppression by various rulers, from Pharaohs to Pashas, have made them. It is for the civilised Englishman to extend to them the hand of fellowship and encouragement, and to raise them, morally and materially, from the abject state in which he finds them … But the Englishman will find, when he once applies himself to his task, that there is, as it were, a thick mist between him and the Egyptian, composed of religious prejudice, antique and semi-barbarous customs, international rivalry, vested interests, and aspirations of one sort or another, some sordid, others, it may be, not ignoble but incapable of realisation.

The Earl of Cromer, *Modern Egypt* (1908)

('Nation' or 'People') Party, which holds that nationality should be territorial and advocates cooperation with the British until social and educational reforms have prepared Egypt for independence. The khedive instigates the founding of the **Constitutional Reform Party**, which despite its name is meant to defend the throne against true parliamentary rule.

1908 In February, Mustafa Kamel dies of an illness at the age of 34. Under new leadership, the Watan Party moves towards **pan-Islamic extremism**.

The khedive appoints **Butros Ghali** as prime minister in November, a Copt of moderate political views whose broadly-based government includes both the nationalist **Saad Zaghloul** of the Umma Party as minister of education, and a member of the Constitutional Reform Party at finance. Being a Christian, however, Ghali becomes a target for Islamic **extremism** – especially because as minister of justice he had been one of the judges on the special tribunal which condemned the Denshaway farmers and so is pilloried as traitor to the nationalist cause.

1910 On 20 February, Prime Minister Butros Ghali is assassinated by **Ibrahim Wardani**, a Muslim with close connections to the Watan Party, who is executed four months later.

1911 Gorst, who is ill, resigns and leaves Egypt in April. He is succeeded as consul by **Lord Kitchener**, whose vision is of an Egypt incorporated into the British Empire.

1911 The Italians begin invading the Ottoman province of Libya, completing their conquest the following year.

1912 The **Aswan Dam** is raised to increase the capacity of its reservoir, meaning the flooding of most of the Nile Valley in Lower Nubia. The Nubians, who had already moved many of their villages to higher ground before the completion of the dam in 1902, are now forced to move their villages again.

1914 On 4 August, Britain and France **declare war** on Germany following the German invasion of **Belgium**.

On 29 October, Ottoman forces attack the Russians at **Odessa** and the British in **Sinai**. Russia responds by declaring war on the Ottoman Empire on 2 November.

Press censorship and **martial law** are introduced in Egypt.

While Egypt's anglophobe khedive **Abbas Hilmi II** is visiting Constantinople, Britain and France declare war on the Ottoman Empire on 5 November.

10: The Liberal Era

1914–52

Now that Britain and the Ottoman Empire were fighting on opposite sides in World War I, the government in London favoured incorporating Egypt into the British Empire. But as that would almost certainly have been resisted by Egypt's ruling elite, the ambiguous status of **British Protectorate** was decided on instead. Egyptian nationalists interpreted the Protectorate as a step towards unfettered independence when the war was over, while for the British the war only made Egypt's strategic importance all the plainer. These were the opposing terms that governed Anglo-Egyptian relations from the end of World War I to the Suez Crisis of 1956.

In fact, Egypt was granted a form of independence in 1922 – in so far as it gained almost complete control over its internal affairs, while a more complete independence came with the **Anglo-Egyptian Treaty** of 1936, limited only by Britain's right to base its military in the country in the event of war. The effect was that, for most of the period covered in this chapter, there were three major players in Egyptian political life: the Wafd, the king and the British. The **Wafd** (nationalist party) and the **king** – who under the 1923 constitution was granted powers equivalent to an American president – each claimed to be the legitimate representative of the Egyptian people and fought a long-running battle to subvert the other's authority. **Britain**, whose aim was to ensure that Egypt remained stable and served British strategic interests, favoured the monarchy or the Wafd as occasion demanded.

This three-cornered arrangement is sometimes said to have undermined the development of a mature political system in Egypt – the king authoritarian and anti-democratic, the Wafd demagogic and corrupt, the British more interested in global than Egyptian matters. But certainly it is true that the period from 1922 to 1952 was an unprecedentedly liberal era in Egyptian history. European-style constitutionalism and pluralism were part of the political landscape, along with a functioning – if imperfect – system of civil and political liberties, and genuine, though irregular, electoral contests involving the participation of all classes.

Though the **battle of Alamein**, a turning-point of World War II, was fought in Egypt's Western Desert, Egypt itself was never a combatant and its people, who were usually far from the fighting, almost entirely escaped its dangers. Nevertheless, the war was to have a considerable effect on the political outlook of Egyptians. The lack of foreign imports and the provisioning of over two million British and Commonwealth soldiers, sailors and airmen passing through Egypt had the effect of stimulating the local **economy**. In addition to nearly quarter of a million Egyptians employed directly by the British forces, many new companies sprang up and new branches of industry developed, providing employment and new horizons for the ever-growing numbers of migrants from the countryside. But though an increased proportion of Egyptians was benefiting from the economic activity brought about by the war, the gap was widening between the landowning and entrepreneurial classes on the one hand and the wage-earning classes on the other, among whom there was a growing class of young, educated and urbanized Egyptians. Additionally, between 1939 and the second half of 1944, the cost of living in Egypt more than trebled. Unskilled rural and urban labourers, as well as the salaried middle and lower classes, suffered severe privations and were relentlessly pressed down. Problems were compounded by the huge job lay-offs which came at the end of the war. The effect was the social radicalization of the nationalist movement and demands for the Egyptianization of the economy.

While the Zionist takeover of **Palestine** contributed to political tensions in Egypt, the issue far from explained the rapid rise of Islamic fundamentalism and nationalist extremism, nor the violence and chaos that overtook Egyptian society after World War II when 'Palestine' joined anti-Britishness as a new rallying cry. The impact of the outside world on Egyptians' lives and the accompanying rapid social and economic changes seem also to have played a part, and not for the first time in Egyptian history were met by a political response which had a religious dimension. The fundamentalist **Muslim Brotherhood**, founded in 1928, was estimated to have a million or more activists by the outbreak of World War II and became stronger still between 1945 and 1948, when it made itself felt in countless demonstrations, marches and protests, influencing lower and middle class Egyptians – among them civil servants, students, workers, policemen, lawyers, soldiers and peasants. Opposed to liberalism, constitutionalism and secularism, the Brotherhood sabotaged meetings, precipitated clashes at public gatherings and damaged property, then went on to terrorist acts and assassinations. Palestine became the Brotherhood's most passionate cause, for which it collected money and arms, and it trained volunteers and sent a battalion of troops to fight alongside the Palestinians in 1948. The Brotherhood remained a radical threat to the political order in Egypt even after it was banned and forced underground, and its founder, **Hassan el Banna**, was murdered by the secret police in November 1948.

Radicalization of students, professionals and skilled workers was not only at the hands of Islamic fundamentalists. Western wartime propaganda, which promoted human rights, together with the Soviet Union's marxist propaganda for social and economic equality, had its effect on this articulate section of the population. They were unable, however, to operate outside their own social strata and failed to penetrate rural villages or the urban poor. But they did influence intellectual and political life through poetry, journalism, fiction and philosophical and political publications, and through demonstrations and strikes, and helped lay the ideological basis – social justice, planned economic development and distrust of the West – that became central to the political, social, intellectual and artistic life of Egypt under **Abdel Nasser** (see p.341).

The activities of the non-parliamentary parties, both marxists and Islamists, with their attacks on the Wafd and the monarchy, helped create the climate in which Nasser could operate and finally strike. By 1952, the old order had broken down, and Egyptians were thankful to be relieved by Nasser's **Free Officers Movement** of the burdens of diversity, pluralism and liberalism.

1914 On 18 December, Egypt becomes a **British Protectorate** and ceases to be part of the Ottoman Empire. Egyptians are not called upon to fight, but many fellahin sign up as navvies and camel drivers, and make a substantial contribution to the war effort by building military installations and transporting supplies.

One day later, Khedive Abbas Hilmi II, who is in Constantinople, is deposed by the British and replaced by his uncle, a son of Ismail, **Hussein Kamel** (r. 1914–17). Underlining the point that Egypt is no longer an Ottoman province, Hussein Kamel assumes the title of **sultan**, while the British consul takes on the title of **high commissioner**.

1915 In February, the British repulse an attempt by Ottoman forces to capture the **Suez Canal** and so invade Egypt.

Anticipating ultimate victory in the Middle East, in March the British Cabinet hears a proposal emanating from the Zionist leader **Chaim Weizmann** that Britain should establish a protectorate over **Palestine** and facilitate the settlement over time of three to four million Jews, who would be granted self-government once forming the overwhelming majority of the population.

In April, Alexandria is the centre of operations for the ill-fated **Gallipoli campaign**, the attempt by British, Australian and New Zealand forces to seize the straits between the Mediterranean and Constantinople.

On 23 May, **Italy** enters the war on the side of Britain, France and Russia.

Armed and supported by the Ottomans and their German allies, the Senussi Bedouin of **Libya** throw off Italian rule in November and attack across Egypt's western frontier. They occupy the border town of **Sollum** and the oases of **Dakhla**, **Farafra**, **Bahariya** and **Siwa**. Hostilities in this quarter continue until February 1917.

1916 In May, the British and French sign the secret **Sykes-Picot agreement**, which carves up the postwar Middle East between the two European powers, even as the British are encouraging the Arabs to rise against the Ottomans with promises of independent states.

The Arabs of the Hejaz under the leadership of **Sherif Hussein** of Mecca and his sons **Feisal**, **Abdullah** and **Ali**, members of the Hashemite family, raise the standard of the **Arab Revolt** against Ottoman rule in June. They receive support from the British in Egypt and men on the spot including **T.E. Lawrence** ('Lawrence of Arabia').

British forces in Egypt repel a second Ottoman attack on the **Suez Canal** during July and August.

1917 The **census** this year shows that Egypt's population stands at 12,751,000.

The British army begins its advance into **Palestine** in March. But no amount of pay can compensate the fellahin working for the British as labourers and camel drivers who now must leave their fields untended and their families neglected back home in Egypt, and instead they cease to volunteer. The British resort to **conscription**, which is harshly enforced, creating bitterness in the countryside and the cities, where life becomes a struggle against **food shortages** and **inflation**.

The **United States** enters World War I in April.

Sultan Hussein Kamel dies on 9 October and is succeeded by his younger brother **Fuad I** (r.1917–36), the sixth son of the khedive Ismail.

On 2 November, foreign secretary **Arthur Balfour** issues a statement of the British government's policy regarding Jewish aspirations in Palestine. The statement, in the form of a letter to the Jewish banker and Zionist Lord Rothschild, is known as the **Balfour Declaration**. But Zionism meets with very little support among the Jews of Egypt, who since Mohammed Ali's time have prospered in its generally tolerant atmosphere and have no desire to emigrate to Palestine, which at this time is inhabited by 600,000 Christian and Muslim Arabs and by 80,000 Jews. Few if any of Palestine's Jews are the remnants of ancient Judaea; instead they are refugees from the Russian pogroms of recent decades.

The British army under **General Sir Edmund Allenby** enters **Jerusalem** on 11 December.

1918 In January, President Woodrow Wilson of the United States announces his **Fourteen Points** embodying the principle of national self-determination, the intended ideal of a postwar settlement, which Egyptian nationalists assume will apply to their country too.

Britain accepts an armistice with the **Ottoman Empire** on 30 October.

> His Majesty's Government view with favour the establishment in Palestine of a National Home for the Jewish people and will use their best endeavours to facilitate the achievement of this object, it being clearly understood that nothing shall be done which may prejudice the civil and religious rights of existing non-Jewish communities in Palestine, or the rights and political status enjoyed by Jews in any other country.

The Balfour Declaration, 1917

World War I ends on 11 November, as Britain and its allies accept an armistice with **Germany**.

With the war over, **Saad Zaghloul** (1860–1927), heading an Egyptian parliamentary delegation (*wafd*), meets the high commissioner **Sir Reginald Wingate** on 13 November and demands full independence. Wingate advises the Foreign Office to receive Zaghloul's delegation, but London brushes his advice aside.

1919 Following agitation by Zaghloul, he and three colleagues are arrested by the British on 8 March, and the following day they are deported to Malta. As news spreads of Zaghloul's deportation, Egypt rises in **revolt** on 10 March. Imams preach in the churches and Coptic priests preach in the mosques, while demonstrating Muslim women remove their veils. But student demonstrations in **Cairo** turn into violent riots, and within 24 hours the capital is at a standstill as government workers and officials as well as professional people join what becomes a general strike. As the disturbances spread, **communications** are disrupted throughout the country. The fellahin, embittered at being conscripted into the labour corps by the British during the war, join in. Telegraph wires are cut, railway lines are torn up, trains and stations are attacked, and unarmed British soldiers and civilians are murdered. On 17 March, the British army finally reacts and the rebellion is quickly put down. Within days the **Delta** is secure, and by the end of the month the revolt is suppressed throughout almost the whole of the country. By then, about 1000 Egyptians are dead, as well as 36 British and Indian soldiers and four British civilians.

Saad Zaghloul and the Wafd

Saad Zaghloul's origins were among the fellahin, but his industry and intelligence carried him from a village school to the university of Al Azhar, where he studied law, eventually becoming minister of education and of justice and vice president of the Assembly before World War I. Though Zaghloul was not a member of the Egyptian government when his delegation of fellow nationalists called on Wingate in November 1918, his image as a simple son of the Nile made him the popular representative of the people, who called him 'the Egyptian'.

When the British deported Zaghloul to Malta in March 1919, the whole of Egypt rose in revolt – not only against the British, but against traditional constraints, so that it was now that some Muslim women first tore off their veils. Britain's interest in Egypt was essentially strategic, which meant protecting the country and in particular the Suez Canal against potential enemies. But in the face of Zaghloul's talent for rousing Egyptian nationalist emotions against any compromise, Britain unilaterally imposed a qualified **independence** on Egypt in 1922. Domestic policy now passed into Egyptian hands, but the years that followed were a wasted opportunity; though reformist by inclination, the **Wafd party** all too often substituted anti-British rhetoric for meaningful steps to improve the welfare of the masses who gave it their support, thereby contributing towards undermining confidence in parliamentary government.

> **"**The present movement in Egypt is not a religious movement, for Muslims and Copts demonstrate together, and neither is it a xenophobic movement or a movement calling for Arab unity.**"**
>
> Saad Zaghloul, 1919

On the recommendation of the new high commissioner, **Lord Allenby** (he is raised to the peerage this year), and amid wild rejoicing throughout Egypt, in April Saad Zaghloul and his fellow deportees are released from detention on Malta in order to attend the **Paris Peace Conference** – only to meet disappointment when the United States recognizes the British Protectorate over Egypt.

British colonial secretary **Lord Milner** arrives in Egypt in December at the head of a commission of inquiry into the disorders and to consult on what form a new **constitution** should take. The **Wafd**, as Saad Zaghloul's new party is called, and most other Egyptian political figures boycott the commission, saying negotiations must be carried out with Zaghloul.

1920 A second attempt at **industrialization** is made when the economic nationalist **Mohammed Talaat Harb** persuades a group of mostly large cotton growers to help found **Bank Misr**, 'an Egyptian bank for Egyptians only', its purpose to provide capital for commercial and industrial development. The bank goes on to finance publishing, printing, film production, air transport, cotton spinning and weaving, and the manufacture of pharmaceuticals.

The League of Nations, meeting at San Remo in May, establishes **Syria** and **Lebanon** as French mandates, and gives Britain mandates over Iraq and Palestine. In Palestine, the decision is met with protests by Muslim and Christian

Arabs, who object to enforced Jewish settlement under the Balfour Declaration.

During the summer, Milner invites Zaghloul to London and offers Egypt **independence**, provided Britain is granted the right to protect Egypt's foreign and religious minorities and British troops can be stationed in the country to safeguard the Suez Canal. The terms are acceptable to the Egyptian prime minister **Adly Pasha**, a moderate nationalist, but Zaghloul hesitates, saying he must consult popular opinion.

1921 After Zaghloul fiercely attacks the Egyptian government and denounces Adly as a traitor for agreeing to Britain's terms, a demonstration by Zaghloul's supporters in **Alexandria** on 23 May turns into a violent three-day riot, which results in widespread destruction of property and costs the lives of thirty Egyptians and fourteen Europeans.

In December, Lord Allenby concludes that no agreement can be reached while Zaghloul is still in Egypt, and has him **deported** once again, this time to the Seychelles.

1922 Against opinion at the Foreign Office but at the insistence of Lord Allenby, who tells the government that Egypt cannot be ruled by force, Britain unilaterally ends the Protectorate on 28 February and **declares Egypt independent**. Its sovereignty is limited, however, by Britain's four **'reserved points'**.

> ❝ In his determination to win national independence for Egypt, Zaghloul introduced patronage system into public life and used violence and public demonstrations as weapons against the opposition. He was domineering in style and personality and asserted absolutist control over party politics, which has been a hallmark of Egyptian political life ever since. ❞
>
> *The Cambridge History of Egypt* (1998)

> The following matters are absolutely reserved to the discretion of His Majesty's government until such time as it may be possible by free discussion and friendly accommodation on both sides to conclude agreements in regard thereto between His Majesty's government and the government of Egypt:
>
> (a) The security of the communications of the British Empire in Egypt.
> (b) The defence of Egypt against all foreign aggression or interference, direct or indirect.
> (c) The protection of foreign interests in Egypt and the protection of minorities.
> (d) The Sudan.
>
> The reserved points in Britain's declaration of Egypt's independence, 28 February, 1922

Sultan Fuad takes the title of king on 1 March.

In October, the fascist leader **Benito Mussolini** comes to power in Italy and begins the ten-year reconquest of **Libya**.

The Turkish nationalist government led by **Mustafa Kemal** (later **Kemal Atatürk**) abolishes the Ottoman sultanate in November, though the ex-sultan continues as caliph.

The same month, in the Valley of the Kings at Luxor, the British Egyptologist **Howard Carter** discovers **Tutankhamun's tomb** – the only royal tomb found with its mummy and treasures intact.

1923 While Zaghloul is still in exile – and in the face of Wafdist hostility – on 19 April moderate Egyptian nationalists agree a **constitution** establishing a parliamentary democracy, though with wide powers vested in the monarchy.

Howard Carter and the curse of Tutankhamun

Tutankhamun's tomb was discovered on 4 November, 1922 by Howard Carter and opened two weeks later, on 26 November, after his patron Lord Carnarvon arrived from England. Years before, Carter had discovered the looted and empty tombs of **Hatshepsut** and **Tuthmosis IV**. But this time, as Carter described his first look inside, 'I was struck dumb with amazement', and when Carnarvon, unable to stand the suspense any longer, enquired anxiously, 'Can you see anything?', it was all Carter could do to get out the words, 'Yes, wonderful things'.

The popular fantasy of **Tutankhamun's curse** began the following spring when Carnarvon died of septicaemia caused by an insect bite. The origins of the curse lay not in the tomb, however, but in newspaper offices around the world. Carnarvon had granted exclusive coverage to *The Times*, including photographs, leaving other newspapers resentful and empty-handed. Their response was simply to invent the story of the curse, a nonsense for which they were free to invent endless headlines, despite the fact that even after 10 years only one of the five people present at the tomb's opening, and only two of the 22 who witnessed the opening of the sarcophagus, had died. Whenever he was asked about the curse, Carter's irritable reply was: 'tommy-rot'.

Martial law, imposed at the outbreak of the war, is lifted in July. Zaghloul and his fellow deportees are allowed to return to Egypt to contest next year's **general election**.

1924 The Turks abolish the **Ottoman caliphate** on 3 March. **King Fuad** of Egypt makes discreet overtures to leading Muslim figures in the hope of becoming caliph, but soon lets the matter drop.

Following the **general election** in January, the first Egyptian constitutional **parliament** opens on 15 March with a large Wafd majority and Saad Zaghloul as prime minister.

During the autumn, Zaghloul visits London for talks with British prime minister **Ramsay MacDonald** in an attempt to sweep away the reserved points, while having regard for Britain's interests. MacDonald is sympathetic to the nationalist cause, but is determined that Britain will continue to protect the Suez Canal, so that when Zaghloul insists that he will accept nothing less than the total withdrawal of British troops from Egypt as a precondition to negotiations, there is nothing left to discuss. Returning from London empty-handed on 16 November, and fearful of losing his popular support, Zaghloul organizes a massive **demonstration** against King Fuad outside **Abdin Palace** in Cairo, where the crowd cries 'Saad or revolution' and demands that the king back the Wafd's rejection of Britain's reserved points.

On 19 November, **Sir Lee Stack**, governor-general of the Sudan and commander-in-chief of the Egyptian army, is

Howard Carter discovered the tomb of Tuntankhamun in 1923, the only royal tomb that had not been looted by the workmen and priests of ancient times

Nationalism and Tutankhamun

Since the beginnings of Egyptology, foreign archeologists were granted concessions that gave them rights over access and to a share of what they found – with some justice, as the expertise and cost were theirs, and also the historical interest. Egyptians themselves had been largely incurious about their past, but the discovery of Tutankhamun's uniquely unviolated and treasure-stuffed tomb soon excited nationalist passions. In the question of finder's versus Egypt's rights, **Howard Carter** found himself cast in the role of an imperialist villain accused of appropriating Egypt's heritage. In 1924 the Mixed Courts ruled in favour of the Egyptian government, which then agreed a compromise with Carter, who was permitted to carry on his valuable work.

But the re-emergence of Tutankhamun after 3300 years also excited debate over who the Egyptians were, for it was not yet taken for granted that Egypt should be defined as an Arab and a Muslim state. **Pharaonism**, a concept to which Saad Zaghloul himself subscribed, saw Egypt as a secular country embracing everyone within its borders regardless of their origins or religion, though it recognized the uniqueness of the Egyptian character as traced back to the glories of pharaonic times. Many of those who espoused Pharaonism were often proponents of **Mediterraneanism** as well, which sought to link Egypt's ancient identity with Europe. A notable supporter of Mediterraneanism was the Muslim writer **Taha Hussein** (1889–1973), who argued that most Egyptians, whether Copt or Muslim, were the direct descendants of the pharaonic population and had little in common with their Arab neighbours. Instead he spoke of Egyptian admiration for European civilization, for its progress and its education, and claimed that Egypt was fundamentally like Europe. This was a notion that appealed to many Muslims and Copts of a liberal democratic persuasion, and it gave recognition to the role of Egypt's Jews and to its Greek and other European residents.

Saad Zaghloul, left, is received at the king's palace by royal chamberlain Ahmed Hassanein – the explorer who discovered Gebel Uweinat (see p.4)

murdered by Wafdist extremists on the streets of Cairo. Lord Allenby, the high commissioner – who had helped put Egypt on the road towards full independence despite the apprehensions of the British government, and who counted Stack as a friend – feels betrayed and angrily issues an **ultimatum** demanding strong measures and compensation. Zaghloul is distressed at events and resigns on 23 November. He never serves as prime minister again.

1925 Fuad I (later **Cairo) University** is inaugurated. At this point, over 90 per cent of Egyptians are illiterate.

Lord Allenby resigns as high commissioner in June and is replaced by **Lord (George) Lloyd**, a staunch defender of British imperial interests in Egypt.

> ❝ He was absolutely certain in his mind that this canal was another world quite independent of that in which he lived. A world that was inhabited by various strange beings without number, among which were crocodiles which swallowed people in one mouthful, and also enchanted folk who lived under the water all the bright day and during the dark of night. Only at dawn and dusk did they come up to the surface for a breath of air, and at that time they were a great danger to children and a seduction to men and women.
>
> And among these strange creatures also were the long and broad fish which would no sooner get hold of a child than they would swallow him up; and in the stomachs of which some children might be fortunate enough to get hold of the signet ring that would bring them to kingship. Now hardly had a man twisted this ring round his finger before two servants of the genie appeared in the twinkling of an eye to carry out his every wish. This was the very ring which Solomon wore and so subjected to his will genies, winds and every natural force he wished.
>
> Now he liked nothing better than to go down to the edge of this canal in the hope that one of these fish would swallow him and so enable him to get possession of this ring in its stomach, for he had great need of it … On the other hand he shrank from the terrors he must undergo before he reached this blessed fish. ❞
>
> Taha Hussein, *An Egyptian Childhood* (1926)

1926 The Muslim writer **Taha Hussein** (1889–1973), professor of classical civilization at Fuad I University and arguably the foremost Egyptian cultural figure of the century, is accused of apostasy after publishing a work of criticism which exposes religiously inspired literary forgeries and describes parts of the Koran as myth. Egypt is sufficiently liberal during this period that a judge dismisses the case, and though the university fires Hussein, he is later reinstated and rises to the positions of dean and rector. Blind since early childhood, Hussein was born and raised in a village between Beni Suef and Minya, where the river and canals were a world of wonder, as he describes in *An Egyptian Childhood*, published this year, the first volume of an autobiographical trilogy which goes on to include *The Stream of Days* and *Memoirs*.

1927 Saad Zaghloul dies on 23 August, and is entombed in a pharaonic-style monument in central Cairo beneath the outstretched wings of Horus. His close associate **Mustafa Nahas** becomes leader of the Wafd.

1928 Prime minister **Sarwat Pasha** agrees a **treaty** with Britain which provides for Egypt to join the League of Nations; for British troops to remain in Egypt for another ten years, after which a new agreement is to be made; for Britain to be represented in Egypt by an ambassador who is to take precedence in the diplomatic corps; and for arrangements in the Sudan to remain unaltered. The Wafd, however, blocks the treaty in parliament, Sarwat resigns, and in March **Mustafa Nahas** becomes prime minister until June – when he resigns after being implicated in a corruption scandal.

> ❝ Nahas was a vociferous ex-judge with a pointed skull and a distinct squint. Although of a gruff and imposing nature he remained a peasant through and through. It was this simplicity that many of his followers found so attractive. He was known as Ragil Tayib, a good and kind fellow. He was forthright in his speech, he called a spade a spade, was absolutely fearless, and difficult to persuade if suspicious. He would accept no opposition from his colleagues, and was prone to listen to all those who whispered in his ears. ❞
>
> Hanna F. Wissa, *Assiout, the Saga of an Egyptian Family* (1994)

Hassan al–Banna, a school teacher, founds the **Muslim Brotherhood** in the Canal Zone at Ismailia, which in time becomes a major political force in Egypt and spreads to other countries of the Arab world.

The Muslim Brotherhood

Hassan al-Banna (1906–48), a charismatic schoolteacher from the provinces, founded the Muslim Brotherhood in reaction to the secular liberal trend in Egypt and to demonstrate that social progress was possible within the bounds of a fundamentalist view of Islam. In this, he was drawing on the 19th-century teachings of **Jamal el Din Afghani** and **Mohammed Abdu**.

Initially, the Brotherhood took the form of a socially conscious Islamic revivalist movement whose activities ranged from running schools and boy scout groups to setting up industrial and commercial projects that provided jobs for the poor and generated income for the Brotherhood itself. But, as Banna's goal was to infuse Islam into every area of life, he opposed Egypt's secular political parties and European-style government and culture, damning them as sinful. Instead he wanted to return Egypt to the supposedly golden age that Islam enjoyed during the reigns of the first four caliphs. To that end Banna established the Muslim Brotherhood's armed **terrorist wing** in 1938. By its uncompromising opposition to any foreign presence, the Brotherhood vied with the Wafd as the champion of Egypt's nationalist aspirations, while at the same time it attracted those who felt bypassed by the benefits of liberalism. As soon as World War II was over, by when the Brotherhood had spread throughout the Middle East, Banna was working with disaffected elements in the army to take over Egypt and install himself as caliph – an ambition denied him in 1948, when he was murdered by the secret police in retaliation for the assassination of the Egyptian prime minister. Officially, the Muslim Brotherhood has been banned in Egypt almost continuously since that time; in reality, it remains extremely potent and has gone a long way towards imposing its fundamentalist ethos on present-day Egypt.

LE CAIRE.

Mosquée Mohamed-Ali.

The mosque of Mohammed Ali atop the Citadel, the fortress overlooking Cairo built by Saladin, became a major tourist attraction

1929 Fear and antagonism grows between native Arabs and immigrant Jews in **Palestine** as the Jewish population approaches 16 percent. Scores of Jews are killed or injured in a week-long riot in **Jerusalem** arising from a dispute over religious practices at the Wailing Wall and reports of the alleged intention of Jews to desecrate Muslim holy places. Egyptians show no interest in importing Palestine's problems into their own domestic politics, however.

1930 Following a huge **general election** victory in December, the Wafd forms its third government on 1 January, its second under Mustafa Nahas. Over the coming months, Nahas and the British negotiate over the reserved points and achieve broad agreement, including over the **Suez** Canal, but neither side makes concessions over the **Sudan** – to which Egyptians have an emotional and imperial attachment, owing to the importance of the Nile – and the talks break down. Nahas **resigns** in June, after disagreements with the king over the Palace's influence in political life and takes his struggle to the streets where the Wafd fosters riots and acts of sabotage. King Fuad appoints **Ismail Sidki**, a defector from the Wafd, as his new prime minister. Sidki arrests Wafd leaders, suppresses pro-Wafd newspapers, uses British troops to quash popular demonstrations, and replaces the 1923 constitution with one which increases the powers of the king while making a Wafd election victory unlikely. He also raises **import duties** to protect Egypt's developing industries – particularly textile manufacturing, which becomes the largest industrial sector by the end of the decade. His actions provide Egypt with a period of convalescence from the Wafd's campaign against Britain and the king, which has encouraged ministers to neglect Egypt's domestic affairs, especially in the cotton sector where exports are suffering from the worldwide **economic depression**.

British engineers complete the **Nag Hammadi barrage** in Upper Egypt, the last of the major Nile barrages to be built.

1932 **Abd al-Aziz ibn Saud**, a descendant of the tribal leader defeated by Egypt's Ibrahim Pasha over a century before, conquers the greater part of the Arabian peninsula and proclaims himself king, naming the country **Saudi Arabia** after himself. But no oil has yet been discovered and the Saudi royal family lives on hand-outs from the British government.

1933 A surge of **emigration** to Palestine by European Jews follows the election of the Nazi Party leader Adolf Hitler as German chancellor.

1934 The **Aswan Dam** is raised for a third time to increase the capacity of its reservoir, which now extends as far south as the Second Cataract at **Wadi Halfa** in the Sudan. Many monuments in **Lower Nubia** are strengthened against prolonged submergence except for a few summer months each year. Most Nubian villages along the Nile are also drowned, and some of their inhabitants move north beyond Aswan, but most prefer to move their villages to higher ground. Their fields and date palm groves cannot be replaced quickly, however, so that large numbers of Nubian men now work most of the year in Egypt, leaving their women and children behind along with the elderly to run their communities.

1935 Mussolini invades **Ethiopia** (Abyssinia) in October. Egypt now faces large numbers of Italian troops stationed in Ethiopia to the south and Libya to the west. The Italian threat convinces all Egyptian parties to form a **United Front** in December, which recognizes the need for British military protection and desires to establish a popular and stable government. With the approval of the king, the United Front secures the reinstatement of the 1923 constitution, and it also informs **Sir Miles Lampson**, high commissioner since 1934, that it wants to begin negotiations towards achieving an Anglo-Egyptian treaty.

Umm Kulsoum and the pan-Arab appeal of Egyptian popular culture

Born around the turn of the 20th century into an impoverished Delta village family, Umm Kulsoum first attracted notice as a Koranic chanter at country weddings. By the 1930s she was earning a Hollywood-size fortune in Cairo, where in place of her religious repertoire she now sang love ballads with lyrics by famous Egyptian poets set to music by modern composers. Her weekly radio broadcasts turned Umm Kulsoum into the embodiment of the Arabic cultural renaissance and earned her the sobriquet of 'Star of the East'. Her exquisitely subtle voice ranged between classical restraint and expressive improvisation and appealed to the sensibilities of both urban and rural Egypt, while throughout the Middle East listeners were roused to ecstasies by her erotically charged phrasing and intonation. Long before the advent of Nasser and Egypt's claim to be the leader of pan-Arabism, Umm Kulsoum had gained legendary status throughout the Middle East and had placed Cairo at the centre of the Arab world.

1936 The great Egyptian singer **Umm Kulsoum** – the Edith Piaf and Maria Callas of Arabic song rolled into one – gives her first live concert over Cairo Radio. With millions tuning in all over the Arab world, she will continue to do so on the first Thursday of every month until her retirement in 1973.

Hitler marches into the **Rhineland** in March.

With the British led by Lampson and the Egyptians by Nahas, negotiations towards an Anglo-Egyptian treaty begin in March. Following a May **general election** victory for the Wafd, Mustafa Nahas again becomes prime minister, and on 26 August he signs the **Anglo-Egyptian Treaty** on behalf of Egypt.

In April, King Fuad dies and is succeeded by his 16-year-old son **Farouk** (r. 1936–52).

Farouk was only 16 when he became king in 1936, the same year as the signing of the Anglo-Egyptian Treaty. To many it seemed like a fresh beginning

In the same month, the Arab population of **Palestine** rises up in revolt against the British and the Zionists in the face of continuing Jewish immigration and the discovery that the Jews are smuggling weapons into the country. The rebellion continues until the eve of World War II, and for the first time Palestine becomes a significant issue in Egyptian politics.

1937 A British commission of inquiry says the Palestine mandate is unworkable and calls for **partition**, but in Egypt Nahas announces that the Wafd rejects the partition of Palestine.

The 1936 Anglo-Egyptian Treaty

The reality of the Italian threat finally brought Egyptian nationalist leaders to accept a defensive treaty with Britain in exchange for independence. The treaty gave the Royal Navy the use of Alexandria harbour and granted the Royal Air Force the right to maintain airfields on Egyptian soil, while it limited British land forces to 10,000 men. These terms effectively met Britain's first two reserved points of 1922, while Britain conceded the third point concerning foreigners and minorities and agreed to work for the early end of the Capitulations. The vexatious fourth point concerning the Sudan was shelved for discussions another day.

The Egyptians celebrated the treaty because it immediately reduced the British presence and was subject to renegotiation after twenty years – when they expected to be free of the British altogether. Meanwhile Egypt gained full control of its police and armed forces, and of its foreign policy; it would be ushered into the League of Nations as a fully sovereign state, and Britain's imperious high commissioner would become an ambassador like any other. However, in what turned out to be an all-important provision of the treaty, in the event of war Egypt was obliged to put all its facilities at Britain's disposal, which effectively meant reoccupation of the country only three years later at the outbreak of World War II.

> ❝ There are no intellectual or cultural differences to be found among the peoples who grew up around the Mediterranean and were influenced by it. Purely political and economic circumstances made the inhabitants of one shore prevail against those of the other. The same factors led them to treat each other now with friendliness, now with enmity.
>
> We Egyptians must not assume the existence of intellectual differences, weak or strong, between the Europeans and ourselves or infer that the East mentioned by Kipling in his famous verse 'East is East and West is West, and never the twain shall meet' applies to us or our country. Ismail's statement that Egypt is a part of Europe should not be regarded as some kind of boast or exaggeration, since our country has always been a part of Europe as far as intellectual and cultural life is concerned, in all its forms and branches.
>
> In order to become equal partners in civilisation with the Europeans, we must literally and forthrightly do everything that they do; we must share with them the present civilisation, with all its pleasant and unpleasant sides, and not content ourselves with words or mere gestures. ❞
>
> Taha Hussein, *The Future of Culture in Egypt* (1938)

The Treaty of Montreux is signed, ending the Capitulations, granting the Mixed Courts jurisdiction in criminal cases and winding up the Courts themselves in 12 years. Egypt joins the **League of Nations**.

1938 American prospectors discover oil in **Saudi Arabia**.

The Wafd, having built its reputation on opposition to the British – to the neglect of policies for domestic reform – is defeated in April **general elections**, its traditional vote split between several political parties.

A British government White Paper published in May envisions the creation of an independent bi-national Arab-Jewish **Palestinian state** in 10 years' time and restricts Jewish immigration to 75,000 over the coming five years, after which no further immigration is to be permitted unless the Palestinian Arabs agree. The White Paper turns the Zionists against the British, but it is welcomed by the Arabs – still two-thirds of the population – and their rebellion dies down.

Egypt's strategic importance in World War II

In a few sudden months in 1940, the whole of the Atlantic coast of Europe from the Arctic Circle to the Spanish frontier had fallen into German hands, while across the English Channel Britain was girding itself against a Nazi invasion from the French ports. At the same time, the Germans and the Italians controlled two thousand miles of coastline around the Mediterranean, which only the Royal Navy's bases at **Gibraltar**, **Malta** and **Alexandria** prevented from becoming an Axis lake. America was neutral and the Soviet Union had signed a non-aggression pact with Germany, so that Britain stood alone against the fascist menace, with the Middle East and the Mediterranean its major battlegrounds. Had the British in Egypt been overwhelmed, then the Royal Navy would have been driven from the Mediterranean and the entire Middle East would have been lost, leaving Germany and Italy – joined by their ally, Japan – to hold much of Europe, Africa and Asia in thrall.

The strategic importance of Egypt in this great conflict was clearly understood by the German grand admiral, when, in support of Rommel's advance towards Alamein in 1942, he proposed to Hitler a naval attack against **Alexandria** and the **Suez Canal**, saying their capture would be more deadly to the British cause than the capture of London. Hitler failed to take his advice, Rommel was halted at Alamein, and with the Russians holding on against the Germans at Stalingrad, the tide of war turned irrevocably against the Axis.

On 3 September, Britain **declares war** on Germany, which has invaded **Poland**. Egypt remains a noncombatant, but in accordance with the 1936 Anglo-Egyptian Treaty all its ports, airfields, roads and other communications facilities are turned over to British use, martial law and censorship are imposed, and enemy aliens are detained.

It is probably during the closing months of the year that Hassan al-Banna forms the **terrorist wing** of the Muslim Brotherhood and begins hiding caches of arms up and down Egypt. Throughout the war he tells Egyptians not to help the British and gives his support to the fascist powers.

1940 In April, the Wafd leader **Mustafa Nahas** puts pressure on the British to restore him to power, delivering a veiled threat to the ambassador Sir Miles Lampson implying that the revolutionary outbreaks of 1919 might be repeated if World War II, like World War I, brings economic problems to Egypt.

A blackout is imposed on **Alexandria** and other Egyptian cities in May, but at the end of the month the Egyptian government declares **Cairo** an open city, meaning it will not be defended against enemy occupation and is therefore entitled under international law to immunity against bombardment and attack. For the rest of the war, the Egyptian capital blazes with lights.

Italy enters the war on the side of Germany on 10 June. The Italians have half a million men in Libya and Ethiopia, while Egypt is defended by 10,000 British soldiers under the command of **Sir Archibald Wavell**, commander-in-chief Middle East.

On 21 June, **France** capitulates to Germany. A growing number of Egyptians begin to believe that the Axis powers, Germany and Italy, will win the war.

Under pressure from Lampson, Farouk dismisses his military chief of staff **Aziz Ali al-Misri** and his prime minister **Ali Maher** for pro-Axis sympathies on 23 June. Maher is replaced by the pro-British **Hassan Sabri**, an independent.

Egypt's cotton exports are badly hit by the war, and to ward off economic disaster Britain agrees in July to buy the entire 1940 **cotton crop** at a price that is extremely favourable to the growers and puts it in store in Alexandria for future sale.

Large British and Australian **reinforcements** begin to arrive in Egypt on 8 September.

An Italian army under Marshal Graziani invades Egypt from Libya on 13 September and takes **Sidi Barrani** on the 18th. But British and Australian forces push the Italians back into Libya in December, taking 24,000 prisoners by the end of the month.

MICHAEL HAAG

British ambassador Sir Miles Lampson towers over Egyptian dignitaries, but his patronizing manner towards Farouk harmed state relations

> Any attempt at defining [the Wafd] would involve a complete description of Egypt. It contained all the generosity, intellectual muddle, good nature, contradictions and mythomania of its millions of supporters. It united the unlimited poverty of some and the insultingly bloated fortunes of others, the demand for change and the demand for conservatism.
>
> Jean and Simmone Lacouture, *Egypt in Transition* (1958)

Hassan Sabri dies while delivering a speech in parliament in November; he is succeeded by the independent **Hussein Sirry**, another pro-British politician.

1941 On 22 January, the Australians capture **Tobruk** – a vital port and supply centre in Cyrenaica (eastern Libya).

German tanks under General **Erwin Rommel** join Italian infantry in Libya for a new Axis offensive eastwards on 30 March. Tobruk is encircled by Axis forces on 13 April, who rush on towards the Egyptian frontier – where fierce fighting follows over the coming months.

A bad harvest during **April** and **May** brings shortages of flour, beans, oil and sugar in Egypt, while attempts at rationing by the pro-British but inept government of Hussein Sirry see staples double over their prewar prices, and agitators among the poor raise the cry that the British army is eating all the food.

Enemy air raids on the city and port of **Alexandria** reach their climax over 5–6 June.

Germany invades the **Soviet Union** on 22 June, breaking the nonaggression pact that had existed between the two nations. Britain now begins shipping vast quantities of arms and weapons to its new Russian ally.

Over the summer, Britain reaches an agreement with Sirry's government that Egypt and Britain share equally in the cost of purchasing this year's **cotton crop**, and that cotton acreage should be reduced by a quarter so that necessary, though less profitable, cereals and other foods are grown instead.

On the anniversary of Saad Zaghloul's death, 23 August, Mustafa Nahas delivers on his threat to Lampson of April 1940 by launching his **anti-British campaign** with inflammatory speeches in Cairo and Alexandria. He accuses the British and Sirry's compliant government of destroying the economy and thereby violating the Anglo-Egyptian Treaty, citing food shortages and the rising cost of staples, but also – without any sense of contradiction – sides with outraged landowners who, at some cost to their own pockets, are obliged by new legislation to grow more food and less cotton. As the disturbances continue into the autumn, British foreign secretary **Anthony Eden** drafts a telegram to Sir Miles Lampson on 24 October, complaining of the ability of the Wafd 'to influence public opinion according to the caprice of Nahas Pasha without incurring the slightest responsibility'. But Eden is less concerned with the immediate security of Egypt than with the perpetuation of British influence well beyond the end of the war – when, in accordance with the Anglo-Egyptian Treaty, Britain will be obliged to evacuate its forces and then, come 1956, to renegotiate the treaty itself. Eden concludes that there is a bargain to be made with Nahas, installing him in the premiership but as the servant of Britain's long-term policy.

Under General **Sir Claude Auchinleck**, who replaced Wavell as commander-in-chief in the summer, the British launch **Operation Crusader** on 18 November – which, over the next nine weeks, drives the German and Italian armies back across Cyrenaica.

The Japanese attack **Pearl Harbor** on 7 December, bringing the United States into the war, though it will be another year before American troops cross the Atlantic.

1942 On 4 February, British armoured cars surround Cairo's **Abdin Palace**, where the ambassador Sir Miles Lampson demands King Farouk's abdication. Farouk keeps his throne by agreeing to appoint **Mustafa Nahas** prime minister.

During May and June, Rommel thrusts eastwards across the whole of Cyrenaica, where **Tobruk** falls on 21 June. The British retreat deep into Egypt, where they finally rally at **Alamein**, only 60 miles from Alexandria. As Rommel's army arrives at Alamein on 1 July, the British fleet at **Alexandria** withdraws through the Suez Canal into the Red Sea, and the rumour goes around Egypt that Britain has lost the entire Middle East. But on 17 July, after over two weeks of battle, Rommel fails to gain any ground and the British under Auchinleck win the **first battle of Alamein**.

British prime minister **Winston Churchill** flies to Egypt in August, where he replaces Auchinleck with general **Sir Harold Alexander** as commander-in-chief Middle East and puts General **Sir Bernard Montgomery** in charge of the Eighth Army at Alamein.

Farouk (later **Alexandria**) **University** is officially opened in September, though it has been operating for a year.

The Abdin Palace 'Incident'

On 2 February 1942, prime minister Hussein Sirry resigned, presenting the British with the opportunity to put pressure on King Farouk to invite Mustafa Nahas to form a Wafdist government. But the monarchy and the Wafd had long been rivals for the control of the destiny of Egypt, and there was no love lost between Farouk and Nahas. Moreover, Lampson had a patronizing way with the young king, whom he regularly referred to as 'the boy'. The problem with Farouk, in Lampson's own words, was that he wanted to be 'an independent king of an independent Egypt'. Not surprisingly, Farouk temporized.

Meanwhile, Rommel had begun a new lunge eastwards across Libya, and students at Al-Azhar were shouting 'Down with the British' in the streets. Arguing that the king's recalcitrance was inconsistent with the overriding requirements of the military alliance, Lampson marched into Abdin Palace and demanded Farouk's abdication. To save his throne, the king agreed to appoint Nahas prime minister.

Yet Lampson's action on the night of 4 February achieved the opposite to its intended effect: it provoked nationalist outrage at foreign interference, destabilized constitutional government and introduced a bitterness between Britain and Egypt that would culminate in the Suez debacle. The sense of shame bit deeply within the Egyptian army, whose supreme commander was the king. 'For the army, this event has been a deep shock', wrote Gamal Abdel Nasser, then a young army officer. 'You see them repenting of not having intervened in spite of their obvious weakness to restore the country's dignity and cleanse its honour in blood. But the future is ours.'

General Erwin Rommel, shown on the cover of the German forces' magazine, came within a day's reach of Cairo and Alexandria, but was beaten at Alamein

The British Eighth Army under Montgomery defeats Rommel in the second battle of Alamein on 5 November.

Taking advantage of Hitler's distraction by Alamein, on 19 November the Soviet Union opens its offensive in the

battle of Stalingrad, which results in the death or surrender of a quarter of a million German troops and lasts until February the following year.

1943 **Makram Ebeid**, recently finance minister in Nahas' Wafdist government, publishes his **'Black Book'** at the end of March, detailing the large-scale corruption of Nahas and his ambitious wife – which includes lining their pockets with government money, selling privileges and concessions, and filling the civil service with cronies and relations. The corruption is excessive even by Egyptian standards, and faith in the Wafd is shaken.

After being driven across North Africa by Britain's Eighth Army, nearly a quarter of a million German and Italian troops surrender in **Tunisia** on 13 May.

In June, **Alexandria**'s Western Harbour becomes 'stiff with ships', part of a massive Allied armada assembling at British and Middle Eastern ports under the command of Admiral Cunningham for **Operation Husky**, the invasion of **Sicily** set to commence on 10 July, its scale larger than the Normandy landings eleven months later. Of the half million troops that would land on Sicily, the slight majority would be British, the rest American, but all under the supreme command of General Dwight D. Eisenhower – an acceptance by Britain that the United States was now the senior partner in the alliance. The war now moves away from Egypt.

The **Alexandria Protocol**, which establishes the framework for the foundation of the **Arab League** – which in turn embodies hopes for Arab unity – is signed on 7 October by Egypt, Iraq, Syria, Lebanon, Saudi Arabia, Yemen and Transjordan. The prime mover is Egypt's prime minister Mustafa Nahas with the support of King Farouk, while the gathering has been facilitated by **Lord Moyne**, Britain's minister of state for the Middle East. Within days, however, Farouk dismisses Nahas, who is so tainted by corruption that the British make no move to save him. On 6 November, Moyne is murdered in **Cairo** by Jewish terrorists, members of the **Stern Gang** – run by future Israeli prime minister Yitzhak Shamir – which sees the British presence in the Middle East as the chief obstacle to the realization of a Jewish state.

1945 **Naguib Mahfouz**, who 43 years later will win the Nobel Prize for Literature, begins his *Cairo Trilogy*, comprising the novels *Palace Walk*, *Palace of Desire* and *Sugar Street*. They lovingly chronicle the life of a lower middle-class family between the world wars as they make the transition from traditional to modern ways. He completes his trilogy before Nasser's coup in 1952, though its volumes are published only in 1956 and 1957.

The Wafd boycotts a January **general election**, which is won by the **Saadists**, a breakaway Wafdist group led by Ali Maher's brother **Ahmed Maher**, who becomes prime minister. On 24 February, Maher announces that his government has secured parliamentary approval for a **declaration of war** on Germany. This step is urged by Churchill, because it is a condition Egypt must fulfil if it is to become a founder member of the United Nations. But Ahmed Maher is assassinated moments later, probably by a member of the Muslim Brotherhood.

Egypt's new prime minister, **Mahmoud Fahmi Nuqrashi**, formally declares war on Germany on 26 February.

Germany capitulates on 8 May, ending the war in Europe, while the Japanese surrender on 14 August brings World War II to an end.

1946 Oil exports from **Saudi Arabia** reach a significant level for the first time, generating fabulous wealth for the country.

Three weeks of massive **demonstrations** and riots by students and workers begin in February, encouraged by the Wafd, the communists and the Muslim Brotherhood, who demand the withdrawal of British troops and the unification of the Sudan with Egypt. The king brings **Ismail Sidki** back as prime minister in February to restrain the opposition. Sidki flies to London in October, where he agrees a draft treaty with the Labour government's foreign minister **Ernest Bevin**, which provides for complete British withdrawal from Egypt (including the Canal Zone) within three years, and for a mutual defence pact. The treaty meets the demands of Egyptian nationalists in all respects, except for its provision that the Sudanese must be consulted before deciding on their future. Unable to carry this point in Egypt, Sidki resigns, Nuqrashi becomes prime minister again, and the draft treaty is shelved.

1947 The British withdraw all their troops to the **Canal Zone**. The government passes the most comprehensive of its **Egyptianization acts**, requiring of companies that 75 percent of all salaried employees and 90 percent of all workers should be Egyptian, and that Egyptians must hold a majority share in all joint stock companies. The purpose is to ensure jobs for young Egyptians, but it raises the problem of what defines an 'Egyptian'. The effect is that many Egyptian-born non-Muslims such as Greeks and Jews find opportunities closed to them.

Egypt's **population** stands at twenty million.

Under strong American pressure, the United Nations General Assembly votes on 29 November for the partition of **Palestine** into separate Arab and Jewish states – against the wishes of its Arab inhabitants, who form 70 percent of the population and own 92 percent of the land. Egypt and other Arab states are among those who vote against partition.

1948 On 14 May, **David Ben Gurion** declares the foundation of the Jewish state of **Israel** with himself as prime minister and **Chaim Weizmann** as its first president. One day later, in defence of the Palestinian Arabs and under the aegis of the Arab League, units of the Egyptian, Transjordanian, Syrian and Iraqi armies **enter Palestine** on the day the British mandate ends.

Britain grants an interim measure of self-government to the **Sudan** in July.

On 28 December, a month after the government bans the Muslim Brotherhood, one of its members assassinates prime minister **Mahmoud el Nuqrashi** inside the ministry of the interior in the presence of the police.

1949 **Gamal Abdel Nasser** forms the secret **Free Officers Movement**, some of whose members have links with the Muslim Brotherhood, others with the communists, yet others no ideology at all – but all are committed to overthrowing the government.

The **Suez Canal Company** agrees that it will not seek to renew its concession when it expires in 1968. Egypt negotiates a greater share of the profits from the canal company and for more Egyptians to work in the Canal Zone.

The Palestine War

Even before the end of the British mandate, Zionist forces had gone into action in Palestine, beginning what Chaim Weizmann was to call 'a miraculous cleaning of the land'. In defence of the Palestinian Arabs and under the aegis of the Arab League, units of the Egyptian, Transjordanian, Syrian and Iraqi armies entered the country on 15 May, 1948, though altogether they could muster barely more than 20,000 troops fit for battle – against 60,000 Jewish soldiers who were better armed and trained.

In Egypt, during the course of the war there were a number of attacks by the Muslim Brotherhood on Jewish-owned shops, department stores and cinemas, but neither the Egyptian public nor the government were engaged in any organized persecution. In December the Brotherhood was banned, but in the same month one of its members assassinated the prime minister, **Mahmud Fahmi Nuqrashi**, and several weeks later the Brotherhood's founder, **Hassan al-Banna**, was killed by the Egyptian secret police: the real battle was being fought not in Palestine but within Egypt.

After Israel and Egypt signed an armistice in February 1949, 2000 Jewish Egyptian internees who had been suspected of Zionist activities were released and their sequestrated property was restored. Their situation was in stark contrast to the Palestinian Arabs, of whom at least 700,000 were driven from their homes by the Zionists. Like others of his generation, **Gamal Abdel Nasser**, who was wounded during the Palestine war, blamed the defeat on Farouk and the corruption and incompetence of his ministers. In 1949 Nasser called a secret meeting of his fellow radical officers; the **Free Officers Movement** pledged itself to overthrowing the Egyptian government within five years.

The **Egyptian Communist Party** is founded and proves influential among Cairo's students, skilled workers and professionals with its ideas of social justice, planned economic development and distrust of the West, but it fails to reach out to the urban poor or to the fellahin in the countryside.

Hassan al-Banna, leader of the Muslim Brotherhood, is assassinated by the Egyptian counter-terrorist police on 13 February.

Egypt signs an armistice with **Israel** on 24 February, which by now has incorporated 80 percent of Palestine into the new Jewish state.

The **Mixed Courts** close at midnight on 14 October, twelve years after the Treaty of Montreux. Everyone in Egypt, regardless of nationality, is now subject to Egyptian civil and criminal law.

1950 After reconciliation between the king and the Wafd, the Wafd wins a January **general election** and Mustafa Nahas once more becomes prime minister.

As the Wafd becomes increasingly unpopular and mired in corruption, Nahas steps up his anti-British demagoguery on 8 October. He unilaterally declares the 1936 Anglo-Egyptian Treaty and 1899 Anglo-Egyptian Condominium over the Sudan null and void, and he proclaims Farouk king of both **Egypt** and the **Sudan**. Jailed members of the Muslim Brotherhood are released and allowed to return to public activity, supposedly in social, cultural and spiritual roles. In fact members of the Muslim Brotherhood and other extremist groups are given arms and training by the Egyptian army with the connivance of the Wafd, which provides them with police protection while they mount attacks against British soldiers in the **Canal Zone**.

11: Egypt under Nasser

1952–70

The old order in Egypt finally broke down on 26 January, 1952. The Palestine disaster, an increasingly discredited monarchy, popular disappointment with the Wafd and anger at the British presence in the Canal Zone all helped to create a feverish and unstable situation which exploded on that frenzied day of arson and murder in Cairo. Six months later, when Nasser and his **Free Officers** struck, first at the army high command, then at King Farouk, their quick and bloodless coup came as a relief and was broadly welcomed, as it seemed to promise a new beginning.

The man behind the coup, **Gamal Abdel Nasser**, went unrecognized as its author at the time. Instead the Free Officers, all men in their early 30s, presented the avuncular, pipe-smoking figure of general **Mohammed Neguib** as their leader, though he had been brought into the conspiracy only a few days before the coup. Neguib was widely respected as a brave and honourable man: he had offered Farouk his resignation at the time of the Abdin incident, ashamed that he had been unable to defend the king who was head of the army, and later he distinguished himself in Palestine, where he was severely wounded. As the first president of the republic and also its prime minister, Neguib's easy-going style endeared him to the public; believing that he was indispensable, he challenged the Free Officers, whose rule he found autocratic and arbitrary, and proposed that there should be an elected assembly and civilian cabinet. Fearing Neguib's growing popularity, Nasser came into the open two years later and swept Neguib aside. By the middle of 1956, he had assumed dictatorial powers.

Perhaps the most pressing problem facing Egypt was the poor quality of its human resources. Despite efforts begun by Mohammed Ali, the mass of Egyptians had hardly benefited from the educational and health advances made in European countries over the past four hundred years. The numbers attending school had doubled between 1933 and 1951 to nearly two million, but that was still no more than 10 percent of the total population. In 1950, it was estimated that 75 percent of the fellahin suffered from bilharzia (disorders of the organs and nervous system caused by exposure to worms breeding in slow-running irrigation canals), while others suffered from eye diseases, hookworm and malaria. The high birth rate was another problem facing the Free Officers: Egypt's population had increased ten-fold in 150 years, making its narrow cultivated area one of the most densely populated regions in the world and putting enormous pressure on the agricultural productivity of the land.

Yet even by 1956, when Nasser assumed supreme power, there had been no revolution. The Free Officers were not committed to any particular ideology: their approach was experimental, common-sensical and pragmatic during their early years. The September 1952 **agrarian reform law**, which limited an individual's land ownership to 200 feddans (a feddan being just over an acre) – freeing up 450,000 feddans for redistribution to the fellahin – had actually been proposed by some large landowners before the coup as a public safety measure. Likewise, plans for what became Nasser's grand project, the construction of the High Dam at **Aswan**, were first developed by parliamentary governments in the late 1940s.

Nasser's policies resulted in a noticeably, though not radically, more equitable distribution of land and wealth in Egypt, but his real radicalism lay in his uncompromising determination to rid Egypt of any lingering foreign influence and to do the same for the entire Arab world – which he envisioned as united under Egyptian leadership. That was the background to his nationalization of the **Suez Canal Company** in July 1956. This act, along with Nasser's pan-Arab strategy, drew a response from **Britain**, **France** and **Israel**, who, as if bent on proving Nasser's worst fears of foreign interference and ill-will, launched an attack on Egypt. The invasion was almost immediately halted by American and Soviet threats, the superpowers in effect declaring that the Middle East was now their sole preserve, and Nasser was handed a spurious victory. For the moment it did seem to the Arab world that it had found a new Saladin, but the exaltation disguised the boundaries between realities and dreams, and now Nasser and Egypt entered upon a period of illusion.

Later, Nasser would speak of his three 'revolutions'. The first was the coup d'état; the second followed the Suez fiasco, when all British and French citizens and many Egyptian Jews were expelled from the country and their property seized; and the third came with Nasser's 1961 socialist measures. But all three were calamities for Egypt – the coup destroyed the institutions of representative politics; the second led to the wholesale expulsion and flight of Egypt's 'foreign' communities, whose families had often been in the country for generations and represented a valuable pool of expertise; and the third began the destruction of the private sector during the 1960s, replacing it with a centralized, bureaucratized and eventually bankrupt Egyptian economy.

1952 In the face of continuing attacks on their troops in the **Canal Zone**, the British suspect that the volatile Egyptian auxiliary police in Ismailia are involved, and demand on 25 January that they surrender their arms and leave the town. The police refuse and open fire on the British, who give an hour's warning then storm their headquarters, killing

43. The events at Ismailia touch off demonstrations in **Cairo** on 26 January, which have the covert support of the Wafdist government. But things quickly get out of control as the crowds are incited to riot and loot by arsonists belonging to Islamic fundamentalist groups. By the afternoon, downtown Cairo is in flames and seven hundred shops, clubs, cinemas, offices, the Opera House and Shepheard's Hotel are destroyed – as is anything associated with the British and foreigners more generally, a number of whom are beaten and burnt to death by the mob. The police, when not joining the crowd, stand by and do nothing, and it is not until 6pm that the army is called in and order is restored.

On 17 January, King Farouk dismisses Nahas and asks **Ali Maher**, known for his strong anti-British views, to form a government, but it does not last long, and over the coming months Maher is followed in rapid succession by three other prime ministers.

> To the people of Egypt. Egypt has lived through one of the darkest periods in its history. The Army has been tainted by the agents of dissolution. This was one of the causes of our defeat in Palestine. Led by fools, traitors and incompetents, the army was incapable of defending Egypt. That is why we have carried out a purge. The Army is now in the hands of men in whose ability, integrity and patriotism you can have complete confidence. The former Army chiefs who are now under arrest will be released when circumstances permit. Egypt will greet our Movement with hope and with joy, and she can be sure that the Army is pledged to protect the national interest. ... The Army, in cooperation with the police, will be responsible for law and order.
>
> Broadcast by Anwar Sadat at 7am on 23 July, 1952

On the night of 22 July, members of the Free Officers Movement under the direction of **Gamal Abdel Nasser** (1918–70) seize power in a coup d'etat; before midnight they capture the Egyptian army GHQ and key members of the high command; at 5am they appoint General **Mohammed Neguib** commander-in-chief of the armed forces; and at 7am on 23 July the coup is announced over the radio by **Anwar Sadat**.

On 26 July, forces loyal to the Free Officers lay siege to Ras el Tin Palace at **Alexandria**, where King Farouk is forced to abdicate in favour of his infant son **Ahmed Fuad** (r. 1952–53), and a regency council is appointed. At 6pm Farouk, together with Queen Narriman and Prince Ahmed Fuad, sails to **Italy** aboard the royal yacht *Mahroussa*, the same vessel that had carried his grandfather Ismail into exile.

On 14 August, the nine-member command committee of the Free Officers Movement transforms itself into the **Revolutionary Command Council** (RCC) by co-opting five more members, among them General Mohammed Neguib, who becomes its public figurehead. In a panic that the Free Officers' coup has been taken as a revolutionary green light by workers, the RCC orders troops to open fire on workmen who have occupied a textile factory at **Kafr el Dawar** near Alexandria and are demanding wage rises; three weeks later, after being tried before a military tribunal, a number of the workers are condemned to up to 15 years' hard labour and two are hanged.

Gamal Abdel Nasser (1918–70)

Nasser was born in Alexandria, where his father, of fellahin stock from Upper Egypt, was a postmaster. While at Ras el Tin school near the royal palace, Nasser took part in his first student demonstration at the age of 11, getting hit in the face with a police baton and spending the night in jail. The 1936 Anglo-Egyptian Treaty put Egypt in charge of its own army, creating the demand for more officers who were now drawn from a wider social class, among them Nasser, Sadat and six other Free Officers, who all entered the military academy in 1937. Nasser read voraciously among the Arab and Western classics, and in history and biography, taking particular interest in the lives of Alexander the Great, Julius Caesar, Rousseau, Voltaire, Napoleon and Gandhi. His heroes were **Ahmed Arabi**, **Mohammed Abdu**, **Mustafa Kamel** and **Saad Zaghloul**, and he described how 'the national struggle of any people, generation after generation, resembles a structure rising one stone on top of the other'.

Nasser was driven by a view of Egypt's history in which he saw the tragedy of its people as forever oppressed, whether by foreigners or by Egyptians, and though in some sense he will always remain a hero of the people, his period of rule is generally judged a calamity. He had the patient and docile fellahin on his side, but he used threats, imprisonment, torture and executions to silence all criticism from other quarters, and by the 1960s had turned Egypt into an oppressive police state. He promoted the hydroelectric High Dam at **Aswan** to industrialize the country, but at the same time he wrecked Egypt's **economy** through his centralizing and socialist measures; and he neglected the problems of his own people while championing the chimerical pan-Arab cause, which led Egypt into the catastrophic 1967 war with **Israel**.

The RCC promulgates the first **Agrarian Reform Law** on 9 September, which limits the amount of land that can be held by any one person to 200 feddans (a feddan amounts to just over an acre) and distributes the excess to landless fellahin.

The RCC **abrogates the constitution** 'in the name of the people' on 9 December.

1953 On 16 January, all **political parties** are dissolved and their funds confiscated. The **Muslim Brotherhood**, which has powerful support in the army and throughout the country, pledges not to interfere in politics.

General Mohammed Naguib (photographed with Sadat behind) was nominal head of the Free Officers' coup, but was soon pushed aside by Nasser

A **Provisional Constitution** is promulgated on 10 February, which gives the RCC supreme authority for three years. Soon afterwards, a new political organization is formed, the **Liberation Rally**, to mobilize political support for the RCC; it is headed by Nasser.

On 12 February, the British and Egyptians agree to allow the people of the **Sudan** to determine their own future, independence or union with Egypt, with the Egyptians convinced that the Sudanese will choose union.

The RCC abolishes the monarchy on 18 June, and declares Egypt a **republic**. General Mohammed Neguib becomes president and prime minister, while Nasser becomes deputy premier and minister of the interior, for the first time revealing himself in a prominent public position. Civilians in the cabinet are almost entirely replaced by military men.

A **Revolutionary Tribunal** consisting of three RCC members, among them Anwar Sadat, is set up in September to try politicians and others of the old regime, though it is opposed by General Neguib.

1954 The **Muslim Brotherhood**, which has continued to be involved in political activity and has clashed with followers of the Liberation Rally, is banned by the RCC on 12 January.

> As the President, Prime Minister and the 'Leader of the Revolution' I was responsible for every action taken by the government. I had no objection to assuming responsibility for actions of which I approved. But I was no longer willing to resume responsibility for actions regarding which I was either not consulted or of which I did not or could not approve.
>
> Mohammed Neguib, *Egypt's Destiny* (1955)

Differences within the Revolutionary Command Council increase after General Neguib calls for the restoration of **parliamentary democracy** in February. He resigns, but after protests from a section of the army, from some members of the RCC – as well as from the Wafd, the left and the Muslim Brotherhood – Neguib is invited by the Council to resume office.

Neguib resigns the post of prime minister on 17 April, which is assumed by **Nasser**, who sets out to destroy the power of the communists and the Muslim Brotherhood.

In July, Britain and Egypt agree that the last British troops are to be withdrawn from the **Canal Zone** in 1956. Posing as fanatical Egyptian nationalists set on disrupting the talks with Britain over the Canal, Egyptian-Jewish terrorists working for Israel explode bombs against Western targets in Cairo and Alexandria in what becomes known as the **Lavon Affair**.

On 26 October, an **assassination attempt** is made on Nasser in Alexandria by a member of the Muslim Brotherhood. The gunman, along with the leaders of the Brotherhood, are arrested and tried; six are hanged and the Brotherhood's supreme leader **Hassan al-Hudaybi** is sentenced to life imprisonment in December. Though the Brotherhood is being broken up for the time being as a political organization, its religious activists continue to promote a fundamentalist view of the Koran while rejecting Western thought among students, young army officers, urban workers and the fellahin. In particular **Sayyid**

The Lavon Affair: Israeli terrorism inside Egypt

The prime minister of Israel in 1954 was **Moshe Sharett**, who had been raised in an Arab village in Palestine and sought a rapprochement with his country's Arab neighbours. Through diplomatic intermediaries in Paris, Sharett and Nasser entered into secret discussions. But the Israeli military and the foreign minister **Pinhas Lavon** pursued their own hard-line policy of discouraging peace with Egypt and preventing it from establishing favourable relations with the West. To make Britain think again about evacuating the Canal Zone and to undermine American confidence in its scheme for an anti-Soviet Arab alliance, Lavon went secretly behind Sharett's back and instructed Israeli intelligence to devise a plan for making it seem that Egypt could not be trusted.

Seven young Egyptian Jews were recruited and trained to make incendiary bombs, and in July 1954 the saboteurs went into action, exploding bombs against Western targets in **Cairo** and **Alexandria** with the intention of making it seem that it was the work of anti-Western Egyptian extremists. The plot was discovered when a bomb exploded in the pocket of a saboteur outside an Alexandrian cinema, setting his trousers on fire. Israeli propaganda presented the arrests as the framing of innocent Jews, while the atmosphere surrounding the trial, which began in December 1954 and ended in January 1955, made Jews worried about their security in Egypt. The Lavon Affair also destroyed Nasser's confidence in Sharett, who admitted that the plot had been hatched by hardliners behind his back. Nasser concluded that Israel's hardliners and not Sharett were determining policy, and, fearing military provocation by Israel, he sought arms – first from Britain, which refused, then from the Soviet bloc, which rapidly sent Egypt the latest tanks, bombers and MiG jet fighters. The spiral had begun towards the **Suez war** of 1956 (see p.355).

> It was a touch of a magic wand which made this man [Neguib] appear to the world at large as a great revolutionary, and the liberator of the Nile. For he was really no more than an ordinary, middle-class man, a good father to his children, whose ambition was to end his career happily shuttling between his office and his fireside. For years the rest of us had worked in secret to prepare Neguib's path to immortality. We raised him to the summit, and then we had to dash him down again.
>
> Anwar Sadat, *Revolt on the Nile* (1957)

Qutb, the Brotherhood's principal ideologue, who is sentenced to ten years in prison, uses his time to write what will become the classic contemporary statement of Islamic fundamentalism, the best-selling *Signposts on the Road* (*Maalim fi al-Tariq*). The book argues that infidels are not only outside Islam but within in the form of secularist rulers like Nasser or the ulama and other clerics, who fail to preserve and enhance 'true' Islamic values, and it calls for a jihad against them.

On 14 November, **Neguib** is dismissed as president on charges of being associated with the Muslim Brotherhood and the communists. He is put under house arrest, and his career is ended. Nasser assumes the presidency of Egypt.

1955 In January, **Iraq** signs a defence agreement with Turkey known as the **Baghdad Pact** and is attacked by Nasser for betraying the pan-Arab cause. **Britain** joins the Pact on 4 April, which Nasser and other Arab nationalists see as an example of imperialist interference in the Middle East.

On 28 February, the Israeli army strikes at Egyptian-held **Gaza** in retaliation for attacks by dispossessed Palestinians. Israel shrugs off condemnation by the United Nations

Egyptian films

The first feature film made in Egypt was *In the Land of Tutankhamun* in 1923, though the accolade for the first Egyptian-made film goes to *Leila*, the 1927 story directed by **Stephen Rosti** of love, misuse, betrayal and downfall – the stuff of Egyptian melodrama that was to fill movie screens thereafter. The Egyptian film industry really took off in the 1930s with the arrival of talkies and the involvement of Bank Misr, which financed productions, sent technicians abroad for training and founded **Misr Studio** in Cairo in 1935.

The 1940s and 1950s were the golden age of Egyptian films. Many of Egypt's great singing stars, already famous through radio and recordings – among them **Abd el Wahab**, the son of a muezzin, **Leila Murad**, the daughter of a Jewish cantor and **Umm Kulsoum** – also appeared in films, helping Egyptian productions to dominate Arab screens. Already before the downfall of the monarchy the director **Youssef Chahine**, born in Alexandria into a Christian Syrian family, began filming *Raging Sky* (1953), the story of a peasant farmer's challenge to a feudal landlord. Its star was 'the first lady of the screen', Egypt's **Faten Hamama**, and playing opposite her was an unknown Syrian-Lebanese Christian called Michel Chairoub. The two fell in love and Chairoub, converting to Islam to marry Hamama, changed his name to **Omar Sharif**. Since then Chahine, widely regarded as Egypt's greatest director, has made nearly fifty films, among them *Saladin* (1963), in which parallels were easily drawn with Nasser, and *The Choice* (1970), both scripted by **Naguib Mahfouz** (see p.365), and *The Sparrow*

Security Council, while Egypt feels humiliated by its military inferiority, which prevents it from hitting back at Israel. Nasser unsuccessfully seeks weapons from Britain before turning to Soviet-bloc Eastern Europe.

From 18 to 24 April, Nasser attends the non-aligned conference at **Bandung** in Indonesia, where he is lauded by such proponents of neutralism as Jawaharlal Nehru of India

(1972) about the 1967 defeat and considered one of his very best. *Destiny* (1997), set in Muslim Andalusia, concerns the early Arab involvement with Greek speculative thought and is a spirited attack on Islamic fundamentalism. Many of Chahine's films are set in Alexandria, 'the city of my childhood, between the two world wars tolerant, secular, open to Muslims, Christians and Jews'.

Egyptian films are seen throughout the Middle East, making Egyptian actors and the Egyptian dialect familiar to Arabs everywhere

and Chou En Lai of China, and comes away feeling that the Arab nationalists' struggle is part of a worldwide movement against domination by the great powers.

In September, Nasser purchases arms from **Czechoslovakia** and is hailed by Arabs throughout the Middle East as another Saladin who will reconquer Palestine. Realizing that the sale must have had the approval of the Soviet

Union, the West is alarmed at the prospect of communist penetration in the region.

1956 On 1 January, the first elected parliament in **Khartoum** rejects unification with Egypt and declares Sudanese independence.

On 9 February, the **World Bank** announces 'substantial agreement' with Egypt over plans for the United States, Britain and the World Bank to finance the construction of a High Dam at **Aswan** to increase Egypt's agricultural area by a third and to provide the hydroelectric power needed for large-scale industrialization. .

In accordance with the July 1954 Anglo-Egyptian agreement, the last British soldiers evacuate the **Canal Zone** on 31 March.

Egypt recognizes communist **China** in May, upsetting the United States Congress just as negotiations for a loan to finance construction of the High Dam at Aswan are reaching a critical stage. In response to the move – and to Nasser's close associations with the Soviet bloc – the US withdraws its offer to help finance construction of the Aswan High Dam, resulting in Britain and the World Bank withdrawing their offers too.

Though it is plain to observers that there is significant opposition to the regime, on 22 June Nasser is elected president with 99.99 percent of the vote in a national referendum, which by the same margin approves a new **constitution** granting him sweeping powers. Also, for what it is worth, **women** are given the vote.

On 26 July, the fourth anniversary of the abdication of King Farouk, Nasser gives a three-hour speech to an enormous crowd in **Alexandria**. He denounces imperialism and accuses the Western powers of seeking to dominate Egypt and the Arab world through Israel and by military pacts, by the manipulation of arms sales and by economic pressure.

The Suez Crisis

Nationalization of the Suez Canal Company made little financial sense for Egypt. Once compensation had been paid to its mostly French and British shareholders, there would not be sufficient revenue from Canal users' fees to finance the High Dam at Aswan, which was always going to be dependent on foreign loans. In fact Nasser's motives were political, for by challenging the Western powers and realizing Egypt's last great nationalist aim of gaining operating control of the Canal, he hoped to bolster his own position, which as yet was far from secure.

Britain's prime minister, **Anthony Eden**, had recently been blaming Nasser for whipping up Arab nationalism throughout the Middle East, and he feared that if the nationalization of the Canal was left unanswered it would be a blow to British influence and interests in the region. A quarter of Britain's trade passed through the Canal and British ships accounted for a third of its users, while most of Britain's oil supply came through Suez. Recalling Britain's prewar appeasement of Germany following its occupation of the Rhineland, Eden began comparing Nasser to Hitler and called for his destruction. For its part, France feared and resented Nasser's support (though largely verbal) for the Algerians in their independence struggle which was tying down 250,000 French troops. Israel, which had failed to prevent the closure of Britain's base in the Canal Zone and was fearful over the loss of the British buffer, had intended to attack Egypt anyway.

Action against Nasser became a shared aim, and **Israel**, **France** and **Britain** formed a conspiratorial alliance to invade Egypt with the intention of regaining control of the Canal and overthrowing Nasser's regime. The military operation was a success, but when the new postwar superpowers, America and the Soviet Union, humiliated Britain and France by demanding their withdrawal, Nasser was handed an unexpected triumph and became the hero of the entire Arab world.

Gamal Abdel Nasser seemed to give Egypt status and purpose, but he drove his country into bankruptcy and led it into a humiliating military defeat in 1967

Asking rhetorically where Egypt is to find the money to finance construction of the Aswan High Dam, he announces the occupation of the **Canal Zone** by the Egyptian army and the nationalization of the Suez Canal Company, 12 years before the expiry of its concession in 1968.

Early in September, Nasser rejects a compromise put forward by a conference of eighteen maritime nations in **London** that the Canal should be managed and developed by an international body until the expiry of the Suez Canal Company's concession.

At a secret meeting held on 23–24 October between representatives of the British, French and Israeli governments at **Sèvres** in France, final plans are made for their joint attack on Egypt. Israel advances into **Sinai** on 29 October, while French pilots in French aircraft with Israeli markings attack Egyptian targets. Under the pretence of keeping Israeli and Egyptian forces apart, British and French troops land at **Port Said** in the Canal Zone on 5 November and begin advancing towards Suez. But on 6–7 November, Britain, France and Israel agree to a **ceasefire** after being put under strong pressure by the United States in particular, though also the Soviet Union. The last British and French forces are withdrawn from Egypt on 22 December; they are replaced by United Nations troops.

1957 All resident British and French citizens are **expelled from Egypt** early in the year, along with many Jews, and their property is seized. All British and French banks and companies, 15,000 establishments in all, are **nationalized**. Soviet Russian trade and aid increases dramatically.

The **Eisenhower Doctrine**, announced in January, declares that international communism is a threat to the Middle East and that financial aid will be given to any government which opposes it. **Lebanon**, **Jordan**, **Saudi Arabia** and **Iraq** back the Doctrine and take America's money; nervous about Egypt since the Suez crisis, they fear growing Soviet influence in the region.

The **Suez Canal**, which had been blocked, is reopened to shipping in April.

In November, the Liberation Rally is replaced by the

National Union with Anwar Sadat as secretary-general; its stated aim is 'the creation of a socialist, democratic, cooperative society free of all political, social and economic exploitation'.

1958 Egypt merges with Syria on 1 February to form the **United Arab Republic** under the leadership of Nasser. The initiative for this move comes from Syria, which is seeking to protect itself from Iraq, Israel and internal communists. In **Damascus**, millions of Syrians throng to hail Nasser as the leader of the Arabs. **Yemen** joins in March. Egypt's National Assembly is dissolved because of the new pan-Arab union, and the 1956 constitution is abrogated.

1959 Naguib Mahfouz publishes *Children of Gebelawi*, a religious and social allegory in which God, Moses, Jesus and Mohammed appear, but the novel is quickly banned in Egypt and Mahfouz is accused of blasphemy. The book also contains what can be interpreted as criticisms of the Nasser regime.

1960 As work starts on the High Dam at **Aswan**, Nasser lays the foundation stone in January. The 30,000-strong Egyptian labour force is supervised by 2000 engineers and technicians from the Soviet Union.

Nasser nationalizes **Bank Misr** on 10 February, whose investment policy he dislikes, despite it being a wholly Egyptian-owned operation established in 1920 in a patriotic effort to direct investment into Egyptian commercial and industrial enterprises.

> **66** Ours is an Arab people and its destiny is tied to the destiny of the unity of the Arab Nation. **99**
>
> Gamal Abdel Nasser

The UNESCO Nubian Rescue Campaign

With Nubia facing complete submersion beneath the waters that would soon back up behind the new High Dam at Aswan, UNESCO responded to urgent appeals by Egypt and Sudan by sponsoring the **Nubian Rescue Campaign** from 1960 to 1980, in which fifty countries took part, providing money, archeologists, engineers and other varieties of expertise. Monuments were dismantled, or, like **Abu Simbel**, were cut from the rock and reassembled at new sites in Egypt and Sudan, while those that could not be moved, such as ancient cemeteries or structures of mudbrick, had their details exhaustively recorded. Five monuments were given as gifts abroad and are now found in New York, Madrid, Berlin, Turin and Leiden. The rest of what survives of Nubia after five thousand years of exploitation by Egypt is now housed in the **Nubia Museum**, opened in 1997, a large sandstone building on a rocky outcrop at Aswan near the First Cataract, that age-old frontier.

The press is nationalized on 23 May, so that its ownership, says Nasser, passes into the hands of 'the people'. Journalism loses all integrity, becoming irresponsible in its foreign reporting and abject in its domestic coverage.

Television is introduced to Egypt on 21 July; like radio, it is state-controlled, and becomes an efficient tool of propaganda in rallying public opinion.

1961 At Nasser's insistence, new faculties specializing in secular subjects are established at the **university of Al-Azhar**.

Nasser decrees sweeping **socialist measures** on 21 July: 400 private firms are nationalized in the banking, insurance, manufacturing, trading, shipping and hotel sectors, while the maximum land holding is halved to 100 feddans.

The Syrians resent Egypt's overbearing attitude and regard Nasser's socialist measures as ruinous to their country's

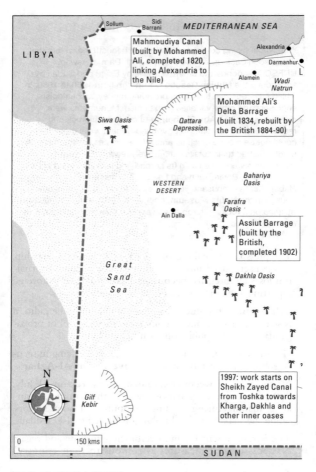

MEDITERRANEAN SEA

Sollum

Sidi Barrani

LIBYA

Alexandria

Darmanhur

Mahmoudiya Canal (built by Mohammed Ali, completed 1820, linking Alexandria to the Nile)

Alamein

Wadi Natrun

Mohammed Ali's Delta Barrage (built 1834, rebuilt by the British 1884-90)

Qattara Depression

WESTERN DESERT

Bahariya Oasis

Farafra Oasis

Ain Dalla

Assiut Barrage (built by the British, completed 1902)

Great Sand Sea

Dakhla Oasis

N

Gilf Kebir

1997: work starts on Sheikh Zayed Canal from Toshka towards Kharga, Dakhla and other inner oases

0   150 kms

SUDAN

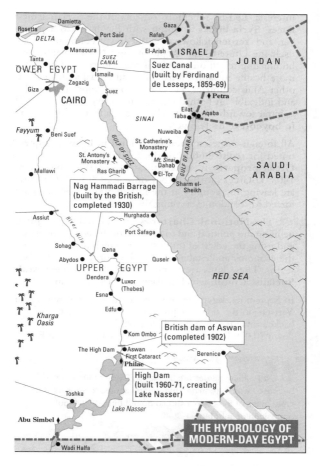

THE HYDROLOGY OF
MODERN-DAY EGYPT

Suez Canal
(built by Ferdinand
de Lesseps, 1859-69)

Nag Hammadi Barrage
(built by the British,
completed 1930)

British dam of Aswan
(completed 1902)

High Dam
(built 1960-71, creating
Lake Nasser)

Rosetta, Damietta, Gaza, Rafah, Port Said, DELTA, Tanta, Mansoura, El-Arish, ISRAEL, JORDAN, SUEZ CANAL, LOWER EGYPT, Ismaila, Giza, Zagazig, CAIRO, Suez, Petra, Eilat, Aqaba, Taba, SINAI, Fayyum, Beni Suef, Nuweiba, GULF OF SUEZ, St. Antony's Monastery, St. Catherine's Monastery, Dahab, GULF OF AQABA, Mt. Sinai, Mallawi, Ras Gharib, El-Tor, SAUDI ARABIA, Sharm el-Sheikh, Assiut, Hurghada, Port Safaga, Sohag, Qena, Abydos, UPPER EGYPT, Dendera, RED SEA, Luxor (Thebes), Esna, Quseir, Edfu, Kharga Oasis, Kom Ombo, The High Dam, Aswan, First Cataract, Berenice, Philae, Toshka, Lake Nasser, Abu Simbel, Wadi Halfa, River Nile

interests. Led by rebellious officers of the Syrian armed forces, **Syria** breaks its union with Egypt on 28 September, and **Yemen** follows suit. But Egypt continues to call itself the United Arab Republic, and Nasser blames this humiliating rebuff on bourgeois reactionaries and becomes more hostile towards monarchies and feudal authorities in other Arab countries. He also becomes more doctrinaire and inflexible in both domestic and foreign affairs as well as bitter towards the West, which starts a form of **economic boycott** of his regime.

All foreign-owned **agricultural land** in Egypt is sequestrated for redistribution to the fellahin in December. All **Greek property** is also confiscated – in 1940 there were 140,000 Greeks in Egypt but only 40,000 in 1961; these are leaving the country at the rate of 500 a week, and are forced to abandon everything they own.

1962 The **National Charter** is proclaimed on 30 June, defining the political and social aims of the government and endorsing the edicts of the past year, which have centralized the economy and established a highly bureaucratized public sector. These aims are to be furthered by the new **Arab Socialist Union**, which replaces the National Union.

In September, Egypt becomes involved in a civil war in the **Yemen** on the side of republican forces fighting the Saudi-backed royalists. The war will drag on for over a decade, tying down 70,000 Egyptian troops but without any gain to Egypt.

> ❝ Political parties are banned in Egypt at the moment because I was determined that our measures to improve the great mass of the people should be put through without opposition or sabotage. ❞
>
> Gamal Abdel Nasser, interviewed in the London *Sunday Times*, 1 July, 1962

> **❝** The old order had been torn down only to be replaced by a regime that harked back to Mameluke rule. Trusting no one, Nasser handed out fiefdoms to his officer friends: governorships of the provinces, directorships of nationalised companies, editorships of newspapers. Like a jealous sultan of old, he chiselled away the memory of his predecessors. Street names changed: Ismailia Square, the hub of [modern Cairo], became Tahrir (or Liberation) Square. King Fuad Avenue was now called 26 July Avenue, after the date of Farouk's departure into exile. The new government claimed all the achievements of the past as its own. Free public education, progressive labour laws, public health and housing, the Arab League; all these things were expanded under the new regime, which neglected to mention that they had been initiated by the old. With the school curriculum sanitised, a whole generation grew up ignorant of its own past, believing that Egypt before the revolution had been a sorry place of oppressed peasants lorded over by imperialist lackeys and wicked feudalists. **❞**
>
> Max Rodenbeck, *Cairo, The City Victorious* (1998)

1963 Nationalization continues apace: all Egypt's export cotton firms and ginning factories are nationalized in April; a further 200 industrial firms follow in August, while in November another 175 companies are taken into public ownership. By now almost the entire private sector has been eliminated: banks, insurance companies, transport, pharmaceuticals, wholesalers and distributors, export and import firms, and mining and manufacturing are all under state control. Rural and urban land are still private, but are placed under tight control. Nasser has reversed all the advances made in the Egyptian economy since the time of Mohammed Ali, turning Egypt into a totalitarian state devoid of enterprise, which sinks into heavy foreign debt.

1964 Nubia's last remaining inhabitants, who number 35,000, are evacuated as the first phase of the **Aswan High Dam** is completed, with the Soviet leader **Nikita Khrushchev** and Nasser attending the ceremony. In elections for a new **National Assembly**, all candidates have to be members of the Arab Socialist Union and half those elected have to be workers or small farmers. The cult of Nasser's personality begins: statues of the president proliferate, and it becomes almost obligatory to mention his name in speeches, newspaper articles, broadcasts and even advertisements, which tend to conclude their copy with 'Long life to our beloved President, Gamal Abdel Nasser. Long live Arab Socialism'.

1965 Aged 46, Nasser is **re-elected** president for another six years in a national plebiscite.

Ex-king Farouk dies in **Rome**, age 45.

Mustafa Nahas dies and his funeral procession in **Alexandria** attracts an ever-swelling multitude which chants 'Bury him with Saad Zaghloul'. The police react quickly and disperse the mourners with tear gas and fire hoses. The affair is not reported in the state-controlled Egyptian press.

1966 After another attempt on his life, Nasser orders the execution of **Sayyid Qutb**, the Muslim Brotherhood's leading ideologue.

Egypt and **Syria**, which are both supplied with arms by the Soviet Union, sign a mutual defence pact after Israeli and Syrian forces clash in the area of the **Sea of Galilee**. Regional tensions rise in the autumn, when Israel launches a major offensive against the **West Bank** in reprisal for Palestinian raids.

1967 Early in the year, it becomes apparent that the Egyptian **economy** is in dire trouble: foreign currency and gold reserves are very low, and the national airline is unable to fly a significant proportion of its fleet because it cannot pay for the spare parts from abroad.

Naguib Mahfouz (b. 1911)

Born in 1911 into a middle-class merchant family living in the old Fatimid heart of Cairo, Naguib Mahfouz has always imbued his novels with a strong sense of atmosphere and history. Indeed he conciously writes as a historian, but one who stands back from his text and lets his characters, with their many voices, re-create a collective memory of their society.

After completing his *Cairo Trilogy* just before Nasser's coup in July 1952, Mahfouz remained silent for several years, as though absorbing the regime's effect on Egyptian society, before publishing *Children of Gebelawi* in 1959 – only to find himself accused of apostasy and to see his novel banned for its religious views. The book also hinted at Mahfouz' disenchantment with Nasser's revolution, not an attitude shared at the time by the generality of Egyptian writers. Mahfouz took his criticisms of the regime further in *Miramar*, published early in 1967 before the Six Day War and set, significantly, in Alexandria, whose cosmopolitan and outward-looking society was in its death throes.

By now it was clear to Mahfouz that, apart from the specific political and economic mistakes made by Nasser's regime, the real damage lay in its moral failure, where rhetoric and reality bore no relation to one another, where terms like 'social equality', 'freedom of the individual' and 'the rule of law' had no meaning, and where cynicism, nihilism, self-interest and self-contempt were the result. Zohra, the peasant girl working at the Miramar pension, earns the admiration or resentment of the men around her by her desire to learn and emancipate herself – this eternally striving female figure appears in Mahfouz' novels under various names, where she represents Egypt. At the end of the book, as Zohra leaves the pension for what she hopes will be a better job, an old man long resident at the Miramar tells her, as Mahfouz may have said of Egypt during the last decade: 'Remember that you haven't wasted your time here. If you've come to know what is not good for you, you may also think of it all as having been a sort of magical way of finding out what is truly good for you.'

Acting on a Soviet intelligence report saying that Israel is mobilizing and plans to invade Syria, in May Nasser moves Egyptian troops into **Sinai** and closes the **Straits of Tiran** across the mouth of the Gulf of Aqaba, preventing Israeli shipping from Eilat reaching the Red Sea. In fact the intelligence report is false, but whether the information is manufactured by the Russians or is planted by the Israelis, its purpose is to provoke a war. Certainly Nasser's steps, which the Egyptians claim are meant as a deterrent to Israel, lead to Israeli mobilization, while at the end of the month **Jordan** signs a mutual defence agreement with Egypt.

The **Six Day War** begins on 5 June, with the Israeli air force destroying the Egyptian, Syrian and Jordanian air forces, mostly on the ground, while Israeli troops cross into **Sinai** and the **West Bank**. Without air cover, the Arab position is hopeless from the start. Cairo Radio falsely announces that 198 Israeli warplanes have been shot down. On 7 June, Israel captures the old city of **Jerusalem** from the Jordanians, who accept a ceasefire. The following day, Cairo Radio announces that the Israeli attack has collapsed and that the Egyptian army will soon be in Tel Aviv. In fact, Israel occupies the whole of **Sinai** and is entrenched on the east bank of the **Suez Canal**, leaving Egypt no choice but to sign a ceasefire.

Following a defeat infinitely worse than the poor performance of the Egyptian army under King Farouk during the

1948 Palestine war, Nasser broadcasts his **resignation** on 9 June. But after genuinely spontaneous mass demonstrations implore him to remain in office, Nasser decides to stay on.

On 10 June, Syria accepts a UN ceasefire after Israel occupies the **Golan Heights**.

1968 Chants of 'Down with the intelligence state!' and 'On 9 June we supported you, Nasser. Today we oppose you!' are heard during widespread student and worker demonstrations against the government in February. They complain too against corruption at the centres of power.

In April, tens of thousands of Copts and Muslims claim to have visions of the Virgin Mary hovering over the Coptic church in the northern Cairo suburb of **Zeitoun**, which they interpret as a consolation for Egypt's defeat in the 1967 war.

> **"** And then [after Nasser's resignation speech], from the twelfth storey of the house in which we were … we heard a swelling tumult, muffled and menacing – like an approaching storm, yet the weather was perfect … from all sides we saw people coming out of their houses like ants, and heads leaning out of windows. We went down. It was dusk and the city was half immersed in the darkness of the blackout. It was an extraordinary spectacle to see all those people hurrying from all sides, shouting, weeping, some wearing pyjamas, some barefoot, women in night dresses, children, all tormented by a suffering beyond endurance and imploring 'Nasser, do not leave us, we need you'. This was the tumult that had reached our ears like the roar of a storm. Women fell to the ground, like the weeping women of antiquity, or like the peasant women of Upper Egypt. Men burst into tears. **"**
>
> Eric Rouleau, the *Le Monde* correspondent in Cairo, 1967

The consequences of the Six Day War

Egypt's calamitous defeat in the Six Day War dealt a mortal blow to public confidence in Nasser's secular, socialist and pan-Arab ideals. The economy was plunged into crisis with the loss of such major income sources as tourism, the Sinai oil fields which were captured by the Israelis, and the Suez Canal, which was blocked and closed to shipping. Investment plummeted and development plans were halted as resources were diverted to rebuild the army and to provide for those displaced from the shattered Canal cities, while Egypt became dependent on subsidies from conservative pro-Western Arab oil states.

The country was already feeling the loss of expertise that went with the flight or expulsion of its large Greek and Jewish communities, but now they were joined by disenchanted Egyptians with marketable skills and university degrees, who emigrated en masse to Saudi Arabia, the Persian Gulf, Europe and North America in search of opportunities. Over the coming years their departure would be felt in Egypt's declining cultural, educational and professional standards, and in the shabbiness and neglect of the built environment. Amid a sense of despair that the nation-state had failed and that Egypt had lost control over its destiny, many Egyptians, both Christian and Muslim, turned to their religious roots. Where once the cry had been pan-Arabism, it now became **pan-Islamism**, with Saudi Arabian petrodollars helping to give it a fundamentalist complexion. Egyptian society became increasingly conservative and conformist; also more intolerant and violent. The imperative of fundamentalist Islam was to establish a theocratic state under **Islamic law** (sharia), an aim opposed by Egypt's Copts, who were vulnerable and became early targets, though soon it became clear that the fundamentalists' real aim was the overthrow of the Egyptian government.

In July, Nasser spends three weeks in the Soviet Union receiving treatment for **diabetes**, from which he has been suffering since 1956.

Egypt begins the **War of Attrition** in September, with cross-Canal artillery attacks and sporadic commando raids to unsettle the Israelis in **Sinai**. Israel replies in kind, driving a million people from the Canal towns, most of them crowding into Cairo.

> The Virgin holds a special place in the hearts of all Egyptians, Christian or Muslim – perhaps as an atavistic throwback to the goddess Isis or simply because she is the symbol of motherhood. Those who saw the apparition claimed that it was swathed in a blue light, others claimed to see the image of a woman wrapped in a mantle and carrying a baby. Thousands of Egyptians lined up outside the church every night until the small hours of the morning, hoping to catch a glimpse of the Virgin. Men and women who had lost sons, husbands and fathers during the [1967] war sought solace in the apparition. Miraculous cures were reported ... A wave of religious fervour swept the country. Coptic monasteries, which had been closing down for lack of candidates, now had waiting lists, and such long ones that they would only admit university students. Koran study groups mushroomed among all classes of society, who turned to religion for consolation. Even [Nasser] explained the defeat as God's will ...The message was clear. In spite of the defeat God was still on the side of the Egyptians and had sent the apparition as a consolation. At least, that was the way in which the population interpreted the apparition. Religious reform, along with other reforms, was necessary, and there was a palpable return to the study of matters religious and a visible resurgence of religious groups.

Afaf Lutfi al-Sayyid Marsot, *A Short History of Modern Egypt* (1985)

1969 Afflicted with circulatory problems and a severe heart condition as well as diabetes, Nasser appoints Anwar Sadat as his sole **vice-president** on 20 December, effectively making him his political heir.

1970 Nasser dies of a heart attack at the age of 52 on 28 September. His funeral is the largest seen in Egypt, with two million mourners filling the streets of **Cairo**, where he is buried in a neo-Mameluke mosque. **Anwar Sadat** (1918–81) is confirmed as president the following month.

12: Contemporary Egypt

1971–2003

After the debacle of the 1967 Six Day War, pan-Arab sentiment in Egypt began to be replaced by **Islamism**, which gained political significance and power from the oil wealth of fundamentalist Saudi Arabia. The banning of political parties had already turned religion into an important panacea for the difficulties of Egyptian daily life, and the new president **Anwar Sadat** used Islam to bolster his position as he reversed his predecessor's policies one after the other. Sadat quickly dropped the name 'United Arab Republic' with its reminder of Nasser's pan-Arab policy, adopting his own Egypt-first policy, which eventually culminated in peace with Israel. He also opened Egypt up to foreign and Arab investment, the open-door policy called **'infitah'**, which began the process of dismantling Nasser's centralized and nationalized economy. Sadat's rule was lighter than Nasser's and the security services less pervasive, but though his instincts were more liberal, he was unsure how to nurture democracy and allowed no real outlet in the press or political institutions for popular opinion. Instead, during the 1980s Egyptian society was gradually Islamized, with Sadat making a point of wearing the traditional *galabiyya* and cultivating a *zabiba* (prayer-bump) on his forehead.

Towards the end of his rule, Sadat became increasingly autocratic and was resented for the pleasure he took in being an international politician, while giving the impression of not wanting to concern himself directly with Egyptian problems. His helicopter became his sole means of transport, symbolizing his remoteness. On the eve of Sadat's assassination the Egyptian **economy** was flourishing, and there was a boom in consumer spending, in tourism and hotel building. But in the streets the visible strength of Islam was becoming more apparent as women wore the hejab concealing their hair and faces, and men wore full beards. Street hawkers were selling tickets to raise money for private mosque construction, while the government was granting tax rebates on the cost of building blocks of flats or offices if a space was set aside for public prayer, vastly increasing the presence of imams in almost every neighbourhood. Meanwhile, militants were plotting armed action with the intention of establishing an Islamic caliphate in Egypt. One of the assassination plotters was a colonel in military security, showing how far they had penetrated the army. Sadat moved late, too late to save his own life, but just soon enough to set in train a review of the security process which helped his successor, **Hosni Mubarak**, to restore order.

Mubarak carried the liberalization of Egypt's economy further, and moved towards greater democracy and freedom. Though criticism of the president and the army remained forbidden, by the mid-1980s Egypt had the liveliest and most varied press in the Arab world. The election laws were relaxed, allowing independents to win seats, which served as a means to bringing the banned **Muslim Brotherhood** into the assembly – where it became the largest opposition party. Mubarak's strategy was to permit such Islamists as the Brotherhood to become involved in the electoral process, provided they exercised their influence in bringing violent groups such as **Gamaa Islamiya** and **Egyptian Islamic Jihad** back into the legal fold. Despite Mubarak's appeasement, however, the 1990s became notable for their wave of Islamist terror and for a society that became increasingly fearful of any expression that could be interpreted as anti-Islamic. Many of Egypt's public figures were targeted, among them **Naguib Mahfouz**, the winner of the Nobel Prize for Literature.

But Egyptian history has broader patterns, too. At Toshka on Lake Nasser, 20 miles north of Abu Simbel, work has begun on a canal which will eventually be over 200 miles long and will link the Nile with the oases of the Western Desert. The oases form a region known as the **'New Valley'** – so called in the expectation that its development will some day match the valley of the Nile for fertility. If the scheme works then life will once again resume in desert lands west of the Nile, where the arts of agriculture which gave rise to Egyptian civilization began 11,000 years ago among the worship of unknown gods.

1971 In January, the **Aswan High Dam** is officially inaugurated by Egypt's new president, **Anwar Sadat**. The dam contains the equivalent in material of 17 pyramids the size of the Great Pyramid of Cheops.

Sadat begins his **'Egypt-first'** policy in September, when he drops the name of United Arab Republic, a hangover from Nasser's pan-Arab enthusiasm for union with Syria. The official name of the country now becomes the **Arab Republic of Egypt**.

In December, a **treason trial** hands out heavy sentences to 91 defendants accused of trying to overthrow the state; among them are Sadat's vice-president, his interior minister, his head of the security service, his minister of information and his minister of war. In fact, all these men had long served under Nasser and are probably guilty of nothing more than protesting against Sadat's increasingly personal leadership.

1972 On 18 July, Sadat expels **Soviet military advisers** as a threat to the stability of Egypt. In doing so, his popularity immediately rises, as he strikes a responsive nationalist chord among the Egyptian people.

The Aswan High Dam: promises and warnings

Completed in 1902, the British dam four miles downstream from Aswan regulated the flow of the Nile during the course of the year. But the Aswan High Dam's reservoir, **Lake Nasser**, reaches back 300 miles to the Second Cataract in Sudan, and can store surplus water over a number of years, balancing low floods against high ones. This has already averted drought, famine and starvation in Egypt, as poor African rainfalls in recent decades have seen the Nile fall to its lowest levels in 350 years. The extra **hydroelectric energy** generated by the dam has also brought electricity to every village in Egypt and has helped towards the industrialization of the country.

In 1997, work began on the **Sheikh Zayed Canal**, which runs from Lake Nasser via the Toshka depression 20 miles north of Abu Simbel towards the oases of Kharga, Dakhla and Farafra. The intention is to turn the Western Desert into a **'New Valley'**, which would increase Egypt's arable area by 28 percent, and where there are plans to grow cotton, wheat and early-season grapes and citrus fruits. But some experts have expressed serious doubts about the viability of the New Valley project, and indeed the unintended consequences of the High Dam are a warning. The dam holds back the silt that would normally be deposited on Egypt's fields, so that artificial fertilizers have to be used instead, with a damaging effect on Egypt's wildlife. The higher ground water level raises salts to the surface of fields, where, no longer washed away by the annual flood, they are causing large areas of the Delta to become infertile. The dam has serious implications for Egyptian military and foreign policy, too, as it leaves Egypt at the mercy of any foreign power capable hitting the dam with a nuclear weapon – which would cause the drowning of the entire Nile Valley, including Cairo.

The growth of Muslim and Coptic activism since the 1967 war leads to **sectarian clashes** in many parts of Egypt in the summer, culminating in attacks on Christian homes and shops and the burning of a Coptic church in November.

1973 On 6 October, during the Muslim holy month of Ramadan and the Jewish observance of Yom Kippur, Egypt launches a surprise attack across the Suez Canal and captures Israel's forward position, the Bar-Lev line, in **Sinai**. The opening phase of the **October War** is an unprecedented Egyptian success that breaks the myth of Israeli military invincibility and erases the humiliation of 1967. Simultaneously, Syrian troops enter the Israeli-occupied **Golan Heights**.

With the October War still in progress, the Arab member states of the **Organization of Petroleum Exporting Countries (OPEC)** meet in Kuwait on 17 October and use the **'oil weapon'** against nations seen as overtly supportive of Israel. OPEC stops oil exports to the United States and the Netherlands (this policy lasts well into 1974), and reduces overall exports by 25 percent. Oil prices soar, and a **worldwide recession** ensues, but over the next four years Egypt receives $27 billion in aid from Gulf Arab countries.

> ❝ The October 1973 War was a major watershed in the development of the Egyptian political system under Sadat. Sadat's ability to take credit for the war, and portray himself as the 'Hero of the Crossing', greatly enhanced his personal legitimacy and made him a leader in his own right ... Sadat used the political capital won in the war and the opportunities created by it to transform Egypt's foreign policy and economic strategy ... His subsequent reversal of Nasser's priorities was of the magnitude of a 'counter-revolution' from above ... [Sadat] produced a foreign policy opening to the West and a corresponding economic Infitah which altered the balance of power in state and society, permitting a virtual 'restoration' of the bourgeoisie. ❞
>
> Raymond A Hinnebusch Jr, *Egyptian Politics under Sadat* (1985)

The singer Umm Kulsoum, pictured here in the 1930s, was the voice of Egypt and the entire Arab world

An Israeli counter-thrust on 18 October crosses the **Suez Canal** south of Ismailia and advances towards **Cairo**. Four days later, all sides accept a **ceasefire** arranged by the United States and the Soviet Union. The war is a political triumph for Sadat, giving him a free hand to alter fundamentally Egyptian domestic and foreign policy, and making possible his later visit to Jerusalem.

1974 With the enactment of **Law 43**, Sadat begins dismantling Nasser's centralized socialist state. The law establishes the *infitah* ('open-door') policy, which aims at attracting foreign (both Western and Arab) and local investment to revive the private sector, though a byproduct is growing income inequality and resentment towards the newly rich with their glaring displays of wealth.

1975 **Umm Kulsoum** dies in Cairo, where the streets fill with well over two million mourners – surpassing even Nasser's funeral.

In April, Sadat appoints his air force chief **Hosni Mubarak** to the vice-presidency.

In an attempt to seize arms to overthrow Sadat and establish an Islamic state, a fundamentalist group called the **Islamic Liberation Organization** attacks Egypt's Military Technical Academy, killing eleven and wounding twenty-seven.

The **Suez Canal**, closed since the 1967 war, is reopened in June.

In September, Egypt and Israel agree to begin disengaging in **Sinai**: Egypt recovers the Sinai oil fields and the Suez Canal, and strategic areas of Sinai are demilitarized.

1976 Sadat initiates a degree of **political pluralism** by allowing the establishment of three platforms of the left, the right and the centre within the **Arab Socialist Union**, the sole party in the country.

1977 On 17 January, the government announces that subsidies on basic commodities such as flour, rice, sugar, cigarettes and butane gas – which currently cost $1.4 billion a year – are to be halved. In the following days, **'Bread Riots'** erupt in Cairo, Alexandria and towns

> "They spoke to me again of you, reminded me, reminded me.
> They woke the fire of longing in my heart and in my eyes.
> They took me back to the past,
> With its ease, with its joys and its sweetness, and its pain and harshness.
> And I remembered how happy I was with you,
> And O my soul I remember why we came apart."
>
> *Fakkaruni (They Made Me Remember)*, a song recorded in 1964 by Umm Kulsoum

around Egypt. The offices of the **Arab Socialist Union** in Alexandria, formerly housing the cotton and stock exchanges, are burnt and later pulled down. Muslim fundamentalists call for the violent overthrow of the state. For the first time since January 1952, the army is called out on the streets to quell a civil disturbance, which leaves 80 dead and 800 wounded around the country. The decision to cut the subsidies is rescinded.

On 9 November, Sadat announces in the People's Assembly his readiness to go to **Jerusalem** to bring peace between Israel and Egypt. Sadat visits the city on 17

President Anwar Sadat with vice-president Hosni Mubarak, who succeeded him after Sadat was assassinated by Islamist fanatics

November and speaks at the Knesset, in effect welcoming Israel to the Middle East. In the talks that follow, Israel agrees to its full withdrawal from **Sinai** but disappoints Egypt by offering nothing but a vague autonomy to Palestinians living on the **West Bank** of the River Jordan.

1978 The Arab Socialist Union is disbanded and the three platforms become fully fledged political parties, the dominant one being the government's own **National Democratic Party**, which can always secure a majority. The **Wafd** is also revived.

On 17 September, Egypt and Israel sign accords for peace in the presence of American president Jimmy Carter at **Camp David**. The accords provide for a new framework for arriving at a Middle East settlement between Egypt and Israel that addresses the Palestine question.

1979 To the anger of Islamic fundamentalists in Egypt, Sadat gives sanctuary to the **Shah of Iran** after he is overthrown by an Islamic revolution. Sadat announces that Egypt is prepared to take the place of Iran as America's guardian of order in the region, and Egypt becomes the world's second largest recipient (after Israel) of American economic aid, reaching $1 billion a year.

The Soviet Union invades **Afghanistan**, and the CIA trains and arms the 'mujahedin' (Islamic fighters) in an effort to resist communism. Young Muslim men from all over the Islamic world, among them 2000 Egyptians, begin going to Afghanistan to join what will end as a victorious jihad against the Soviet infidels.

On 26 March, Egypt and Israel sign their **peace treaty** against a background of violent left-wing and Islamic fundamentalist opposition. In response to this latest instance of Sadat's 'Egypt-first' policy, other Arab leaders (whom Sadat calls 'dwarfs') exclude Egypt from the **Arab League**.

1980 A referendum held on 22 May approves amendments to the **constitution**, allowing Sadat to remain in office indefinitely and, in what he sees as a gesture to gain the support of the fundamentalists, to make Islamic *sharia* law the principal source of legislation.

1981 Sectarian riots between Muslims and Copts on 17 June in **Cairo** leave at least 20 dead and 100 injured. Following continued disturbances, both sectarian and in opposition to Sadat's reconciliation with Israel, over 1500 people are arrested on 5 September, including journalists, lawyers, politicians and Muslim clerics. Coptic clerics are arrested, too, for their aggressive response against intimidation by Muslim fanatics, among them the dynamic Coptic pope **Shenouda III**, the 117th patriarch since St Mark, who is incarcerated at a monastery in the Wadi Natrun. Sadat, who thought he had succeeded in using the Islamists for his own ends, now sees them as a serious threat and announces that he will devote all his time to countering the fundamentalist menace.

Army officers who are members of **Egyptian Islamic Jihad**, a secret fundamentalist group, **assassinate Anwar**

> ❝ I killed him but I am not guilty. I did what I did for the sake of religion and of my country. I killed the pharaoh. ❞
>
> Lieutenant Khaled Islambouli, leader of Sadat's assassins

The assassination of Anwar Sadat

The news of Anwar Sadat's murder was met with silence in the streets of Cairo, and the reaction throughout Egypt was generally one of indifference. Most Egyptians felt that their president had not cared about them: while Sadat had bathed in Western admiration, in Egypt there was widespread resentment at his autocratic style of government, and many ridiculed his pomposity. In his long and meandering public speeches, he liked to describe himself as the 'Pious President' and the 'Father of the Great Egyptian People', but he gave the impression of being above the nation, not of it.

Not that his killers enjoyed much sympathy for their cause – there were no demonstrations in their favour when they were executed the following April. Their leader was **Lieutenant Khaled Islambouli**, who was born in Mallawi in Upper Egypt, where both his father and his uncle were lawyers, while he himself had graduated from the military academy with honours. Islambouli and his fellow conspirators, all high-ranking officers from notable provincial families, were just the sort of people who had promising futures within the existing order, yet Islamic Egyptian Jihad had drawn up detailed plans for an Islamic caliphate with six regional councils, all in Upper Egypt apart from one at Giza, and expected that Sadat's murder would touch off fundamentalist uprisings throughout the country. In fact in the aftermath of the assassination there were only localized outbreaks, the major one in **Assiut** in Upper Egypt, a lesser one in **Mansoura** in the Delta. The new president, Hosni Mubarak, immediately arrested a further 2000 people and imposed a state of emergency that remains in force to this day.

Islambouli was able to say he had killed Sadat but was not guilty of a crime because his group had obtained a *fatwa* (ruling) from a blind Egyptian cleric, **Sheikh Omar Abdel Rahman**, stating that it was lawful to kill a ruler who had disobeyed the ordinances of God. The blind sheikh, accused of having links with both Egyptian Islamic Jihad and another terrorist fundamentalist organization, Gamaa Islamiya, then fled to America, where he has since been jailed for his part in the 1993 attempt to blow up the World Trade Center in New York.

Sadat at a Cairo military parade ground during the eighth anniversary celebrations of the October War on 6 October. Vice-President **Hosni Mubarak** (b. 1928) assumes command and is confirmed as president in a referendum later in the month. Sadat is buried in a concrete pyramid a few yards from where he fell.

1982 On 25 April, President Hosni Mubarak hoists the Egyptian flag over **Sinai** as Israel evacuates the peninsula.

1984 Egypt holds its first relatively free **elections** since 1952; the banned but tolerated Muslim Brotherhood takes part by placing several of its candidates on the Wafd party lists. This follows on Hosni Mubarak's policy of dealing with Islamic fundamentalism by drawing a distinction between the 'moderates' who agree to work within the law and the 'radicals' or 'activists' who rely on violence to achieve their aim of an Islamic state. Mubarak offers the moderates toleration if they will take responsibility for bringing the radicals back within the legal fold. The **Muslim Brotherhood** agrees to work within the legal system and is permitted to work for an Islamic state through educational and publishing activities, and though it remains banned as a political party it is permitted to field candidates in elections, provided that they are sponsored by one of the legal political parties.

1985 **Pope Shenouda III**, one of the religious leaders arrested by Sadat, is released from detention in time to celebrate Coptic Orthodox Christmas in Cairo at midnight on 6–7 January.

The **Muslim Brotherhood** embarks on a political strategy of systematically and openly infiltrating other parties, with the intention of becoming the leading opposition group in the Assembly.

Acting on a tip-off, police raid a bookshop near al-Azhar mosque and seize 2000 copies of a work that a court goes on to ban, describing it as 'negating the morality of Egyptian society'; the book is *The Thousand and One Nights*.

1986 A **mutiny** on 25–26 February by 17,000 conscripts of the Central Security Forces in Cairo and at their barracks near the Pyramids of Giza is quelled by the army on the orders of Field Marshal **Abu Ghazala**, the defence minister. His decisive action makes it clear that he is the second most powerful man in the country, and that Mubarak's regime depends on the army's continuing approval.

1987 Palestinians begin a six-year *intifada* (uprising) against the Israeli occupation of the West Bank and Gaza.

Mubarak is **elected** president for a second term, while in the National Assembly the **Muslim Brotherhood** succeeds in its aim to become the main opposition to the government's National Democratic Party. The Brotherhood uses its legislative power to press for *sharia* to be the sole source of law for Egypt.

UNESCO launches an international fund-raising appeal in support of the Egyptian government's plan to build a new world-class **library** at Alexandria.

The **International Monetary Fund** releases figures showing that Egypt is the largest debtor nation in the Middle East and Africa. In part this is due to the government's major social welfare programme, which includes food and energy subsidies costing $8 billion a year. The memory of the 1977 Bread Riots makes Mubarak loath to interfere, while the West is concerned that destabilization of the government will harm Egypt's accords with Israel and have an adverse effect on Western policy generally in the Middle East.

1988 Since the completion of the High Dam at Aswan the Nile no longer lays down an annual layer of silt, so that for the first time in Egypt's history mud is an exhaustible resource, and building with **mud brick** is banned.

CORBIS

Naguib Mahfouz, the Arab world's most successful and best-known novelist, won the Nobel Prize for Literature in 1988

Novelist **Naguib Mahfouz**, author of *The Cairo Trilogy*, *Children of Gebelawi*, *Miramar* and numerous other works, wins the Nobel Prize for Literature.

1989 Egypt rejoins the **Arab League**.

An extensive **metro system** begins operating beneath the streets of Cairo.

1990 Saddam Hussein's Iraq invades **Kuwait** in August.

1991 In the January **Gulf War**, a coalition led by the United States and including Egypt drives Iraqi forces out of Kuwait.

1992 In March, joint Egyptian and French underwater **archeological investigations** begin in and around the Eastern Harbour of Alexandria, where over the coming years archeologists find remains of the fallen Pharos and the Ptolemies' royal palaces, which since ancient times had subsided into the sea.

On 8 June, **Farag Fouda**, an outspoken secularist writer, is shot dead in Cairo by a member of **Gamaa Islamiya** (Islamic Group). On 30 September, the group warns **tourists** not to visit Egypt.

An **earthquake** in October causes damage to medieval mosques and other monuments in Cairo, destroys thousands of homes and kills 500 people – divine retribution for Egypt's godless state, say Islamic fundamentalists.

1993 **Egyptian Islamic Jihad** ceases terrorist operations within Egypt, while, under the leadership of the Egyptian surgeon **Ayman el Zawahari**, a faction of the group joins up with Saudi millionaire Osama bin Laden's **Al Qaeda** ('The Base') in Sudan and then Afghanistan, where it vows to carry out operations on an international scale.

On 7 January, a bomb is thrown near a tourist bus in **Cairo**, the first attack in the capital. There are no injuries. On 26 February, another bomb goes off in a Cairo cafe, killing two foreigners and an Egyptian.

Farag Fouda's battle against 'dark thought'

During the 1980s and early 1990s, when Egypt's leading political, intellectual and cultural figures – not to mention the Egyptian government – were appeasing the Islamists, the writer **Farag Fouda** waged an almost lone battle against what he called the 'thinkers of darkness', the fundamentalists who claimed that 'Islam is the solution'. A champion of civil liberties, Fouda joined the Wafd Party in 1978 but left in 1984 when it betrayed its liberal heritage by entering into an electoral alliance with the Muslim Brotherhood. He argued that the Brotherhood remained hostile to democracy and plurality, and that it was behind the militant Islamic groups that were resorting to violence.

After 1984, Fouda wrote eight books exposing the bogus piety of political Islam and describing its destructive effect on intellectual integrity. He wrote against the Islamists for attacking artists and art and for inciting their followers in the universities to ban music concerts and destroy statues, and he foresaw a day when Islamists might destroy statues of Rameses II, Saad Zaghloul and other great Egyptian figures – foreshadowing the **Taleban**'s destruction of venerable statues of the Buddha in Afghanistan. In the late 1980s, when Gamaa Islamiya began attacking Copts, Fouda blamed Al-Azhar for teaching that Muslims can only have true affection for other Muslims, and that it was *halal* ('permitted') to attack people of other beliefs. 'The worst thing that has plagued our nation', Fouda wrote, 'is the entrance of the religious scholars into politics, which has led to strange opinions and perverted thoughts.' In 1992 a council of scholars at Al-Azhar branded Fouda 'a follower of the non-religious current and extremely hostile to anything Islamic' – a judgement cited a few months later by his murderer, a member of Gamaa Islamiya.

Also in February, an attempt is made to blow up the **World Trade Center** in New York; the blind **Sheikh Omar Abdel Rahman**, who absolved Sadat's assassins and who is the spiritual guide to Gamaa Islamiya, is involved in the conspiracy.

Israel and the **Palestine Liberation Organization (PLO)** sign the **Oslo Accords** in September, agree upon mutual recognition, and begin the peace process in which Egypt plays an important part. The Palestinian *intifada*, which began in 1987, ends.

Mubarak begins his **third term** of office in October.

1994 Nobel prize-winning author **Naguib Mahfouz** almost loses his life when he is stabbed by an Islamist after condemning the *fatwa* issued by Ayatollah Khomeini, leader of the Iranian revolution, to kill Salman Rushdie for writing *The Satanic Verses*.

1995 The assassination of Israeli prime minister **Yitzhak Rabin** by a Jewish fundamentalist is followed by the election of **Binyamin Netanyahu**'s hard-right government.

A court in **New York** convicts Sheikh Omar Abdel Rahman of conspiracy to blow up the World Trade Center, and various bridges and tunnels in the city.

Underwater archeological expeditions are revealing much of ancient Alexandria, which slipped into the Mediterranean after earthquakes and subsidence

Jet-age hajj: Muslims sometimes like to celebrate their pilgrimage to Mecca by painting scenes from it on their houses

In June, President Mubarak is the target of an Islamist **assassination attempt** in Addis Ababa, Ethiopia, upon his arrival at the summit of the Organization of African Unity.

1996 After publishing his revisionist studies of the Koran and the history of Islam, **Nasr Abu Zaid**, a Cairo University professor, has his conviction for apostasy upheld by the High Court, which orders him, as he is no longer considered to be a Muslim, to divorce his wife, **Ibtihal Younes**, also a professor at the university. Facing harassment and death threats in Egypt, the couple flee to Holland.

1997 As Egypt's population reaches 65 million, on 9 January President Mubarak inaugurates the **New Valley scheme**, which is to draw water from Lake Nasser and bring huge areas of the Western Desert to life.

Jailed leaders of Gamaa Islamiya call for a **truce** with the government in March, saying that violence is contrary to Islam.

On 18 September, gunmen kill six foreigners and three Egyptians outside the Egyptian Museum in **Cairo**. The violence reaches a peak in November, when six members of a Gamaa Islamiya splinter group kill 58 foreign tourists and four Egyptians at the mortuary temple of Hatshepsut across the river from **Luxor**. Tourist numbers fall immediately and take two years to recover, causing hardship to those one in five Egyptians directly or indirectly involved in tourism.

1998 The 22-member Arab League approves a pan-Arab **counter-terrorism treaty**, providing for cooperation in extraditing and cracking down on militants. It makes clear that it does not regard the Lebanese-based **Hezbollah** or the Palestinian **Hamas** to be terrorist groups, and calls for sanctions against Israel for what it describes as 'state terrorism' against **Palestinians**. The Saudi Arabian-born **Osama bin Laden** announces the formation of the **World Islamic Front for Jihad against Jews and Crusaders**, which declares a holy war against the United States. Bin Laden's right-hand man is the Egyptian Jihad leader **Ayman el Zawahari**, while other members of Bin Laden's umbrella group include **Mohammed Islambouli**, brother of Anwar Sadat's assassin. In August, Al Qaeda groups, including Saudis and Egyptians, blow up the US embassies in **Kenya** and **Tanzania**.

1999 Ayman el Zawahari's Jihad faction announces that it possesses **chemical and biological weapons** that it will use against Israel and the United States.

> ❝ We are not terrorists; we have not used bullets or machine guns, but we have stopped an enemy of Islam from poking fun at our religion. No one will even dare to think about harming Islam again. ❞
>
> Sheikh Youssef al-Badri, the cleric whose preachings inspired the case against Abu Zaid

Mubarak begins his **fourth term** of office in October.

2000 In September, the Palestinians begin a second *intifada* against the Israelis following a provocative visit by Ariel Sharon to the al-Aqsa mosque in **Jerusalem**. Sharon, the Israeli defence minister, is known to favour further illegal Jewish settlements in the Occupied Territories.

Egypt and 11 September

Osama bin Laden was the charismatic Saudi millionaire behind the 11 September attacks, but the strategist and ideologue behind Bin Laden was the Egyptian **Ayman el Zawahari**. Bin Laden's narrow aim was to establish a theocratic state in Saudi Arabia until Zawahari convinced him that there was a larger battle to be fought by attacking American interests and those of other infidels everywhere in the world.

Zawahari was born into a prominent provincial family of politicians, doctors and religious sheikhs, and himself became a surgeon, having already joined the Muslim Brotherhood at 15. During the Afghan jihad, Zawahari served the mujahedin as a doctor, and by the 1990s he emerged as leader of Egyptian Islamic Jihad, which had earlier assassinated President Sadat. Then as head of EIJ's international faction, he returned to Afghanistan and joined forces with Bin Laden. Fifteen of the nineteen hijackers on 11 September were Saudis, but the pilot of the first plane to hit the World Trade Center was **Mohammed Atta**, a member of EIJ and the son of a well-off Cairo lawyer.

After 11 September, the government cracked down more heavily than ever on Islamic groups – giving rise to accusations of illegal detentions, of detainees being tortured and sometimes beaten to death in custody, of people disappearing altogether, and of families too terrified to enquire or complain. The number of political prisoners in Egypt now stands at 20,000, the same as in Nasser's time.

In December, **Egypt**, **Lebanon** and **Syria** sign an initial agreement for a $1 billion project to build a **gas pipeline** that will transport Egyptian natural gas under the Mediterranean to the northern Lebanese port of Tripoli, which is also to be linked to Syria. Another pipeline will carry gas to Turkey and on to European markets.

2001 Presidents **Bashar al-Assad** of Syria and **Hosni Mubarak** of Egypt, together with **King Abdullah of Jordan**, inaugurate a $300 million **electricity line** linking the grids of the three countries in March.

On 11 September, Al-Qaeda suicide crews hijack American airliners and use them as flying bombs to destroy the twin towers of the World Trade Center in **New York** and damage the Pentagon in **Washington DC**, killing around 3000 people.

Figures released in October show that in the immediate aftermath of the 11 September attacks, Egypt suffers a 50 percent fall in **tourist numbers** – a devastating blow, as tourism is a mainstay of the economy, contributing 11.3 percent to gross domestic product and generating $4.3 billion in 2000. These figures are not expected to recover for two years.

2002 On 30 July, sixteen leading members of the **Muslim Brotherhood**, mostly academics, doctors and engineers, are convicted by the Supreme Military Court and each jailed for three to five years. Though the Brotherhood is banned, it continues to be tolerated by the government on the principle that it has been around for so long that it has acquired a tired and unfashionable image. With seventeen seats in the National Assembly, the Brotherhood is the largest opposition party in the country.

The **Bibliotheca Alexandrina**, the new Alexandria Library, is inaugurated on 16 October.

Censorship and the new Alexandria Library

Designed in the shape of a solar disc rising at an angle along the city's Mediterranean shore, the new Alexandria Library is a deliberate architectural statement that the ancient powerhouse of knowledge has been reborn in modern Egypt. The Library's priority is to accumulate collections on Egypt and especially Alexandria and its ancient Library, but with the Mediterranean and the Arab world also emphasized.

Given its capacity to house eight million volumes, over ten times as many as its famous predecessor, and containing a reading room (the largest in the world), built to accommodate thousands of scholars on seven cascading levels, and with plans to make much of its material available worldwide over the Internet, the library has the potential to be a major force for intellectual advance. But nothing was yet available over the Internet when the new Library opened, and its shelves were largely empty due to lack of funds.

These are difficulties that can be put right with time and money, but the real problem Alexandria's new Library faces is **censorship**. In recent years, Egypt's writers and scholars have been persecuted and even murdered, while books and films are routinely banned. Egypt's best existing library is at the American University in Cairo, an institution accredited in the United States, but which in recent years has been forced by the Egyptian government censor to remove hundreds of titles from its shelves, variously for discussing sex, criticizing President Mubarak or offending Muslim fundamentalists' views of the Prophet Mohammed; one of the banned titles was N.J. Dawood's English translation of the Koran, published by Penguin Books. When Suzanne Mubarak, the president's wife and patron of the Bibliotheca Alexandrina, was asked for reassurance that the Library would not suffer from the same kind of censorship, she answered 'Inshallah' – God willing.

Books

Books

T he range of works on Egypt is vast, particularly on ancient Egypt, though the Old and New Kingdoms are far better covered than other periods. There is a scarcity of writing about the Arab and Turkish periods, and the situation only improves after Napoleon's expedition at the end of the 18th century. The following list, while highly selective, does represent all periods, and though readily available titles have been favoured, some aspects of Egyptian history are represented by titles that will require some searching out at libraries. Wherever the title in question is in print, the UK publisher is given first, followed by the US publisher. Where a title is available in one country only, the country in question is indicated. Where a title is published by a single firm in both territories, only the name of one is given.

General ancient history

John Baines and Jaromir Malek, *Atlas of Ancient Egypt* (Phaidon, o/p; Checkmark). An atlas, yes, with superb maps and site plans, but also a wide-ranging encyclopedia on religion, art, pyramid building, burial customs, Nubia, women in society and so on, by two leading authorities in Egyptology.

James Henry Breasted, *A History of Egypt from the Earliest Times to the Persian Conquest* (Simon Publications; 2 vols). This first attempt at an all-encompassing narrative history of ancient Egypt down to 525 BC was first published in New York in 1905 and has gone through subsequent editions there and in London. Breasted, a great American Egyptologist, presents a vigorous and highly readable historical review which largely compensates for the out-of-dateness of his detail.

Rosalie and Antony E. David, *A Biographical Dictionary of Ancient Egypt* (Routledge; Univ of Oklahoma). A useful Who's Who of Egyptians down to the Arab conquest in the 7th century AD, and also covering important foreigners with whom they came into contact as well as classical writers who left vivid descriptions of the country.

Sir Alan Gardiner, *Egypt of the Pharaohs, An Introduction* (Oxford University Press). Though dedicated to Breasted, Gardiner's book (published in 1961) is more than an updating of narrative history – rather it emphasizes how knowledge of the past is achieved through the study and interpretation of ancient texts, many of which are quoted, allowing Egyptians of the past to speak for themselves.

Herodotus, *The Histories* (Penguin). Herodotus travelled to Egypt in about 447 BC, and the material he gathered there fills a good third of his great history of the Greeks and their world. He spoke with priests, asked how the pyramids had been built, enquired into the process of embalming the dead, observed the habits of peasant men and women, and sought the origins of the Nile, to present a vivid ethnographical and historical account of a country, unreliable but wonderful for its insatiable curiosity.

Barry J. Kemp, *Ancient Egypt, Anatomy of a Civilization* (Routledge). Modern Egyptologists, rather than simply writing history, tend to prefer to interpret it with tendentious or moralizing results, but in this case the effect is stimulating.

Michael Rice, *Egypt's Legacy, The Archetypes of Western Civilization* (Routledge). Another go at interpreting what the ancient Egyptians were up to, this time with the benefit of some Jungian insights which can be stimulating – indeed, entertaining – but leave you unsure if Rice is entirely sound on matters strictly Egyptological.

Ian Shaw (ed.), *The Oxford History of Ancient Egypt* (Oxford University Press). Published in 2000, this is the latest attempt to encompass the whole of ancient Egyptian history up to the end of the Roman period in a single volume. Chapters are arranged chronologically, though each chapter is more an essay than a strict narrative and does not always cover as much ground as one would like before fluttering off into some discursive realm. The predynastic and dynastic periods are handled very well, the Graeco-Roman period less so.

Aspects of ancient Egypt

Karl W. Butzer, *Early Hydraulic Civilization in Egypt* (University of Chicago Press). A fascinating if specialized examination of the effect of the Nile and its annual floods on the fortunes of Egypt's dynasties, and how flood levels, flood control and irrigation techniques directly determined agricultural productivity, population size and national wealth.

I.E.S. Edwards, *The Pyramids of Egypt* (Penguin). Written by the late Keeper of Egyptian Antiquities at the British Museum, this definitive, orthodox account of what the pyramids were for and how they were built is an antidote to the theories of amateurs and cranks.

Henri Frankfort, *Ancient Egyptian Religion: An interpretation* (Dover). Frankfort shows how the bewildering diversity and contradictions of Egyptian religion resolve into certain common and comprehensible themes, as meaningful today as in the ancient past.

George Hart, *A Dictionary of Egyptian Gods and Goddesses* (Routledge). As close to exhaustive as a pocket-sized volume can ever be, this comprehensive god-spotters' guide shows what they looked like, provides potted biographies and takes you through their various pseudonyms, guises and powers.

Erik Hornung, *Idea into Image* (Rizzoli; Timken). The ancient Egyptians, like ourselves, asked themselves questions about being and non-being, the meaning of death, the nature of the cosmos and of man, and about the basis of human society and the legitimization of power. In these essays Horning shows how they knew that their answers could never be definitive, so that the provisional, the flexible and the pluralistic became the essence of their philosophical outlook.

Lise Manniche, *Sexual Life in Ancient Egypt* (Kegan Paul). If the popular perception of ancient Egyptians is that they were humourless and obsessed with death, the blame lies with dull and puritanical museum keepers and censorious modern authors. The truth is that the ancient Egyptians were at least as naughty as anyone else – as you might have expected of a people in a warm and sunny climate who went around more than half-naked all their lives.

Kurt Mendelssohn, *The Riddle of the Pyramids* (Thames and Hudson, o/p). Though not an Egyptologist, Mendelssohn was emeritus professor of physics at Oxford when he wrote this book, which proposes that the sheer scale of pyramid building demanded that they be constructed in a continuous production line process whether or not there was a specific demand for any particular one. Furthermore, he argues, this process, transcending the lifetime and power of any individual, served to create the infrastructure, bureaucratic and institutional, of the Egyptian state. Though an amateur, Mendelssohn is far from being a crank, and his ideas excited serious argument in the academic journals.

A.J. Spencer, *Death in Ancient Egypt* (Penguin, o/p). As well as examining the varieties of mummies, tombs and funeral rites, the reasons for their existence, and how they changed in response to religious developments, this book also shows how modern Egyptological techniques are able to trace family relationships among the dead, identify prevalent diseases and sometimes provide complete pathological case histories of individuals.

The predynastic period

Michael A. Hoffman, *Egypt Before the Pharaohs: The prehistoric foundations of Egyptian civilization* (Knopf, o/p). Thirty years ago, very little was available on the predynastic period; now it is one of the fastest growing areas of Egyptological research, and thanks very largely to Hoffman it is also gaining public attention. As Hoffman himself writes, he has attempted to do for prehistory what Breasted did for the history of ancient Egypt – that is, to produce a first readable narrative account of the roots of Egyptian culture during those thousands of years before the first pharaoh ascended his throne.

The Old Kingdom

No history specific to the Old Kingdom has yet been written, so readers should refer to the relevant section of general histories, such as Barry Kemp's *Ancient Egypt: Anatomy of a Civilization* or *The Oxford History of Ancient Egypt* (see p.396).

The First Intermediate Period, the Middle Kingdom and the Second Intermediate Period

For the First and Second Intermediate Periods, a general history is again recommended. For the Middle Kingdom, Herbert Winlock's *The Rise and Fall of the Middle Kingdom* (o/p), written in the 1940s by the Egyptologist who did so much of the original fieldwork for the period, remains the best general history.

The New Kingdom

Cyril Aldred, *Akhenaten, Pharaoh of Egypt* (Thames & Hudson, o/p). This is a comprehensive, authoritative and enthralling account of Akhenaten and his wife Nefertiti, of their revolutionary sun disc religion and the extraordinary art it produced, and of the calamitous aftermath.

Erik Hornung, *The Valley of the Kings* (Timken, o/p). A beautifully photographed and learned tour through the tombs of the Valley of the Kings by the noted Swiss Egyptologist.

K.A. Kitchen, *Pharaoh Triumphant, The Life and Times of Ramesses II* (Aris & Phillips). Written by the eminent expert on Rameses the Great, this has all the readability and narrative drive of a good historical biography, and is no less vivid for treating a subject who lived over three thousand years ago.

David O'Connor and Eric H. Cline, *Amenhotep III: Perspectives on his reign* (University of Michigan). A multifaceted examination of the times of

Amenophis III during the apogee of the New Kingdom and the Egyptian Empire.

The Third Intermediate and Late Periods

K.A. Kitchen, *The Third Intermediate Period in Egypt* (Aris and Phillips, o/p). Now in its third edition, this book is the definitive source, but the general reader is best advised to go to the relevant chapters of a general history.

Graeco-Roman Egypt

Edwyn Bevan, *A History of Egypt under the Ptolemaic Dynasty* (Ares, o/p). Though undeniably useful, this survey is somewhat dry.

Alan K. Bowman, *Egypt after the Pharaohs, 332 BC–AD 642* (British Museum; University of California). Drawing together the Egyptian, Greek and Roman strands of the story, Bowman presents a masterly survey, excellently illustrated, of that thousand-year period between the last of the pharaohs and Islamic conquest when Alexandria was the queen of the Mediterranean and Egypt played a vital role in the Graeco-Roman and Christian worlds.

P.M. Fraser, *Ptolemaic Alexandria* (Oxford University Press). That a single person within a single lifetime could have written so comprehensive, rich and authoritative a book almost defies belief. Quite simply, this is *the* book on Alexandria during Greek rule: its history, topography, philosophy, religion, literature, architecture, politics, social structure – you name it. A snip at £120/$200.

Michael Grant, *Cleopatra* (Phoenix; Sterling). An immensely readable and entirely authoritative biography of the great Ptolemaic queen.

Naphtali Lewis, *Greeks in Ptolemaic Egypt* (American Society of Papyrologists). A remarkable book constructed out of life histories derived from careful study of salvaged papyri. The texts have the quality of present-day interviews, giving a lively impression of everyday life in Ptolemaic Egypt.

J. Grafton Milne, *A History of Egypt under Roman Rule* (Ares, o/p). Like Bevan's book on the Ptolemies (which was originally part of the same series), this is worthy – if somewhat dry.

Plutarch, *The Age of Alexander* and *Makers of Rome* (Penguin). Read the former for the 1st century AD Greek historian Plutarch's life of Alexander the Great, and the latter for his life of Mark Antony as it became entangled with that of Cleopatra.

Christian Egypt, past and present

B.L. Carter, *The Copts in Egyptian Politics 1918–1952* (Routledge, UK, o/p; AUC, Cairo). An exploration of the political relationship between the Muslim majority and the Coptic minority in Egypt during the days when the Copts played an important role in the Wafd and the liberal constitutional order, and before the experiment failed and Copts retreated again in the face of Egypt's newly aggressive Islamic identity.

Henry Chadwick, *The Early Church* (Penguin). The story of the emergent Church, with chapters on such early architects of Christianity as Clement of Alexandria and Origen, on the persecutions, Gnosticism, the Arian controversy, and the Councils of Nicaea and Chalcedon.

E. J. Chitham, *The Coptic Community in Egypt: Spatial and Social Change* (University of Durham, Centre for Middle Eastern and Islamic Studies, Occasional Papers Series). Dry but informative account of the conditions under which the Copts live in Egypt today.

Eusebius, *The History of the Church* (Penguin). The early history of Christianity up to its legalization by Constantine the Great, as told by an eyewitness to the terrible persecutions in Egypt.

Otto F. A. Meinardus, *Monks and Monasteries of the Egyptian Deserts* (AUC, Cairo). This is the standard work on Egyptian monasticism from its flowering in the deserts during the 4th century AD, its subsequent influence throughout the Christian world, and to the renaissance of the Coptic faith in Egypt today.

Helen Waddell, *The Desert Fathers* (Arrow; Vintage). An account, drawn from their own writings, of the 4th-century solitaries who founded the monastic and ascetic traditions in the West.

Barbara Watterson, *Coptic Egypt* (Scottish Academic Press). A good general introduction to the political, religious and art history of the native Christians of Egypt from the 1st century AD to the present day.

General histories of medieval and modern Egypt

Carl F. Petry (ed.), *The Cambridge History of Egypt, volume 1: Islamic Egypt, 640–1517*; **M.W. Daly** (ed.), *The Cambridge History of Egypt, volume 2: Modern Egypt, from 1517 to the end of the twentieth century* (Cambridge University Press). Though valuable in many respects – not least because it offers a readily accessible general history from the Islamic period onwards – the *Cambridge History of Egypt* has its limitations. The second volume especially is poor, with sloppy editing, frequent mis-datings and contradictions, while essays too often tend towards the shallow, the tendentious and the politically correct, meaning that it cannot be trusted as the essential reference work it pretends to be.

Max Rodenbeck, *Cairo, The City Victorious* (Picador; Vintage). By telling the story of Cairo since its origins, Rodenbeck succeeds in telling much of the story of Egypt from the Arab conquest to the present day, making this a good general history – though it is strongest on present-day reportage.

The Arab period

Alfred J. Butler, *The Arab Conquest of Egypt* (Oxford University Press; Darf). This definitive work gives a detailed and prolonged account of Egypt's last years under Byzantine rule, which serves as a prologue to its central subject, the circumstances of the Arab conquest.

Bernard Lewis, *The Arabs in History* (Oxford University Press). A swift, though reliable, gallop through Arab history from pre-Islamic times to the near-present.

The Crusades

Joinville and Villehardouin, *Chronicles of the Crusades* (Penguin). The Seventh Crusade was a remarkably inept enterprise led by the bumptious French king Louis – or Saint Louis, as he became. Joinville, who was there, tells it with the straight face of a true believer, though one cannot help but smile.

Sir Steven Runciman, *A History of the Crusades* (Penguin, 3 vols). A wonderful account of adventure, daring, stupidity and violence, interwoven with the life and gossip of the Crusader courts in the East. The real consequence of the Crusades was felt not in the Middle East but in the transfer of power and cultural hegemony from Byzantium to Western Europe, so marking the beginning of the modern world.

The Mameluke and Ottoman periods

Robert Irwin, *The Middle East in the Middle Ages: The early Mamluke sultanate 1250–1382* (University of Southern Illinois). While being academically absolutely pukka, this volume is an excellent read, telling the exciting story of the rise of the Mamelukes, their repulse of the Mongols and their triumph over the Crusaders.

Michael Winter, *Egyptian Society under Ottoman Rule 1517–1798* (Routledge). A good, solid account of the period by one of the leading experts in the field.

French invasion

Vivant Denon, *Travels in Upper and Lower Egypt during the Campaign of General Bonaparte*, trans. E.A. Kendal (Darf UK). A vivid firsthand account, first published in 1803, of Napoleon's expedition to Egypt.

Alan Moorehead, *The Blue Nile* (Penguin; Harper). Apart from being a marvellous history of the river during the 18th and 19th centuries, a full quarter of the book is devoted to Napoleon's expedition to Egypt.

19th and 20th centuries

Correlli Barnett, *The Desert Generals* (Cassell; Indiana University Press). Originally published in 1960, this is the first and still the best complete account of the desert campaign of 1940–43, demonstrating in particular the vital role of Auchinleck rather than Montgomery in turning the tide against the Germans at Alamein.

Ahron Bregman and Jihan el-Tahri, *The Fifty Years War: Israel and the Arabs* (BBC, o/p; TV Books). Written by a Jew and an Arab, this largely succeeds in being a balanced and inside account of the hostility between both sides.

Artemis Cooper, *Cairo in the War, 1939–1945* (Penguin; Hamish Hamilton). During World War II the second city of the British Empire was, in effect, Cairo. Almost everyone who was anyone was there, usually because the Germans had thrown them out of everywhere else. The collection of politicians, generals, spies, writers, poets, socialites, dancing girls and so on – not to mention Rommel on the doorstep – made Cairo a very exciting place indeed.

The Earl of Cromer, *Modern Egypt* (MacMillan o/p). For 24 years, Cromer – or Evelyn Baring, as he formerly was – ruled Egypt absolutely in all but title, and wrote this justification of the British presence a year after his resignation. Though this account is long out of print, it's worth tracking down.

Lord Killearn, *The Killearn Diaries 1934–1946* (Sidgwick & Jackson, o/p). The bluff and commanding high commissioner turned ambassador tells in his own words the trials of trying to make Egyptians see reason *à la Anglaise*.

Alexander Kitroeff, *The Greeks in Egypt 1919–1937* (Ithaca, o/p).

Invited to Egypt by Mohammed Ali, the Greeks were a dynamic minority in the country and did much to build up Alexandria as a great city and trading port. In fact the book looks back into the 19th century, while an epilogue carries the story to the Greeks' final expulsion from Egypt in the 1960s.

Gudrun Krämer, *The Jews in Modern Egypt 1914–1952* (University of Washington Press). Along with the Greeks, the Jews of Egypt contributed enormously to the modern development of the country, but their attachment to the country was overwhelmed by the wars with Israel.

Peter Mansfield, *The Arabs* (Penguin). A reliable survey of the Arab world in general and also country by country, providing a quick survey of recent Egyptian history and concerns.

Peter Mansfield, *The British in Egypt* (Weidenfeld and Nicolson, o/p). An excellent political history of the British presence in Egypt from 1882 to 1956.

Anthony McDermott, *Egypt from Nasser to Mubarak: A flawed revolution* (Routledge, o/p). Seeing Egypt and its institutions from the inside as a journalist with the *Guardian* and the *Financial Times*, McDermott concludes that Nasser was a catastrophe for his country and that neither Sadat nor Mubarak has really succeeded in pulling it out of the hole.

Afaf Lutfi al-Sayyid Marsot, *Egypt in the Reign of Muhammad Ali* (Cambridge University Press). Despite its academic guise, this is a slightly chatty, slightly unreliable, but generally useful survey of Mohammed Ali's reign.

E.R.J. Owen, *Cotton and the Egyptian Economy, 1820–1914: A study in trade and development* (Oxford University Press, o/p). An extremely interesting book, believe it or not, about the biggest money-earner in the country at the time – "white gold", they called it.

J.C.B. Richmond, *Egypt 1798–1952: Her advance towards a modern identity*, (Methuen, o/p). A fairly brief but solid account of modern Egyptian history by an apologetic British diplomat.

Sir Thomas Russell Pasha, *Egyptian Service 1902–1946*, London 1949. Just as J. Edgar Hoover was head of the FBI for so long and knew so many secrets that nobody dared remove him, so Russell Pasha remained for decades at the head of the Cairo police, even after the Anglo-Egyptian Treaty of 1936 and the conclusion of World War II. His services were indispensable to the Egyptians, especially his campaign against drugs, and this account of his exploits is both excellent and entertaining.

Anwar Sadat, *Revolt on the Nile* (Alan Wingate o/p). This early book by Sadat reads like a boy scout's account of being accidentally caught up in a revolution. It is quite sweet, really, and entirely sycophantic towards Nasser.

Anthony Sattin, *Lifting the Veil: British society in Egypt 1768–1956* (Dent, o/p). An enjoyable account of the social life of the British in Egypt during the days when a tea party really mattered.

Janice J. Terry, *The Wafd, 1919–1952* (Third World Centre for Research and Publishing, UK, o/p). The only specialized account of Egyptian political history during the liberal constitutional period.

Hugh Thomas, *The Suez Affair* (Weidenfeld, o/p; Penguin, o/p). A good, informed account of the Suez Crisis of 1956, often using interviews with insiders.

Art, religion, culture and society

The Koran (Penguin). N. J. Dawood's translation is generally considered to be the most accurate, if not the most literarily accomplished, translation of the Koran into English – notwithstanding which, Egyptian fundamentalists have had it banned.

Hassan Fathy, *Architecture for the Poor* (AUC, Cairo). In this classic work, the late Egyptian architect demonstrates the practicability and beauty of building with mud brick, maintaining traditional forms against the phoney orientalizing decoration and concrete brutality of architecture found in Egypt today. Though lauded internationally, Fathy received no support from the Egyptian government and little from Egyptians generally – and now building with mud brick has been banned. He might have got somewhere had he called his book *Architecture for the Rich*.

Robin Fedden, *Egypt: Land of the valley* (Hippocrene, o/p). Fedden taught at Cairo University before and during World War II, and has written with deep knowledge and affection an interpretation of all that is most characteristic and permanent in the life, landscape and monuments of Egypt. A marvellous introduction to the country.

Edward William Lane, *The Manners and Customs of the Modern Egyptians* (East-West, o/p). First published in 1836, this is a classic account by an outsider who, by living among the Egyptian people, succeeded in writing the most perceptive record of life in an Islamic community during the 19th century.

Elaine Pagels, *The Gnostic Gospels* (Penguin; Vintage). An account of the meaning of Jesus and the origin of Christianity based on Gnostic gospels found at Nag Hammadi in Upper Egypt in the late 1940s.

Justin Wintle, *The Rough Guide History of Islam* (Rough Guides). From its 7th-century origins in the Arabian interior, Islam has spread to span more than half the world. Its remarkable development is related in a similar format to this *Rough Guide History of Egypt*, with a continuous time-line, informative sidebars, and chapter introductions, each providing ways of accessing elements and periods of the story as desired.

The oases and desert exploration

R. A. Bagnold, *Libyan Sands: Travel in a dead world* (Immel, UK). An account of Bagnold's motoring travels from the Nile and across the Sahara by one of the great desert explorers of the 1920s and 1930s, who went on to found the Long Range Desert Group during World War II.

Ahmed Fakhry, *Siwa Oasis* (AUC, Cairo). A history and guide to this most famous and beautiful of Egypt's oases, where Alexander the Great heard himself proclaimed a god.

Ahmed Mohammed Hassanein, *The Lost Oases* (Thornton Butterworth, u/p). Before Bagnold and others motored or flew across the Sahara, there was Hassanein, the first man to cross the Great Sand Sea, who did so by camel in the 1920s to discover the lost oasis of Uweinat (see pp.4–5).

Egyptology

Howard Carter, *The Tomb of Tut-Ankh-Amen*. Carter was a wonderful writer, and his account is fully equal to the wonder of his discovery. It was first published in three volumes in 1923; numerous reprints have appeared in various forms over the years, most usually the first volume only, or sometimes an abridgement of all three volumes.

Jean-Yves Empereur, *Alexandria Rediscovered* (British Museum Press, o/p; Braziller). The exciting recent underwater discoveries of ancient Alexandria are included here among dry-land excavations, presented by the French archeologist in charge of the project. The photographs, maps and reconstructed cityscapes are all excellent. The same author's *Alexandria: past and present* (Thames and Hudson) is also worth investigating.

Laura Foreman, *Cleopatra's Palace: in search of a legend* (Weidenfeld and Nicholson; Random House). Lavishly illustrated, Foreman's book uncovers the dramatic tale of Cleopatra's palace, now underwater as the result of an ancient earthquake. It has a foreword by Franck Goddio, the underwater archeologist responsible for discovering the site – whose own *Alexandria: the submerged royal quarters* (Periplus), though now out of print, is worth tracking down.

Geoffrey T. Martin, *The Hidden Tombs of Memphis* (Thames and Hudson). Saqqara has been described as the greatest archeological site in the world, so far only partly touched by the excavator's trowel and with many more secrets to reveal. In proof comes this publication, detailing discoveries from the time of Tutankhamun and Rameses II.

H.V.F. Winstone, *Howard Carter and the Discovery of the Tomb of Tutankhamun* (Constable, o/p). Written with elegance and sensitivity,

Winstone's book captures the difficult but remarkable character of Carter and thrillingly retells the story of his discovery of Tutankhamun's tomb.

Travel and guides

Karl Baedeker, *Egypt and the Sudan*. The 1929 edition – the last true Baedeker guide to Egypt, and including the discovery of Tutankhamun's tomb – is the best guide ever written about the country, and by far the greater part of it is still entirely useful today. Secondhand copies with beautifully coloured maps go for £100/$150 upwards; recent monotone reprints will cost about one-third as much.

Amelia Edwards, *A Thousand Miles up the Nile* (Summersdale; J. P. Tarcher). Edwards, who was a bestselling novelist in her day, wrote this lively and vivid account of her voyage up the Nile in the 1870s, a journey which awakened a lifetime fascination with ancient Egypt and spurred her to campaign against the deplorable way in which its monuments were being destroyed. She founded the Egyptian Exploration Society, which established the first chair in Egyptology in Britain, filled by Sir Flinders Petrie at University College London.

E. M. Forster, *Alexandria, A History and a Guide* (Michael Haag, o/p). First published in Alexandria in 1922, this is one of the best guides to anywhere ever written – it addresses not the all-but-invisible physical remains of ancient Alexandria, but the cultural, intellectual and spiritual heritage of the city, which lies at the heart of Western civilization.

Jocelyn Gohary, *Guide to the Nubian Monuments on Lake Nasser* (AUC, Cairo). The necessary handbook if you sail upon Lake Nasser to visit the salvaged Nubian monuments or visit the Nubian Museum at Aswan.

Jill Kamil, *Coptic Egypt: History and Guide* (AUC, Cairo). A good simple account, directing you to the important churches and monasteries and guiding you round the Coptic Museum in Cairo.

Deborah Manley, *The Nile, A Traveller's Anthology* (Cassell, o/p). By far the best recent anthology of writings on Egypt, from ancient times to the present.

Richard P. Parker, Robin Sabin and Caroline Williams, *Islamic Monuments in Cairo: A practical guide* (AUC, Cairo). Indispensable if you want to get to know the Islamic monuments of Cairo and enter properly into the historical atmosphere of the medieval city.

References

References

The following references provide publication details for quotations used. All quotations from the Bible come from the King James Version, 1611; all those from the Koran are from the edition translated by N.J. Dawood, Penguin, London 1990.

p.5: Ahmed Hassanein, *The Lost Oases*, Thornton Butterworth, London 1925, p.204ff; p.6: Herodotus, *The Histories*, Penguin, London 1996, p.87; p.9: Michael A. Hoffman, *Egypt before the Pharaohs*, Alfred A. Knopf, New York 1979, p.14; p.11: in Sir Alan Gardiner, *Egypt of the Pharaohs*, Oxford University Press, Oxford 1961, p.404; p.16: Henri Frankfort, *Ancient Egyptian Religion*, Columbia University Press, New York 1948, p.30ff; p.28: *The Wisdom Book of Ptah-Hotep*, cited in Lise Manniche, *Sexual Life in Ancient Egypt*, Kegan Paul International, London and New York, 1987, p.97; p.30: Ipuwer, *Admonitions of a Sage*, cited in Gardiner, *Egypt of the Pharoahs*, p.109; p.38: *Prophecy of Neferti*, cited in John A. Wilson, *The Burden of Egypt*, University of Chicago Press, Chicago 1951, p.107; p.42: Michael Rice, *Egypt's Legacy*, Routledge, London 1997, p.127; p.49: Herodotus, *Histories*, p.141; p.53: Manetho, *Aegyptiaca*, quoted by Josephus in his *Against Apion*, cited in Gardiner, *Egypt of the Pharoahs*, p.155f; p.55: A.J. Spencer, *Death in Ancient Egypt*, Penguin, Harmondsworth 1982, p.116ff; p.56. adapted from citation in Wilson, *Burden of Egypt*, p.164; p.61: James Henry Breasted, *A History of Egypt*, Charles Scribner's Sons, New York 1905, p.170; p.63: in Ian Shaw, editor, *The Oxford History of Ancient Egypt*, Oxford University Press, Oxford 2000, p.232; p.70: Breasted, *History of Egypt*, p.320f; p.72: in Gardiner, *Egypt of the Pharaohs*, p.199ff; p.75: in David O'Connor and Eric H. Cline, editors, *Amenhotep III: Perspectives on his reign*, The University of Michigan Press, Ann Arbor 1998, p.19; p.79: Cyril Aldred, *Akhenaten: Pharaoh of Egypt*, Thames and Hudson, London 1968, p.11; p.80: in Aldred, *Akhenaten*, p.180; p.89: in Geoffrey T. Martin, *The Hidden Tombs of*

Memphis, Thames and Hudson, London 1991, p.36; p.88: Amelia Edwards, *A Thousand Miles up the Nile*, London 1877, p.412; p.89: K.A. Kitchen, *Pharaoh Triumphant*, Aris and Phillips, Warminster 1982, p.119; in Kitchen, *Pharaoh Triumphant*, p.59; p.92: Kitchen, *Pharaoh Triumphant*, p.99; p.97: in Gardiner, *Egypt of the Pharaohs*, p.285; p.99: Erik Hornung, *The Valley of the Kings*, Timken Publishers, New York 1990, p.46; p.109: in Rice, *Egypt's Legacy*, p.175; p.110: Cited in K.A. Kitchen, *The Third Intermediate Period in Egypt*, Aris and Phillips, Warminster, 1986, p.331; p.112: Adapted from Gardiner, *Egypt of the Pharaohs*, p.346; p.117: Herodotus, *Histories*, p.152; p.118: in Gardiner, *Egypt of the Pharaohs*, p.359; p.120: Herodotus, *Histories*, p.164; p.123: Herodotus, *Histories*, p.144; p.130: Robin Lane Fox, *Alexander the Great*, Allen Lane, Penguin, London 1973, p.196; p.135: Herondas, *Mimes*, I, 23–6, in Naphtali Lewis, *Greeks in Ptolemaic Egypt*, Oxford University Press, Oxford 1986, p.10; p.136: Edwyn Bevan, *A History of Egypt under the Ptolemaic Dynasty*, Methuen, London 1927, p.32; p.138: E.M. Forster, *Alexandria: A history and a guide*, Michael Haag, London 1982, p.145; p.144: Polybius, *History*, v, 107, in P.M. Fraser, *Ptolemaic Alexandria*, Oxford University Press, Oxford 1972, vol. 1, p.75; p.145: Adapted from Fraser, *Ptolemaic Alexandria*, vol. 1, p.681ff, and Alan K. Bowman, *Egypt after the Pharaohs*, London 1986, p.31; p.146: W.W. Tarn and G.T. Griffith, *Hellenistic Civilisation*, third edition, St Martin's Press, London and New York, 1952, p.28ff; p.147: Adapted from Bevan, *Egypt under the Ptolemaic Dynasty*, p.263ff; p.148: Polybius, *History*, xxix, 27, adapted from *The Oxford History of Ancient Egypt*, p.421, and from Lewis, *Greeks in Ptolemaic Egypt*, p.164; p.149: P.M. Fraser, *Ptolemaic Alexandria*, vol. 1, p.79; p.153: Bevan, *Egypt under the Ptolemaic Dynasty*, p.359ff; p.156: Plutarch, *Life of Mark Antony*, in *Makers of Rome*, Penguin, London 1965, p.293; p.159: Plutarch, *Life of Mark Antony*, translated by Sir Thomas North, 1579, in Forster, *Alexandria*, p.231; p.165: Tacitus, *The Histories*, Penguin, Harmondsworth 1956, p.124; p.171: in Forster, *Alexandria*, p.50; p.174: Plotinus, *The Enneads*, translated by Stephen Mackenna, abridged edition, Penguin, London 1991, p.55; p.175: J. Grafton Milne, *A History*

of Egypt under Roman Rule, Methuen, London 1924, p.69; p.176:
Edward Gibbon, *The Decline and Fall of the Roman Empire*, Allen Lane,
Penguin, London 1994, p.313; p.178: Eusebius, *The History of the
Church*, Penguin, Harmondsworth 1965, p.337ff; p.182: in Forster,
Alexandria, p.236; p.186: Stanley Lane-Poole, *A History of Egypt in the
Middle Ages*, Methuen, London 1901, p.46; p.200: Alfred J. Butler, *The
Arab Conquest of Egypt*, first edition 1902, second edition, Oxford
University Press, Oxford 1978, p.291ff; p.201: in Butler, *Arab Conquest*,
p.347ff; p.202: in Forster, *Alexandria*, p.61ff; p.205: in *Otto Meinardus,
Monks and Monasteries of the Egyptian Deserts*, The American
University in Cairo Press, Cairo 1989, p.55; p.208: Robin Fedden, *Egypt:
Land of the Valley*, John Murray, London 1978, p.100f; p.219: Bertold
Spuler, *The Muslim World*, E.J. Brill, Leiden 1960, vol. 1, p.88ff; p.222: in
Max Rodenbeck, *Cairo: The city victorious*, Picador, London 1998, p.81;
p.223: in Desmond Stewart, *Great Cairo, Mother of the World*, American
University in Cairo Press, Cairo 1996, p.98; p.233: in Bernard Lewis,
Islam from the Prophet Muhammed to the Capture of Constantinople,
Oxford University Press, Oxford 1987, p.97ff; p.234: in Bernard Lewis,
The Arabs in History, Hutchinson, London 1970, p.155; p.237: Robert
Irwin, *The Middle East in the Middle Ages*, Croom Helm, Beckenham
1986, p.136; p.240: in Stewart, *Great Cairo*, p.121; p.247: Edwards, *A
Thousand Miles up the Nile*, p.388; p.251: in *The Cambridge History of
Egypt*, vol. 2, p.76; p.252: in *The Cambridge History of Egypt*, vol. 2,
p.84; p.253: in Jean Thiry, *Bonaparte en Egypte*, Berger-Levrault, Paris
1973, p.126: author's translation; p.259: Alan Moorehead, *The Blue
Nile*, Hamish Hamilton, London 1962, p.140; p.261: Vivant Denon,
*Travels in Upper and Lower Egypt during the Campaign of General
Bonaparte*, translated by E.A. Kendal, London 1803; reprinted by Darf
Publishers, London 1986, p.213; p.263: Josiah Condor, *The Modern
Traveller*, London 1827, vol. 5, p.164; p.264: in Edward Said,
Orientalism, Penguin, Harmondsworth 1985, p.84; p.266: John Lewis
Burckhardt, *Travels in Nubia*, London 1819, p.243; p.267: in Afaf Lutfi
al-Sayyid Marsot, *Egypt in the Reign of Muhammed Ali*, Cambridge
University Press, Cambridge 1984, p.114; p.272: in Harold Temperley,

England and the Near East, Longmans, London 1964, p.89; p.275: in Marsot, *Egypt in the Reign of Muhammad Ali*, p.256; p.279: in A.E.M. Ashley, *Life and Correspondence of Palmerston*, London 1879, p.338; p.283: in Tom Little, *Modern Egypt*, Benn, London 1967, p.163; p.285: in J.C.B. Richmond, *Egypt 1798–1952*, Methuen, London 1977, p.109; p.286: in Richmond, *Egypt*, p.111; p.287: in Richmond, *Egypt*, p.127; p.289: Evelyn Baring, Earl of Cromer, *Modern Egypt*, Macmillan, London 1908, vol. 1, p.287; p.290: Adapted from Alan Moorehead, *The White Nile*, Penguin, Harmondsworth 1973, p.249; p.293: Winston Churchill, *My Early Life*, Collins, London 1930, p.192; p.296: Cromer, *Modern Egypt*, vol. 2, p.130f; p.297: in Gordon Waterfield, *Egypt*, Thames and Hudson, London 1967, p.119; p.298: B.L. Carter, *The Copts in Egyptian Politics*, Croom Helm, Beckenham 1986 and The American University in Cairo Press, Cairo 1988, p.12; p.298: in Richmond, *Egypt*, p.151; p.307: in Peter Mansfield, *The Arabs*, Penguin, Harmondsworth 1985, p.172; p.309: in Gudrun Krämer, *The Jews in Modern Egypt*, 1914–1952, University of Washington Press, Seattle 1989, p.231; p.310: in *The Cambridge History of Egypt*, vol. 2, p.293; p.311: The Royal Institute of International Affairs, Information Department Papers No. 19, *Great Britain and Egypt 1914–1936*, London 1936, p.14; p.316: Taha Hussein, *An Egyptian Childhood*, The American University in Cairo Press, Cairo 1990, p.5; p.317: Hanna F. Wissa, *Assiout, the Saga of an Egyptian Family*, The Book Guild, Lewes 1994, p.250; p.325: in William H. McNeill and Marilyn Robinson Waldman, editors, *The Islamic World*, The University of Chicago Press, Chicago and London, 1983, p.418ff; p.329: Jean and Simmone Lacouture, *Egypt in Transition*, Methuen, London 1958, p.91; p.331: Foreign Office files, Public Record Office; p.334: Correlli Barnett, *The Desert Generals*, second edition, George Allen & Unwin, London 1983, p.217; p.336: Janice J. Terry, *The Wafd 1919–1952*, Third World Centre for Research and Publishing Ltd, London 1982, p.292; p.339: in Artemis Cooper, *Cairo in the War*, Hamish Hamilton, London 1989, p.329; p.344: Anwar Sadat, *Revolt on the Nile*, Allan Wingate, London 1957, p.119; p.345: Mohammed Neguib, *Egypt's Destiny*, Doubleday, Garden City, NY 1955, p.131;

p.348: Neguib, *Egypt's Destiny*, p.200; p.349: in Peter Mansfield, *The British in Egypt*, Weidenfeld and Nicolson, London 1971, p.309; p.351: Sadat, *Revolt on the Nile*, p.111; p.358: in Waterfield, *Egypt*, p.164; p.362: in Elizabeth Monroe, *Britain's Moment in the Middle East 1914–1956*, Chatto and Windus, London 1963, p.218; p.363: in Rodenbeck, *Cairo*, p.217ff; p.366: in Waterfield, *Egypt*, p.195; p.367: in *Middle East Record*, London 1967, p.554; p.369: Afaf Lutfi al-Sayyid Marsot, *A Short History of Modern Egypt*, Cambridge University Press, Cambridge 1985, p.126; p.375: Raymond A. Hinnebusch Jr, *Egyptian Politics under Sadat*, Cambridge University Press, Cambridge 1985, p.54; p.377: in Rodenbeck, *Cairo*, p.337; p.379: in Anthony McDermott, *From Nasser to Mubarak*, Croom Helm, Beckenham 1988, p.55; p.380: in McDermott, *From Nasser to Mubarak*, p.57; p.389: in *The Atlantic Monthly*, January 1999

Index

Entries in colour represent feature boxes

b

i

k

j

l

m

around the world

in twenty years

London Mini Guide ★ London Restaurants ★ Los Angeles ★ Madeira ★
Madrid ★ Malaysia, Singapore & Brunei ★ Mallorca ★ Malta & Gozo ★ Maui
★ Maya World ★ Melbourne ★ Menorca ★ Mexico ★ Miami & the Florida
Keys ★ Montréal ★ Morocco ★ Moscow ★ Nepal ★ New England ★ New
Orleans ★ New York City ★ New York Mini Guide ★ New York Restaurants
★ New Zealand ★ Norway ★ Pacific Northwest ★ Paris ★ Paris Mini Guide
★ Peru ★ Poland ★ Portugal ★ Prague ★ Provence & the Côte d'Azur ★
Pyrenees ★ The Rocky Mountains ★ Romania ★ Rome ★ San Francisco ★
San Francisco Restaurants ★ Sardinia ★ Scandinavia ★ Scotland ★
Scottish Highlands & Islands ★ Seattle ★ Sicily ★ Singapore ★ South Africa,
Lesotho & Swaziland ★ South India ★ Southeast Asia ★ Southwest USA ★
Spain ★ St Lucia ★ St Petersburg ★ Sweden ★ Switzerland ★ Sydney ★
Syria ★ Tanzania ★ Tenerife and La Gomera ★ Thailand ★ Thailand's
Beaches & Islands ★ Tokyo ★ Toronto ★ Travel Health ★ Trinidad &
Tobago ★ Tunisia ★ Turkey ★ Tuscany & Umbria ★ USA ★ Vancouver ★
Venice & the Veneto ★ Vienna ★ Vietnam ★ Wales ★ Washington DC ★
West Africa ★ Women Travel ★ Yosemite ★ Zanzibar ★ Zimbabwe

also look out for our maps, phrasebooks, music guides and reference books

ROUGH GUIDES TWENTY YEARS

ROUGH GUIDE **HISTORIES**

£7.99 each

Uniquely accessible pocket histories
— History Today

Essential pocket histories for anyone interested in getting under the skin of a country